The Language of Argument

FOR

Molly Theresa McDonald

(The Argument for Adoption)

Sponsoring Editor: Phillip Leininger
Project Editor: Pamela Landau
Designer: Gayle Jaeger
Production: Marion Palen/Delia Tedoff
Compositor: Haddon Craftsmen
Printer and Binder: R. R. Donnelley

THE LANGUAGE OF ARGUMENT, Fourth Edition
Copyright © 1983 by Harper & Row, Publishers, Inc.

Library of Congress Cataloging in Publication Data

McDonald, Daniel Lamout.
  The language of argument.

  1. College readers.   2. Persuasion (Rhetoric)
3. English language—Rhetoric. I. Title.
PE1417.M43   1983   808'.0427   82-12037
ISBN 0-06-044361-8

The Language of Argument

FOURTH EDITION

DANIEL McDONALD
University of South Alabama

HARPER & ROW, PUBLISHERS, New York
Cambridge, Philadelphia, San Francisco,
London, Mexico City, São Paulo, Sydney

1817

Contents

v

Argument for Analysis

PART III   237

Eight Rules for Good Writing

Subjects Discussed in this Book

Preface

The purpose of this text remains the same: to teach students how to read argument and to provide materials around which they can write their own argumentative essays. The selections cover a range of provocative issues. Some are notably persuasive; some are not.

Only five titles have been retained from the previous edition. I kept four because a poll indicated they were particularly popular with teachers who use the book. The fifth, the essay on vitamin E, I kept because my students asked me to.

Besides revising "Eight Rules for Good Writing" (which was new in the Third Edition), I have added two sections that counsel students on the forms in which they are most likely to make an argument—the business letter and the platform speech.

To promote student writing, I have included a section called "Argument for Analysis." This has 36 short (or relatively short) works: essays, advertisements, letters, photographs, cartoons, editorials, and so on. Students can be asked to write on any of these, giving either an analysis of the argument or a response to it. Teachers could conceivably assign a different title to each student in their class.

I am grateful to colleagues who made useful suggestions for improving this book, particularly Gene Knepprath (California State University, Sacramento) and Jon Lighter (University of Tennessee, Knoxville). I must acknowledge the contribution of Michael Hanna (University of South Alabama), who offered valuable counsel about platform speaking. I thank all the authors for permission to reprint their essays. And for letting me use their previously unpublished work, I express particular appreciation to George J. Koelzer and Will Dwyer II, eloquent advocates both.

The editor who selects and annotates controversial essays must work to keep his own opinion out of his textbook. Once again, I have tried.

Daniel McDonald

Forms of Argument
PART I

Japonica
Glistens like coral in all of the neighbouring gardens,
And to-day we have naming of parts.

HENRY REED

Logic and Composition

Good English is not merely correct English.

ROBERTSON AND CASSIDY, *The Development of Modern English*

Good writing is that which gets the result you want. And a knowledge of the techniques of persuasion will help you to win whatever you're after.

A study of logic will make you concerned about both your audience and the writing patterns that have a good or bad effect on them. It will keep you from speculating vaguely on some topic that is not subject to evidence and will help you know when you are making sense.

WIN YOUR AUDIENCE

To make a persuasive case, you have to know the character of your audience. This will help you to choose your words and shape your style.

One body of readers—say, a group of fraternity men—will respond to a direct appeal in strong language; another group—say, members of a Baptist congregation—will reject your whole argument if you use a word like "crap." One group will respond to wit; another, to biblical quotation; and still another, to a spread of statistics. There are particular readers who will be offended if you write "Ms.," "ain't," "Negro," "symbiotic," "de jour," or "and/or." Most audiences will be bored if you write vaguely about "Responsibility" or "Tomorrow's Promise," but there are church and civic groups who may favor high-flown rhetorical generalities. To make your case effectively, you have to know your audience.

A central feature in argument is creating a personal voice to express your views. Too often individuals with an impressive case fail to be persuasive because of an inadequate writing style which makes them sound like a computer, a demanding top sergeant, a condescending aristocrat, or a stubborn child.

Most readers respond favorably to a concerned and courteous tone. Whatever your personal character, let your writing reflect a warm, human personality. When addressing a committee, refer to the members in your presentation. ("I'm sure you ladies and gentlemen recognize how complex this question is.") When writing a business letter, try to use a direct, personal

3

voice. ("I'm sorry about your problem, Mr. Majors, and I hope we can do more for you next time.") Routinely, work to avoid a brittle or hostile tone. Don't write, "You must do this," when you can say, "We would like to have you do this promptly." Never write, "I will not do this," when you can say, "For these reasons I cannot do this now." Don't protest, "You seem incapable of understanding my argument"; say, "I am sorry I did not make myself understood."

This tone can be difficult to maintain. At times you will want to express righteous indignation or ego-gratifying scorn. Although the outburst may be personally satisfying, remember that anger never persuaded anyone. In argument, nice guys finish first.

The point deserves repetition. An Alabama attorney looking back on a lifetime of courtroom experience said, "When I was young, I thought that lawyers won cases. Later I believed that facts won cases. Now I think that clients win cases. When the facts are not overwhelmingly against him, the jury will find for the person they like best."

DEFINE THE ISSUE

A study of logic shows the importance of defining your issue. Some topics that you may want to discuss are in flatly non-arguable form. They would produce vague speeches and incoherent essays.

Some issues rely more on definition of terms than on evidence. When two people argue whether Senator Ted Kennedy is handsome, for example, they are not disagreeing about his hair, teeth, or clothes, but about a definition of "handsomeness." If they can agree on a definition, they will probably agree about Senator Kennedy as well. Similarly, the question of whether capital punishment is wrong hinges not so much on the character of the act (the pain, the possibility of error, the protection afforded society) as on the definition of "wrongness."

Aesthetic and moral questions often are not susceptible to evidence because individuals cannot agree on the terms of argument. The meaning of any word is what people agree it is. (A telephone is called a "telephone" because English speakers regularly use that word to denote it.) And in these special areas, people are not in accord. What is handsomeness? What is beauty? Theoreticians have sought objective standards, but the quest seems fruitless. Is a Greek temple more beautiful than a Gothic cathedral? Is Whistler's "Mother" handsomer than da Vinci's *Mona Lisa* or Andy Warhol's *Marilyn Monroe?* Who can say? The decision rests on a subjective judgment, which does not lend itself to argument. Taste is indisputable.

Like beauty, the idea of goodness is not subject to easy definition. Seeking an objective basis for calling actions right and wrong, authorities have cited scriptural precedents; they have based systems on the inalienable rights of each human being; they have insisted that nature provides a moral example. But such definitions have won no universal acceptance. If two disputants could agree that morality resides, say, in a natural law, they might then *begin* to argue about capital punishment. In general usage, however, moral terms remain so ill-defined that such issues often cannot be argued meaningfully at all. (If you have to write on beauty or morality, focus your essay on some concrete example—say, arson or pop art or Miss January—and work in as many "for example" and "for instance" references as you can.)

Moral and aesthetic questions are further removed from argument because they often produce emotional responses. Two individuals who agree in defining "handsomeness" might, for example, still disagree about Senator Kennedy because one objects to his liberal politics or to the Chappaquiddick incident. It is, of course, unreasonable to let emotions color such a judgment, but the attitude is not uncommon. You might be completely persuaded that capital punishment is cruel and barbaric, yet, at a given moment, argue that hanging is too good for a child murderer or a political assassin.

Vagueness of definition precludes argument in other areas as well. Saab has been proclaimed "the most *intelligent* car ever built" and Royal Copenhagen as "the only *elegant* musk oil cologne." The advertisement insists "Only Tareyton has the *best* filter!" Are these claims true? Until the key words are defined, the statements are no more subject to evidence than is "Razzle dagons, popple stix." Nonsense is neither true nor false.

Many modern areas of controversy hinge on the definition of terms. Do animals "talk"? Can children "sin"? Is running a "religious" experience? Is prostitution a "victimless" crime? Do computers "think"? It depends on how you define the words.

It is only when terms are defined and mutually accepted that you can begin gathering evidence to prove something. You can, for example, argue whether Jim Brown or O. J. Simpson was the better football player, because their records, the merits of their supporting and opposing teams, and the qualities of a good running back are generally agreed on. Is it true that smoking causes lung cancer, that Vice-President Agnew took bribes, that Gordon's is the largest-selling gin in the world? The questions can at least be argued.

MAKE YOUR CASE

Finally, the study of argument will let you know when you are making sense. It will tell you if your sample is sufficient to support an inductive conclusion, if the expert you want to quote is a reliable authority, if your words express the meanings you want, and if your statistics are relevant.

A survey of logic will make you a more perceptive reader. You will be better able to recognize strengths and weaknesses in particular arguments. It will be harder for people to lie to you.

> <

The essays in this book will show you writing patterns to imitate and avoid. You cannot become a good writer simply by knowing how words are spelled and where commas go. You need a clearly defined subject, a personal voice, and an effective presentation of your information. *What you have to say is of the essence of good writing.* And the study of logic should make what you have to say more persuasive and meaningful.

EXERCISES

Can you argue the truth of these assertions?

1. "Blessed are the pure in heart; for they shall see God."
2. Mexico City's Copper Dome is higher than the Empire State Building.
3. It is wrong to say "between you and I."
4. Babe Ruth was a better baseball player than Dizzy Dean.
5. Patty Hearst was brainwashed.
6. "The child is father to the man."
7. Abortion is a sin.
8. "The crux of the biscuit is the apostrophe."
9. "Everything tastes more or less like chicken."
10. Dogs are better pets than cats.
11. "The style is the man himself."
12. Olympia Spalanzani is a doll.
13. Stolichnaya—"the only vodka imported from Russia."
14. One way to relieve the gasoline shortage is to legalize marijuana.
15. "The climate of the Caymans is conducive to concinnity."

CHARLES HARTSHORNE

Concerning Abortion: An Attempt at a Rational View

My onetime colleague T. V. Smith once wrote a book called *Beyond Conscience,* in which he waxed eloquent in showing "the harm that good men do." To live according to one's conscience may be a fine thing, but what if A's conscience leads A to try to compel B and C to live, not according to B's or C's conscience, but according to A's? That is what many opponents of abortion are trying to do. To propose a constitutional amendment to this effect is one of the most outrageous attempts to tyrannize over others that I can recall in my long lifetime as an American citizen. Proponents of the antiabortion amendment make their case, if possible, even worse when they defend themselves with the contention "It isn't my conscience only—it is a commandment of religion." For now one particular form of religion (certainly not the only form) is being used in an attempt to tyrannize over other forms of religious or philosophical belief. The separation of church and state evidently means little to such people.

IN WHAT SENSE "HUMAN"?

Ours is a country that has many diverse religious groups, and many people who cannot find truth in any organized religious body. It is a country that has great difficulty in effectively opposing forms of killing that *everyone* admits to be wrong. Those who would saddle the legal system with matters about which consciences sincerely and strongly differ show a disregard of the country's primary needs. (The same is to be said about crusades to make things difficult for homosexuals.) There can be little freedom if we lose sight of the vital distinction between moral questions and legal ones. The law compels and coerces, with the implicit threat of violence; morals seek to persuade. It is a poor society that forgets this difference.

What is the *moral* question regarding abortion? We are told that the fetus is alive and that therefore killing it is wrong. Since mosquitoes, bacteria, apes and whales are also alive, the argument is less than clear. Even plants are alive. I am not impressed by the rebuttal "But plants, mosquitoes, bacteria and whales are not human, and the fetus is." For the issue now becomes, *in what sense* is the fetus human? No one denies that its origin is human, as is its *possible* destiny. But the same is true of every unfertilized egg in the body of a nun. Is it wrong that some such eggs are not made or allowed to become human individuals?

Granted that a fetus is human in origin and possible destiny, in what further sense is it human? The entire problem lies here. If there are pro-life activists who have thrown much light on this question, I do not know their names.

One theologian who writes on the subject—Paul Ramsey—thinks that a human egg cell becomes a human individual with a moral claim to survive if it has been fertilized. Yet this egg cell has none of the qualities that we have in mind when we proclaim our superior worth to the chimpanzees or dolphins. It cannot speak, reason, or judge between right and wrong. It cannot have personal relations, without which a person is not functionally a person at all, until months—and not, except minimally, until years—have passed. And even then, it will not be a person in the normal sense unless some who are already fully persons have taken pains to help it become a human being in the full value sense, functioning as such. The antiabortionist is commanding some person or persons to undertake this effort. For without it, the fetus will *never* be human in the relevant sense. It will be human only in origin, but otherwise a subhuman animal.

The fertilized egg is an individual egg, but not an individual human being. For such a being is, in its body, a multicellular organism, a *metazoan*—to use the scientific Greek—and the egg is a single cell. The first thing the egg cell does is to begin dividing into many cells. For some weeks the fetus is not a single individual at all, but a colony of cells. During its first weeks there seems to be no ground for regarding the fetus as comparable to an individual animal. Only in possible or probable destiny is it an individual. Otherwise it is an organized society of single-celled individuals.

A possible individual person is one thing; an actual person is another. If this difference is not important, what is? There is in the long run no room in the solar system, or even in the known universe, for all human eggs—even all fertilized eggs, as things now stand—to become human persons. Indeed, it is mathematically demonstrable that the present rate of population growth must be lowered somehow.

It is not a moral imperative that all possibilities of human persons become actual persons.

Of course, some may say that the fertilized egg already has a human soul, but on what evidence? The evidence of soul in the relevant sense is the capacity to reason, judge right and wrong, and the like.

GENETIC AND OTHER INFLUENCES

One may also say that since the fertilized egg has a combination of genes (the units of physical inheritance) from both parents, in this sense it is already a human individual. There are two objections, either one in my opinion conclusive but only one of which is taken into account by Ramsey. The one he does mention is that identical twins have the same gene combination. The theologian does not see this as decisive, but I do.

The other objection is that it amounts to a very crude form of materialism to identify individuality with the gene-combination. Genes are the chemical bearers of inherited traits. This chemical basis of inheritance presumably influences everything about the development of the individual—*influences*, but does not fully determine. To say that the entire life of the person is determined by heredity is a theory of unfreedom that my religious conviction can only regard as monstrous. And there are biophysicists and neurophysiologists who agree with me.

From the gene-determined chemistry to a human person is a long, long step. As soon as the nervous system forming in the embryo begins to function as a whole—and not before—the cell colony begins to turn into a genuinely individual animal. One may reasonably suppose that this change is accompanied by some extremely primitive individual animal feelings. They cannot be recognizably human feelings, much less human thoughts, and cannot compare with the feelings of a porpoise or chimpanzee in level of consciousness. That much seems as certain as anything about the fetus except its origin and possible destiny. The nervous system of a very premature baby has been compared by an expert to that of a pig. And we know, if we know anything about this matter, that it is the nervous system that counts where individuality is concerned.

Identical twins are different individuals, each unique in consciousness. Though having the same genetic makeup, they will have been differently situated in the womb and hence will have received different stimuli. For that reason, if for no other, they will have developed differently, especially in their brains and nervous systems.

But there are additional reasons for the difference in development. One is the role of chance, which takes many forms. We are passing through a great cultural change in which the idea, long dominant in science, that chance is "only a word for our ignorance of causes" is being replaced by the view that the real laws of nature are probabilistic and allow for aspects of genuine chance.

Another reason is that it is reasonable to admit a reverse influence of the developing life of feelings in the fetus on the nervous system, as well as of the system upon the feelings. And since I, along with some famous philosophers and scientists, believe in freedom (not solely of mature human beings but—in some slight degree—of all individuals in nature, down to the atoms and farther), I hold that even in the fetus the incipient individual is unconsciously making what on higher levels we call "decisions." These decisions influence the developing nervous system. Thus to a certain extent we *make our own bodies* by our feelings and thoughts. An English poet with Platonic ideas expressed this concept as follows:

> *The body from the soul its form doth take,*
> *For soul is form and doth the body make.*

The word soul is, for me, incidental. The point is that feelings, thoughts, experiences react on the body and partly mold its development.

THE RIGHTS OF PERSONS

Paul Ramsey argues (as does William Buckley in a letter to me) that if a fetus is not fully human, then neither is an infant. Of course an infant is not fully human. No one thinks it can, while an infant, be taught to speak, reason, or judge right and wrong. But it is much closer to that stage than is a three-month fetus. It is beginning to have primitive social relations not open to a fetus; and since there is no sharp line anywhere between an infant and a child able to speak a few words, or between the latter and a child able to speak very many words, we have to regard the infant as significantly different from a three-month or four-month fetus. Nevertheless, I have little sympathy with the idea that infanticide is just another form of murder. Persons who are already functionally persons in the full sense have more important rights even than infants. Infanticide can be wrong without being fully comparable to the killing of persons in the full sense.

Does this distinction apply to the killing of a hopelessly senile person (or one in a permanent coma)? For me it does. I hope that no one will think that if, God forbid, I ever reach that stage, it must be for my sake that I should be treated with the respect due to normal human beings. Rather, it is for the sake of others that such respect may be imperative. Symbolically, one who has been a person may have to be treated as a person. There are difficulties and hazards in not so treating such individuals.

Religious people (I would so describe myself) may argue that once a fetus starts to develop, it is for God, not human beings, to decide whether the fetus survives and how long it lives. This argument assumes, against all evidence, that human life-spans are independent of human decisions. Our medical hygiene has radically altered the original "balance of nature." Hence the population explosion. Our technology makes pregnancy more and more a matter of human decision; more and more our choices are influencing the weal and woe of the animals on this earth. It is an awesome responsibility, but one that we cannot avoid. And, after all, the book of Genesis essentially predicted our dominion over terrestrial life. In addition, no one is proposing to make abortion compulsory for those morally opposed to it. I add that everyone who smokes is taking a hand in deciding how long he or she will live. Also everyone who, by failing to exercise reasonably, allows his or her heart to lose its vigor. Our destinies are not simply "acts of God."

I may be told that if I value my life I must be glad that I was not aborted in the fetus stage. Yes, I am glad, but this expression does not constitute a claim to having already had a "right," against which no other right could prevail, to the life I have enjoyed. I feel no indignation or horror at contemplating the idea that the world might have had to do without me. The world could have managed, and as for what I would have missed, there would have been no such "I" to miss it.

POTENTIAL, NOT ACTUAL

With almost everything they say, the fanatics against abortion show that they will not, or cannot, face the known facts of this matter. The inability of a fetus to say "I" is not merely a lack of skill; there is nothing there to which the pronoun could properly refer. A fetus is not a person but a *potential* person. The "life" to which "pro-life" refers is nonpersonal, by any criterion that makes sense to some of us. It is subpersonal animal life only. The mother, however, *is* a person.

I resent strongly the way many males tend to dictate to females their behavior, even though many females encourage them in this. Of course, the male parent of a fetus also has certain rights, but it remains true that the female parent is the one most directly and vitally concerned.

I shall not forget talking about this whole matter to a wonderful woman, the widow of a philosopher known for his idealism. She was doing social work with young women and had come to the conclusion that abortion is, in some cases, the lesser evil. She told me that her late husband had said, when she broached the subject to him, "But you can't do that." "My darling," she replied, "we *are* doing it." I see no reason to rate the consciences of the pro-lifers higher than this woman's conscience. She knew what the problem was for certain mothers. In a society that flaunts sex (its pleasures more than its serious hazards, problems and spiritual values) in all the media, makes it difficult for the young to avoid unwanted pregnancy, and does little to help them with the most difficult of all problems of self-discipline, we tell young persons that they are murderers if they resort to abortion. And so we should not be surprised that Margaret Mead, that clearsighted observer of our society (and of other societies), should say, "Abortion is a nasty thing, but our society deserves it." Alas, it is too true.

I share something of the disgust of hard-core opponents of abortion that contraceptives, combined with the availability of abortion, may deprive sexual intercourse of spiritual meaning. For me the sacramental view of marriage has always had appeal, and my life has been lived accordingly. Abortion is indeed a nasty thing, but unfortunately there are in our society many even nastier things, like the fact that some children are growing up unwanted. This for my conscience is a great deal nastier, and truly horrible. An overcrowded world is also nasty, and could in a few decades become truly catastrophic.

The argument against abortion (used, I am sorry to say, by Pearl Buck) that the fetus may be a potential genius has to be balanced against the much more probable chance of its being a mediocrity, or a destructive enemy of society. Every egg cell is a possible genius and also a possible monster in human form. Where do we stop in calculating such possibilities?

If some who object to abortion work to diminish the number of unwanted, inappropriate pregnancies, or to make bearing a child for adoption by persons able to be its loving foster parents more attractive than it now is, and do this with a minimum of coercion, all honor to them. In view of the population problem, the first of these remedies should have high priority.

Above all, the coercive power of our legal system, already

stretched thin, must be used with caution and chiefly against evils about which there is something like universal consensus. That persons have rights is a universal belief in our society, but that a fetus is already an actual person—about that there is and there can be no consensus. Coercion in such matters is tyranny. Alas for our dangerously fragmented and alienated society if we persist in such tyranny.

DISCUSSION QUESTIONS

1. Why did the author call his essay "an attempt" at a rational view of abortion?
2. Define the words "soul," "person," "human," and "moral."
3. The author refers to persons opposing abortions as "proponents of the antiabortion amendment," "antiabortionists," "activists," "hard-core opponents of abortion," "the fanatics against abortion," and advocates of "the most outrageous attempt to tyrannize over others." How else might these people be described?
4. The author describes himself as "an American citizen" and as one of the "religious people." How else might he be described?
5. "I may be told that if I value my life I must be glad that I was not aborted in the fetus stage. Yes, I am glad, but this expression does not constitute a claim to have already had a 'right,' against which no other right could prevail, to the life I have enjoyed. I feel no indignation or horror at contemplating the idea that the world might have had to do without me. The world could have managed, and as for what I would have missed, there would have been no such 'I' to miss it." In this kind of passage, an author is telling about both an issue and himself. What does this section tell you about him?
6. The author talks about preserving the lives of unfertilized human-eggs, fertilized eggs, fetuses, babies, adults who fail to exercise, adults who smoke, and hopelessly senile people. How parallel are these examples? What is the author's point in mentioning such instances?
7. He also refers to the life of plants, bacteria, mosquitoes, whales, dolphins, apes, and chimpanzees. Do these help his case? Do any of the examples complicate his case?
8. The author refers to fertilized eggs, a colony of cells, possible persons, and potential persons. How would a prolife advocate describe such entities?
9. If the entire abortion issue were described as "semantic," would it be less crucial and dramatic? Is it essentially semantic?

Breakdown in Family Life

The truth is evident; we can no longer deny the fact . . . morals in the United States have and are declining at a frightening speed.

Immorality in all its corrupting aspects is sweeping through our country like a wild and uncontrollable hurricane.

What once was considered debased, sinful, and forbidden (not too long ago) is now accepted and unfortunately tolerated by the good. Pagan Rome in her most corrupt and lurid days did not surpass the immorality of our times.

The collapse of moral society stems chiefly from the breakdown in family life. Countless marriages are not of God. Sensuality, parental irresponsibility, alcoholism, and the absence of religion are the chief spearheads of destruction. There are too many faithless husbands—as well as faithless wives, and too many abandoned children.

The following groups play a major part in the moral decay of family life:

PLEASURE-MAD PARENTS

These parents are occupied solely with earthly enjoyments. They spend their best years racing from one passing pleasure to another. They usually have little religion—or no religion at all. Their children are brought up in a materialistic atmosphere. Stress is placed on what to get out of life. God and religion are left out of the picture. A large percentage of our young criminals emerge from such homes. Is it any wonder?

WORKING PARENTS

This group also plays a vital part in moral destruction. Both the father and mother work, only to try to "get ahead," too often to keep up with the neighbors.

The youngest children are placed in day care centers. They

Source: Reprinted from *The Wanderer* (March 7, 1981), p. 2.

are at the tenderest years when they need the watchful care and the deepest love of a mother. The older children are left to shift for themselves until evening when the tired parents return home.

Unsupervised children feel free to go to any place and every place. They never miss the opportunity to explore, not only playgrounds and parks, but stores, movies, and every available door that is open to them. They spend long hours in bookstores or at newsstands, browsing through every magazine and comic book. Immorality flaunts in too many of these comics. Many magazines today illustrate every form of obscenity. Many of these same youths become victims of drugs and end in serious trouble. They not only wreck their own lives but shatter the lives of others.

A concrete example of a home without unity and with parents not fulfilling their duty, and the wrecking of a young life was heard in the trial of a recent young criminal.

The youth stoutly declared that his downfall began in his own home, where there was no family love, understanding, or religion. He strongly pointed out: "My father's sole interests were work and money. He always came home disgruntled and quarrelsome. I longed for his attention, understanding, and companionship. I wanted his guidance, but I was too afraid to approach him. My mother was always nagging and impatient with the four children; she complained of all the housework that she had to do; she never—or seldom— showed any warmth or affection for us. Bored with the duties at home, she went to work as a secretary. It was just the time when all her children were most impressionable and needed her most.

"Neither of my parents ever tried to understand me; my problems were my own. My desires, my love, my longings, dreams, fears, weaknesses, and strengths were kept locked within me. Nothing about me ever seemed of importance to them.

"I went outside my home for companionship and comfort. My choice of friends was not wisely selective; anyone was suitable. Soon I lost interest in school, played truant, got in with a gang of tough boys. We did anything for excitement. We stole, drank, fought, gambled, and took dope. Soon I became an addict. From here I went from bad to worse; one crime followed another until finally I took the life of two of my companions. It would all have been different if my home life had but been a happy one. Now I am but a condemned murderer. Only death will give me relief."

If family life is to survive, not only must indifferent parents change their attitude and views of life, but every home and every person must struggle to make the family a community of love, each one sharing and giving of self, all united in joy and sorrow, each recognizing lawful authority, giving obedience and respect when it is due, all promoting peace, order, and love.

Religion must play the major role in every home. Love of God and love of neighbor must be the motivating force in every home. It would be well and most pleasing to God to have the enthronement of the Sacred Heart in all Catholic homes. Some families might consider the family Rosary; others, reading Sacred Scripture, while some might prefer inspirational prayers. All are pleasing to God and will strengthen every member of a household.

Pope John Paul, in view of the dangers engulfing family life, recently pleaded with all Christians:

"Work and pray to foster the spirit of love within families, to make every home a church."

DISCUSSION QUESTIONS

1. "Immorality in all its corrupting aspects is sweeping through our country like a wild and uncontrollable hurricane." What is the author referring to here?
2. What evidence is offered to support this claim? What could be?
3. If American homes often contain alcoholic, materialistic, and indifferent parents, how can the author object to children being sent to day-care centers?
4. What evidence is offered to indicate that, in families where both father and mother work, they are doing so "to keep up with the neighbors"? Is an alternative explanation possible?
5. Consider the language of the young murderer:

   > *Soon I became an addict. From here I went from bad to worse; one crime followed another until finally I took the life of two of my companions. It would all have been different if my home life had but been a happy one. Now I am but a condemned murderer. Only death will give me relief.*

   What conclusion can you draw from these words? Does this sound like ghetto or criminal language? What does it sound like?
6. If family life is to survive, the author writes, "every person must struggle to make the family a community of love, each one sharing and giving of self, all united in joy and sorrow, each recognizing lawful authority, giving obedience and respect when it is due, all promoting peace, order, and love." Is it possible to argue with such a claim?

STEPHEN JAY GOULD

Evolution as Fact and Theory

Kirtley Mather, who died last year at age 89, was a pillar of both science and the Christian religion in America and one of my dearest friends. The difference of half a century in our ages evaporated before our common interests. The most curious thing we shared was a battle we each fought at the same age. For Kirtley had gone to Tennessee with Clarence Darrow to testify for evolution at the Scopes trial of 1925. When I think that we are enmeshed again in the same struggle for one of the best documented, most compelling and exciting concepts in all of science, I don't know whether to laugh or cry.

According to idealized principles of scientific discourse, the arousal of dormant issues should reflect fresh data that give renewed life to abandoned notions. Those outside the current debate may therefore be excused for suspecting that creationists have come up with something new, or that evolutionists have generated some serious internal trouble. But nothing has changed; the creationists have not a single new fact or argument. Darrow and Bryan were at least more entertaining than we lesser antagonists today. The rise of creationism is politics, pure and simple; it represents one issue (and by no means the major concern) of the resurgent evangelical right. Arguments that seemed kooky just a decade ago have re-entered the mainstream.

CREATIONISM IS NOT SCIENCE

The basic attack of the creationists falls apart on two general counts before we even reach the supposed factual details of their complaints against evolution. First, they play upon a vernacular misunderstanding of the word "theory" to convey the false impression that we evolutionists are covering up the rotten core of our edifice. Second, they misuse a popular philosophy of science to argue that they are behaving scientifically in attacking evolution. Yet the same philosophy demonstrates that their own belief is not science, and that "scientific creationism" is therefore meaningless and self-contradictory, a superb example of what Orwell called "newspeak."

In the American vernacular, "theory" often means "imperfect fact"—part of a hierarchy of confidence running downhill from fact to theory to hypothesis to guess. Thus the power of the creationist argument: evolution is "only" a theory, and intense debate now rages about many aspects of the theory. If evolution is less than a fact, and scientists can't even make up their minds about the theory, then what confidence can we have in it? Indeed, President Reagan echoed this argument before an evangelical group in Dallas when he said (in what I devoutly hope was campaign rhetoric): "Well, it is a theory. It is a scientific theory only, and it has in recent years been challenged in the world of science—that is, not believed in the scientific community to be as infallible as it once was."

Well, evolution *is* a theory. It is also a fact. And facts and theories are different things, not rungs in a hierarchy of increasing certainty. Facts are the world's data. Theories are structures of ideas that explain and interpret facts. Facts do not go away when scientists debate rival theories to explain them. Einstein's theory of gravitation replaced Newton's, but apples did not suspend themselves in mid-air pending the outcome. And human beings evolved from apelike ancestors whether they did so by Darwin's proposed mechanism or by some other, yet to be discovered.

Moreover, "fact" does not mean "absolute certainty." The final proofs of logic and mathematics flow deductively from stated premises and achieve certainty only because they are *not* about the empirical world. Evolutionists make no claim for perpetual truth, though creationists often do (and then attack us for a style of argument that they themselves favor). In science, "fact" can only mean "confirmed to such a degree that it would be perverse to withhold provisional assent." I suppose that apples might start to rise tomorrow, but the possibility does not merit equal time in physics classrooms.

Evolutionists have been clear about this distinction between fact and theory from the very beginning, if only because we have always acknowledged how far we are from completely understanding the mechanisms (theory) by which evolution (fact) occurred. Darwin continually emphasized the difference between his two great and separate accomplishments: establishing the fact of evolution, and proposing a theory—natural selection—to explain the mechanism of evolution. He wrote in *The Descent of Man:* "I had two distinct objects in view; firstly, to show that species had not been separately created, and secondly, that natural selection had been the chief agent of change . . . Hence if I have erred in . . . having exaggerated its [natural selection's] power . . . I have at least, as I hope, done good service in aiding to overthrow the dogma of separate creations."

Thus Darwin acknowledged the provisional nature of natural selection while affirming the fact of evolution. The fruitful theoretical debate that Darwin initiated has never ceased. From the 1940s through the 1960s, Darwin's own theory of natural selection did achieve a temporary hegemony that it never enjoyed in his lifetime. But renewed debate characterizes our decade, and, while no biologist questions the importance of natural selection, many now doubt its ubiquity. In particular, many evolutionists argue that substantial amounts of genetic change may not be subject to natural selection and may spread through populations at random. Others are challenging Darwin's linking of natural selection with gradual, imperceptible change through all intermediary degrees; they are arguing that most evolutionary events may occur far more rapidly than Darwin envisioned.

Scientists regard debates on fundamental issues of theory as a sign of intellectual health and a source of excitement. Science is—and how else can I say it?—most fun when it plays with interesting ideas, examines their implications, and recognizes that old information may be explained in surprisingly new ways. Evolutionary theory is now enjoying this uncommon vigor. Yet amidst all this turmoil no biologist has been led to doubt the fact that evolution occurred; we are debating *how* it happened. We are all trying to explain the same thing: the tree of evolutionary descent linking all organisms by ties of genealogy. Creationists pervert and caricature this debate by conveniently neglecting the common conviction that underlies it, and by falsely suggesting that we now doubt the very phenomenon we are struggling to understand.

Using another invalid argument, creationists claim that "the dogma of separate creations," as Darwin characterized it a century ago, is a scientific theory meriting equal time with evolution in high school biology curricula. But a prevailing viewpoint among philosophers of science belies this creationist argument. Philosopher Karl Popper has argued for decades that the primary criterion of science is the falsifiability of its theories. We can never prove absolutely, but we can falsify. A set of ideas that cannot, in principle, be falsified is not science.

The entire creationist argument involves little more than a rhetorical attempt to falsify evolution by presenting supposed contradictions among its supporters. Their brand of creationism, they claim, is "scientific" because it follows the Popperian model in trying to demolish evolution. Yet Popper's argument must apply in both directions. One does not become a scientist by the simple act of trying to falsify another scientific system; one has to present an alternative system that also meets Popper's criterion—it too must be falsifiable in principle.

"Scientific creationism" is a self-contradictory, nonsense phrase precisely because it cannot be falsified. I can envision observations and experiments that would disprove any evolutionary theory I know, but I cannot imagine what potential data could lead creationists to abandon their beliefs. Unbeatable systems are dogma, not science. Lest I seem harsh or rhetorical, I quote creationism's leading intellectual, Duane Gish, Ph.D., from his recent (1978) book *Evolution? The Fossils Say No!* "By creation we mean the bringing into being by a supernatural Creator of the basic kinds of plants and animals by the process of sudden, or fiat, creation. We do not know how the Creator created, what processes He used, *for He used processes which are not now operating anywhere in the natural universe* [Gish's italics]. This is why we refer to creation as special creation. We cannot discover by scientific investigations anything about the creative processes used by the Creator." Pray tell, Dr. Gish, in the light of your last sentence, what then is "scientific" creationism?

THE FACT OF EVOLUTION

Our confidence that evolution occurred centers upon three general arguments. First, we have abundant, direct, observational evidence of evolution in action, from both the field and the laboratory. It ranges from countless experiments on change in nearly everything about fruit flies subjected to artificial selection in the laboratory to the famous British moths that turned black when industrial soot darkened the trees upon which they rest. (The moths gain protection from sharp-sighted bird predators by blending into the background.) Creationists do not deny these observations; how could they? Creationists have tightened their act. They now argue that God only created "basic kinds," and allowed for limited evolutionary meandering within them. Thus toy poodles and Great Danes come from the dog kind and moths can change color, but nature cannot convert a dog to a cat or a monkey to a man.

The second and third arguments for evolution—the case for major changes—do not involve direct observation of evolution in action. They rest upon inference, but are no less secure for that reason. Major evolutionary change requires too much time for direct observation on the scale of recorded human history. All historical sciences rest upon inference, and evolution is no different from geology, cosmology, or human history in this respect. In principle, we cannot observe processes that operated in the past. We must infer them from results that still survive: living and fossil organisms for evolution, documents and artifacts for human history, strata and topography for geology.

The second argument—that the imperfection of nature reveals evolution—strikes many people as ironic, for they feel that evolution should be most elegantly displayed in the nearly perfect adaptation expressed by some organisms—the chamber of a gull's wing, or butterflies that cannot be seen in ground litter because they mimic leaves so precisely. But perfection could be imposed by a wise creator or evolved by natural selection. Perfection covers the tracks of past history. And past history—the evidence of descent—is our mark of evolution.

Evolution lies exposed in the *imperfections* that record a history of descent. Why should a rat run, a bat fly, a porpoise swim, and I type this essay with structures built of the same bones unless we all inherited them from a common ancestor? An engineer, starting from scratch, could design better limbs in each case. Why should all the large native mammals of Australia be marsupials, unless they descended from a common ancestor isolated on this island continent? Marsupials are not "better," or ideally suited for Australia; many have been wiped out by placental mammals imported by man from other continents. This principle of imperfection extends to all historical sciences. When we recognize the etymology of September, October, November, and December (seventh, eighth, ninth, and tenth, from the Latin), we know that two additional items (January and February) must have been added to an original calendar of ten months.

The third argument is more direct: transitions are often found in the fossil record. Preserved transitions are not common—and should not be, according to our understanding of evolution (see next section)—but they are not entirely wanting, as creationists often claim. The lower jaw of reptiles contains several bones, that of mammals only one. The non-mammalian jawbones are reduced, step by step, in mammalian ancestors until they become tiny nubbins located at the back of the jaw. The "hammer" and "anvil" bones of the mammalian ear are descendants of these nubbins. How could such a transition be accomplished? the creationists ask. Surely a bone is either entirely in the jaw or in the ear. Yet paleontologists have discovered two transitional lineages of therapsids (the so-called mammal-like reptiles) with a double jaw joint—one composed of the old quadrate and articular bones (soon to become the hammer and anvil), the other of the squamosal and dentary bones (as in modern mammals). For that matter, what better transitional form could we desire than the oldest human, *Australopithecus afarensis,* with its apelike palate, its human upright stance, and a cranial capacity larger than any ape's of the same body size but a full 1,000 cubic centimeters below ours? If God made each of the half dozen human species discovered in ancient rocks, why did he create in an unbroken temporal sequence of progressively more modern features—increasing cranial capacity, reduced face and teeth, larger body size? Did he create to mimic evolution and test our faith thereby?

AN EXAMPLE OF CREATIONIST ARGUMENT

Faced with these facts of evolution and the philosophical bankruptcy of their own position, creationists rely upon distortion and innuendo to buttress their rhetorical claim. If I sound sharp or bitter, indeed I am—for I have become a major target of these practices.

I count myself among the evolutionists who argue for a jerky, or episodic, rather than a smoothly gradual, pace of change. In 1972 my colleague Niles Eldredge and I developed the theory of punctuated equilibrium [*Discover,* October]. We argued that two outstanding facts of the fossil record—geologically "sudden" origin of new species and failure to change thereafter (stasis)—reflect the predictions of evolutionary theory, not the imperfections of the fossil record. In most theories, small isolated populations are the source of new species, and the process of speciation takes thousands or tens of thousands of years. This amount of time, so long when measured against our lives, is a geological microsecond. It represents much less than 1 per cent of the average life span for a fossil invertebrate species—more than 10 million years. Large, widespread, and well-established species, on the other hand, are not expected to change very much. We believe that the inertia of large populations explains the stasis of most fossil species over millions of years.

We proposed the theory of punctuated equilibrium largely to provide a different explanation for pervasive trends in the fossil record. Trends, we argued, cannot be attributed to gradual transformation within lineages, but must arise from the differential success of certain kinds of species. A trend, we argued, is more like climbing a flight of stairs (punctuations and stasis) than rolling up an inclined plane.

Since we proposed punctuated equilibria to explain trends, it is infuriating to be quoted again and again by creationists—whether through design or stupidity, I do not know—as admitting that the fossil record includes no transitional forms. Transitional forms are generally lacking at the species level, but are abundant between larger groups. The evolution from reptiles to mammals, as mentioned earlier, is well documented. Yet a pamphlet entitled "Harvard Scientists Agree Evolution Is a Hoax" states: "The facts of punctuated equilibrium which Gould and Eldredge . . . are forcing Darwinists to swallow fit the picture that Bryan insisted on, and which God has revealed to us in the Bible."

Continuing the distortion, several creationists have equated the theory of punctuated equilibrium with a caricature of the beliefs of Richard Goldschmidt, a great early geneticist. Goldschmidt argued, in a famous book published in 1940, that new groups can arise all at once through major mutations. He referred to these suddenly transformed creatures as "hopeful monsters." (I am attracted to some aspects of the non-caricatured version, but Goldschmidt's theory still has nothing to do with punctuated equilibrium.) Creationist Luther Sunderland talks of the "punctuated equilibrium hopeful monster theory" and tells his hopeful readers that "it amounts to tacit admission that anti-evolutionists are correct in asserting there is no fossil evidence supporting the theory that all life is connected to a common ancestor." Duane Gish writes, "According to Goldschmidt, and now apparently according to Gould, a reptile laid an egg from which the first bird, feathers and all, was produced." Any evolutionist who believed such nonsense would rightly be laughed off the intellectual stage; yet the only theory that could ever envision such a scenario for the evolution of birds is creationism—God acts in the egg.

CONCLUSION

I am both angry at and amused by the creationists; but mostly I am deeply sad. Sad for many reasons. Sad because so many people who respond to creationist appeals are troubled for the right reason, but venting their anger at the wrong target. It is true that scientists have often been dogmatic and elitist. It is true that we have often allowed the white-coated, advertising image to represent us—"Scientists say that Brand X cures bunions ten times faster than . . ." We have not fought it adequately because we derive benefits from appearing as a new priesthood. It is also true that faceless bureaucratic state power intrudes more and more into our lives and removes choices that should belong to individuals and communities. I can understand that requiring that evolution be taught in the schools might be seen as one more insult on all these grounds. But the culprit is not, and cannot be, evolution or any other fact of the natural world. Identify and fight your legitimate enemies by all means, but we are not among them.

I am sad because the practical result of this brouhaha will not be expanded coverage to include creationism (that would also make me sad), but the reduction or excision of evolution from high school curricula. Evolution is one of the half dozen "great ideas" developed by science. It speaks to the profound issues of genealogy that fascinate all of us—the "roots" phenomenon writ large. Where did we come from? Where did life arise? How did it develop? How are organisms related? It forces us to think, ponder, and wonder. Shall we deprive millions of this knowledge and once again teach biology as a set of dull and unconnected facts, without the thread that weaves diverse material into a supple unity?

But most of all I am saddened by a trend I am just beginning to discern among my colleagues. I sense that some now wish to mute the healthy debate about theory that has brought new life to evolutionary biology. It provides grist for creationist mills, they say, even if only by distortion. Perhaps we should lie low and rally round the flag of strict Darwinism, at least for the moment—a kind of old-time religion on our part.

But we should borrow another metaphor and recognize that we too have to tread a straight and narrow path, surrounded by roads to perdition. For if we ever begin to suppress our search to understand nature, to quench our own intellectual excitement in a misguided effort to present a united front where it does not and should not exist, then we are truly lost.

DISCUSSION QUESTIONS

1. Trace the outline of this essay. Does the clarity of organization make it a more effective argument?
2. The author says the phrase "scientific creationism" is meaningless and self-contradictory. How is it self-contradictory? Can any word be meaningless?
3. The author says, "A set of ideas that cannot, in principle, be falsified is not science." What does this mean? Why can't the creationist view be falsified?
4. Trace the evidence that the author gives to show evolution is a fact. Does it help his case that different kinds of evidence converge to support him?
5. The author finds himself quoted as a scientist who is rejecting evolution. Wouldn't this justify an angry response? Why doesn't the author make one?
6. Is the author's argument weakened by his use of words like "hegemony," "ubiquity," "therapsids," "quadrate," "squamosal," "stasis," "speciation," and "equilibria"?

Poster distributed by the American Lung Association.

DISCUSSION QUESTIONS

1. What evidence does this poster offer to support the claim "Smoking spoils your looks"?
2. Do cigarettes in her ears spoil Brooke Shields' looks?
3. Do you think a cigarette lodged (more traditionally) in her hand or her mouth would spoil her looks?
4. If "looks" are not central to the case, what is the real argument that Ms. Shields and the American Cancer Society are offering?

Induction

What I tell you three times is true.
LEWIS CARROLL, *The Hunting of the Snark*

Induction is the process of arriving at a general conclusion on the basis of incomplete evidence. Most of the things you know, you know by induction.

You believe, for example, that polar bears are white. But because you haven't seen all polar bears, your judgment is based on limited evidence. The two or three polar bears you have seen were white. Those shown in *National Geographic* and in Disney movies were white. Everyone you know agrees they are white. From this information, you reasonably decide that all polar bears are white.

This process is induction. You consider evidence you have seen or heard to draw a conclusion about things you haven't seen or heard. The intellectual movement from limited facts—called a *sample*—to a general conviction is called an inductive leap. Most conclusions regarding past, present, and future events are based on this kind of leap. You believe that Balboa discovered the Pacific Ocean, that taking Tylenol eases a headache, and that the Democrats will win the next presidential election. Because you can never secure all the evidence relating to these questions, you reasonably make judgments from the evidence you have.

It is equally reasonable, on hearing induced conclusions, to inquire about the number and kinds of facts that went into them. For a claim to be creditable, its sample must be (1) known, (2) sufficient, and (3) representative. If you are told simply that the FBI is directed by Jewish conspirators, you can withhold belief on the ground that the sample is not known. No evidence is given to support the accusation. If you hear a famous athlete's low IQ cited to demonstrate that all athletes (or all members of the athlete's race or nationality) are intellectually weak, you can respond that the sample is not sufficient. One example proves nothing about a large group. And if you hear the cruelties of the Spanish Inquisition used as evidence of the repressive views of Catholics in general, you can insist that the sample is not representative. Spanish practice in the fifteenth century is hardly typical of worldwide Catholicism today.

26

You should recognize such unsubstantiated claims when you see them and work to keep them out of your own writing.

IS THE SAMPLE KNOWN?

You frequently hear statements that lack evidence. Advertisements announce that "Ban is preferred by seven out of ten American women" and that "four out of five top movie stars use Lustre-Creme shampoo." Rumor whispers that Viceroy filters are made of harmful fiberglass and that fluoridated drinking water can cause brain damage. Such claims can be dismissed if no evidence is ever offered to support them.

A variation popular with sensational writers is to make an extravagant claim and point to conclusive evidence—which happens to be unavailable. They charge that Warren Harding was murdered by his wife and that Franklin Roosevelt was poisoned by the Russians at Teheran; then they regret that evidence is lost in the past. They affirm the existence of abominable snowmen, the true "Shakespeare," Atlantis, and the Loch Ness monster; then they lament that proof remains out of reach. They know that UFOs are extraterrestrial spaceships and that a massive conspiracy led to the attempted assassinations of President Reagan and Pope John Paul II— then they protest that government officials and law-enforcement agencies are withholding crucial evidence. These too are inductions with an absent sample.

IS THE SAMPLE SUFFICIENT?

Induction with an insufficient sample is common. You regularly hear charges like these:

> Most labor leaders are crooks. Look at Tony Boyle, Frank
> Brewster, Jimmy Hoffa, and Roy Williams.
> The Medicaid system is unfair. Let me tell you what happened
> to my father-in-law.
> Don't talk to me about Puerto Ricans. I lived next to a Puerto
> Rican family for two years.

Clearly, the indicated samples—*four* labor leaders, *one* relative, and *one* family—are inadequate evidence on which to base any broad conclusion.

Advocates of a particular view commonly try to broaden the effect of limited examples by declaring them "typical" or "average." They remain limited examples. *In argument, the words "typical" and "average" deserve immediate suspicion.*

IS THE SAMPLE REPRESENTATIVE?

A sample is said to be unrepresentative when it is not typical of the whole class of things being studied. It is easy to see that you cannot gauge your town's attitude toward a proposed liquor tax by polling only the citizens at a corner tavern or only members of the local Baptist church.

Nevertheless, conclusions based on an unrepresentative sample can be quite deceptive on first hearing; for example, "Women are better drivers than men; they have fewer accidents." Here the sample is large enough—a substantial body of accident statistics—but it is not broad enough to be meaningful. The conclusion concerns *all drivers,* but the sample group includes only *drivers who have had accidents.* To be representative (i.e., typical of the whole area under discussion), the sample must include all four groups involved:

1. *men*
2. *women*
3. *drivers who had accidents*
4. *drivers who had no accidents*

With this broad sample you could see that there are fewer women in automobile accidents because there are fewer women driving. The isolated accident statistics are meaningless if not compared to those for all drivers.

Similarly, if you hear that 60 percent of all lung cancer victims were moderate-to-heavy smokers or that 80 percent of all San Quentin convicts came from homes that served liquor, you can draw no significant conclusion. The implied judgments describe *everyone,* but the samples include only *cancer victims* and *convicts;* there are no general statistics with which to make comparison. Perhaps 60 percent of all adults are moderate smokers and 80 percent of all homes serve liquor. Then, of course, the narrower statistics become meaningless.

Any induced conclusion is open to question, then, if its sample is too small or unduly weighted in some way. The Nielsen rating service claims to know the audience size for American television programs. But because its information comes from 1100 audiometers (one for every 50,000 homes), the sufficiency of the sample is doubtful. *The Hite Report* on female sexuality is based on responses to questionnaires mailed to chapters of the National Organization for Women, abortion-rights groups, and university women's centers; on information from women who saw notices in the newspaper, the *Village Voice,* and in *Mademoiselle, Bride's,* and *Ms.* magazines and who wrote in for the questionnaires; and on responses from female readers of *Oui* magazine, which ran the questionnaire in its entirety. Clearly, the representativeness of the sample is open to question. The 100,000 questionnaires produced some 3000 responses.

Any poll with a selective sample—that is, where some individuals choose to respond to it and others do not—is unrepresentative.

POLLING

People can misuse a poll to make it support a favored opinion. They can announce the results of surveys that were never taken. (Politicians have for years made good use of "private polls" to enhance the prestige of a lagging candidate.) They can phrase a poll question to draw the response they seek. (An evangelical questionnaire asked, "Do you approve of PORNOGRAPHIC and obscene classroom textbooks being used under the guise of sex education? Yes   No") Or they can inflate others' polls. (In 1972, Washington television station WTTG asked viewers to write in their opinion of President Nixon's decision to mine North Vietnamese harbors: The final count showed 5157 supporting the president and a much smaller number opposing him. Later investigation showed that some 4000 of the votes favorable to Mr. Nixon came directly from the Committee to Re-elect the President.)

What is an adequate sample on which to base a reliable judgment? There is no easy answer. This varies with both the character of the question and the degree of probability one seeks.

You should remember, however, that a small sample—if generally representative—can sustain a broad conclusion. George Gallup assesses the opinions of the American public by polling 1500 individuals. But because his sample is chosen so that every adult American has an equal chance of being interviewed, the Gallup Poll, like similar polls, is a reliable source of information. The mathematical probability is that, 95 times out of 100, a selection of 1500 anonymous people will give results no more than 3 percentage points off the figures that would be obtained by interviewing the whole population.

Over the past twenty-three national elections, the Gallup predictions were an average of 2.3 percent off the exact results.

In the 1980 presidential election, however, both the Gallup and the Harris polls were 4 percent off the final total. Apparently, many voters made up their minds at the last minute, after these polls had been completed. Both Mr. Carter's and Mr. Reagan's personal pollsters, who surveyed opinion right up to election eve, predicted the final results exactly.

OCCAM'S RAZOR

Even in everyday experience you commonly use very limited information to draw a tentative conclusion. This is not unreasonable. If you see a girl not wearing her engagement ring and behaving despondently, you may speculate that she has broken her engagement. The evidence is not sufficient for you to offer condolences, but it will keep you from making jokes about marriage.

If you hear from a friend that a new movie is disappointing, you will probably choose not to see it—at least until you hear a contrary report. Your conclusion is based on a tiny sample, but it is all the sample you have. As your sample grows, so will your degree of conviction.

With induction, you should remember *Occam's razor,* the maxim that when a body of evidence exists, the simplest conclusion that expresses all of it is probably the best. A perfect illustration occurred in 1967 when New Orleans District Attorney James Garrison sought to prove that Clay Shaw, a local businessman, was involved in the assassination of President Kennedy. He submitted that Shaw's address book carried the entry "Lee Odom, P.O. Box 19106, Dallas, Texas," and that the number "PO 19106," when properly decoded, became "WH 15601," the unlisted phone number of Jack Ruby, slayer of Kennedy's assassin Lee Oswald. (The process involved "unscrambling" the numerals and—since P and O equal 7 and 6 on a telephone dial—subtracting 1300.) Thus Garrison used the entry in Shaw's address book as inductive evidence leading to a sensational conclusion. But Occam's razor suggests a simpler explanation, one that proved to be a fact: Shaw was acquainted with a businessman named Lee Odom, whose Dallas address was P.O. Box 19106.

You should remember Occam's razor when you read the many books and articles that "reexamine" famous crimes. Routinely, they conclude that people like Lee Harvey Oswald, Alger Hiss, Lizzie Borden, Bruno Hauptmann, Carl Coppolino, James Earl Ray, Sam Sheppard, the Rosenbergs, Alice Crimmins, and Sacco and Vanzetti were really innocent. The true criminal was either a shadowy figure whom nobody saw or members of some complex and incredible conspiracy. Occam's razor submits that the person with the motive and the opportunity and the weapon is probably guilty.

> <

As you read, examine carefully the facts underlying conclusions. Are they given? Are they sufficient and representative? As you write, support your generalizations as much as you can.

EXERCISES

How reliable are these inductive arguments?

1. In a study of a possible relationship between pornography and antisocial behavior, questionnaires went out to 7500 psychiatrists and psychoanalysts, whose listing in the directory of the American Psychological Association indicated clinical experience. Over 3400 of these professionals responded. The result: 7.4 percent of the psychiatrists and psychologists had cases in which they were convinced that pornography was a causal factor in antisocial behavior; an additional 9.4 percent were suspicious; 3.2 percent did not commit themselves; and 80 percent said they had no cases in which a causal connection was suspected.

2. "Proven most effective against colds."—Listerine Antiseptic advertisement.
3. I'm not going to sign up for Professor Feldman's class. Several of my friends had the course and disliked it.
4. How can you argue that large families frustrate the individual child? Benjamin Franklin was the eighth child of his parents. There were six in the Washington family, and Abraham Lincoln had seven brothers and sisters. The Jeffersons numbered ten; the Madisons, twelve; the Longfellows, eight; and the Beethovens, twelve.
5. I don't care what you say about stereotypes. Most of the blondes I know *are* dumb.
6. Cola drinkers were asked to compare glasses of Coke and Pepsi for better taste. The Coke was in a glass marked Q, and the Pepsi in a glass marked M. A majority of those tested said they preferred the taste of Pepsi.
7. Certainly it's obvious from the newspaper reports that rich and famous people have a higher proportion of divorces than the general public.
8. A study of 3400 New York citizens who had had recent heart attacks showed that 70 percent of them were 10 to 50 pounds overweight. Clearly, obesity is the cause of heart disease.
9. Arguing that eighteenth-century English poetry was essentially prosaic, Matthew Arnold offered a passage from "Pope's verse, take it almost where you will":

> *To Hounslow Heath I point and Banstead Down;*
> *Thence comes your mutton and these chicks my own.*

10. Don't tell me that homosexuals aren't sick. I'm a psychiatrist with a large number of homosexual patients, and all are deeply disturbed. Every one of them.
11. Four out of five dentists who were surveyed recommended Trident sugarless gum for their patients who chew gum.

ESSAY ASSIGNMENTS

Write an essay either affirming or opposing one of these statements. The arguments you encounter in your background reading will probably be inductive, and so will your essay.

1. Prisoners should be brainwashed.
2. ESP has been proved to exist.
3. Absurd drama is a waste of time.
4. Rock music is a national danger.
5. Jogging is a perfect exercise.
6. American Catholicism is approaching heresy.
7. X is worth saving. (Fill in the X.)

ANN JONES
Putting Away Alice Crimmins

When the police arrived at the apartment in Kew Gardens, Queens, they found Edmund Crimmins, a husky aircraft mechanic thickened by too much beer-drinking, and his twenty-six-year-old wife, Alice. Eddie, separated from his wife, had been summoned by her frantic 9:00 A.M. phone call: the children, five-year-old Eddie and four-year-old Alice Marie, called Missy, had disappeared from their bedroom. Detective Gerard Piering, in the absence of senior detectives, fell into command of his first major case; and according to all reports, he took one look at Alice Crimmins and disliked her. Alice Crimmins was what the newspapers called a "shapely" woman in toreador pants, her strawberry blond hair carefully teased and lacquered, her makeup perfectly applied. She cast herself in the same mold as Candy Mossler and Lana Turner, but she was a working-class housewife. To Jerry Piering, Catholic father of six, she did not look like "Mother." When he gave orders to question Eddie and Alice Crimmins separately, he announced to his partner, "I'll take the bitch." That afternoon he took Alice Crimmins to a vacant lot half a mile away to look at her dead daughter. Missy was lying on her side in the sun, her pajama top knotted around her neck, her body swarming with flies. Alice Crimmins staggered, swooned, and fell into the arms of a detective; but she didn't cry. To Piering her reaction was too theatrical—not like a real mother; he was sure he had his murderer. That evening when reporter Kenneth Gross went on assignment to the Crimmins apartment, other reporters and photographers popping flashbulbs in Alice Crimmins's face told him what the police had told them: "The bitch killed her kids."

The police continued to question Eddie Crimmins and to check out tips on prowlers and known sex offenders, but they focused on Alice Crimmins. They tapped her telephone and bugged the new apartment that she and Eddie, temporarily reconciled by crisis, shared; but in three years of listening in on the life of Alice Crimmins, they found no bit of incriminating evidence to use against her.

Source: From *Women Who Kill* by Ann Jones. Copyright © 1980 by Ann Jones. Reprinted by permission of Holt, Rinehart and Winston, Publishers.

Perhaps that's why they turned nasty and began to harass her in other ways. When she went to bed with another man in her apartment, the listening police phoned Eddie and told him to go home. Whenever she got a new job under her maiden name—she was an executive secretary and reportedly an excellent one—the police visited her employer and told him who she was. They leaked word to the press that although their bugging tapes wouldn't be admissible in court, they proved that Alice had killed her children. Soon it was "common knowledge" among the police and the press that Alice Crimmins was guilty of murder, though so far there wasn't any evidence to prove it. There was plenty of evidence, however, on the tapes and off, that Alice Crimmins had had sexual relations with several different men. What's more, she never denied it, never was ashamed of it, and even when she knew the police were watching her constantly, she never made the slightest effort to change her ways. "If she were my wife," said Detective Piering, "I'd kill her." Instead, on September 13, 1967, he arrested Alice Crimmins for the murder of her daughter. She was tried and convicted of manslaughter.

During the trial there was scarcely a fact that was not in dispute. A good deal of what should have constituted the physical evidence in this case existed only in the memory of Detective Piering. Whether the children could have been taken or enticed through the bedroom window and whether they had eaten veal or manicotti for supper became issues of crucial significance, but only Piering had seen the layer of dust on the bureau under the window and the manicotti carton in the trash. He had made no note at the time, no photographic record. He just remembered. The testimony of the star witnesses for the prosecution, Joseph Rorech and Sophie Earomirski, was equally problematical. Rorech, once a high-rolling contractor rapidly going bankrupt and an ex-boyfriend of Alice Crimmins, testified that she had confessed killing Missy in anger, and through the help of another boyfriend, summoned a hit man to silence little Eddie, who had witnessed the killing. Alice screamed that Rorech was lying.

There was no incontrovertible proof on either side; everything depended on whose word was believed. Could one believe the testimony of star witness Sophie Earomirski, the middle-aged housewife who came forward eighteen months after the children's disappearance to say that at 2:00 A.M. on July 14, 1965, she had seen Alice Crimmins, a little boy, a dog, and a big man throwing a bundle into the back of a car? The defense pointed out that Sophie Earomirski had filed a workman's compensation claim for brain damage—she had jumped and struck her head at work when a "yellow mouse" ran up her arm—had attempted suicide with an overdose of tranquilizers,

and had once been found with her head in the oven. (She was checking on dinner, she said.) Sophie Earomirski marched into court like a
soldier, and after telling her improbable tale, she marched out again
with her fist raised in triumph while the appreciative courtroom
crowd cheered her on. She was photographed like that—the moment's
hero—for all the papers. Nothing made it quite so clear that what was
going on was not a search for justice but a war on Alice Crimmins.

Crimmins reacted accordingly: scornful, unashamed, hurt,
and defiant. Outside the courtroom she masked the grief she refused
to share with the public behind a desperate, brittle gaiety. Inside the
courtroom, she was angry; and when she took the stand her cold
anger told against her. Later she told reporter Gross that when she re-
read her own testimony she thought she sounded like a bitch. "But
the thing is," she explained, "I was angry. I just wanted to get to the
point. That man, the prosecutor, he kept asking me those questions
about sex. I wanted to get to the point. He only wanted to know about
sex." Her own attorneys wanted her to change her hairdo, her dress,
her style; they wanted her to break down and cry for the jury, but she
would not. The prosecution took her angry composure for hardness
and worse.

To the press she was a sexy swinger. The pulp *Front Page Detective* featured the story of "Sexpot on Trial," calling her an "erring
wife, a Circe, an amoral woman whose many affairs appeared symp-
tomatic of America's Sex Revolution." The New York *Daily News*
called her "the Queens housewife with hamster morals." Her name
was rarely mentioned without some descriptive swipe: curvy, comely,
shapely, flame-haired, blonde. And always she was identified by an
occupation she had filled for only six months: the ex-cocktail waitress—a term used pejoratively to sneer at Alice Crimmins and a
whole category of women workers at once. Before long the terms lost
their meaning and became merely slurs so that on a single page of a
newspaper she might be identified as a "sllekly [*sic*] attractive red-
head" in one column and a "shapely blonde" in the next. But they all
added up to bitch and the capacity to kill. A Queens housewife who
attended several sessions of the trial told *New York Times* reporter
Lacey Fosburgh that she found it hard to believe that any woman
could kill her children, but "a woman like that . . . well . . . it makes
it easier to understand." One of the jurors agreed: "A tramp like that
is capable of anything." There was no question that Alice Crimmins
was a woman "like that"; her own attorney said she was "amoral"
and acknowledged that the jury had been forced to listen to a lot of
"filth."

But Alice Crimmins, who thought the prosecution never did get to the point, got a new defense team and fought back. In May 1968 the Appellate Division reversed her conviction and ordered a new trial because three of the jurors admitted visiting the scene without permission. The prosecution retaliated by carrying the case before a second grand jury which, in July 1970, returned indictments charging Alice Crimmins with manslaughter in the death of her daughter and murder in the death of her son. (Indicting her a second time for murder in her daughter's death would have constituted double jeopardy.) On March 15, 1971, she went on trial again.

The court heard the same conflicting, inconclusive evidence that had filled the newspapers before; and a few additional witnesses added to the confusion. The alleged hit man identified by Crimmins's ex-boyfriend Joseph Rorech took the stand for the defense; Vincent Colabella, serving a twenty-year sentence in Atlanta penitentiary on drug charges, testified that he had never seen Alice Crimmins before but that a former Queens assistant district attorney had offered to let him "go home free" if he would say that he had gone to the Crimmins apartment and found both children already dead. A woman testified that she had seen the same group—woman, boy, dog, and man with bundle—that Sophie Earomirski claimed to have spotted from her window. Marvin Weinstein testified that he and his family, leaving a friend's Kew Gardens apartment at 2:00 A.M., may well have been the group that Earomirski saw. The friend, Anthony King, said the Weinstein family hadn't been at his house. Mrs. Weinstein came in to court to say that they had so; and another of King's acquaintances testified that King was a notorious liar.

So it went, back and forth, until Dr. Milton Halpern, New York City's chief medical examiner and undoubtedly the world's most famous "coroner," testified unequivocally that Missy Crimmins had died within two hours of eating her last meal, which consisted in part of "macaroni." Somehow, in that snarl of charge and countercharge, Helpern's testimony seemed a decisive scientific fact that pinned the murder on Alice Crimmins and the vanished manicotti carton— despite her own insistence that she had fed the children veal at 7:30 and seen them alive at midnight. Meanwhile, the press raked over Alice Crimmins's sex life again, and there was nothing to prevent twelve graying, middle-aged male jurors, who were never sequestered, from taking it all in. The judge instructed them to use their common sense, and on April 23, 1971, they announced their verdict: guilty of murder in the first degree—the most severe judgment they could have reached. Crimmins was sentenced to life imprisonment on the murder charge and five to twenty years for manslaughter; bail was denied as attorney Herbert Lyon, who always maintained that she had been tried for her morals and not for murder, began the complicated legal battle to free her.

Two years later, on May 7, 1973, the Appellate Division overturned both convictions because of various "errors and improprieties" by the prosecution prejudicial to the defendant. The court threw out the murder conviction altogether and ordered that Crimmins be retried on the manslaughter charge. Having served two years in prison, Crimmins was released, but in February 1975 the State Court of Appeals reversed the decision of the Appellate Court. (The Appeals Court did agree to throw out the murder conviction because the state could not prove beyond reasonable doubt that little Eddie Crimmins, found five days after his disappearance and too badly decomposed for autopsy, had in fact been murdered.) But it upheld the manslaughter conviction—although in order to do so it had to establish a new interpretation of the law. Formerly errors in trial procedure had been considered prejudicial to the defendant if there was a "rational possibility" that the jury would have acquitted the defendant if the error had not occurred. The Appeals Court now maintained that an error was prejudicial only if there was "significant probability" that without it the case would have gone the other way. Two dissenting justices argued that by accepting the new standard the court was "dangerously diluting the time-honored standard of proof beyond a reasonable doubt, cornerstone of Anglo-Saxon criminal jurisprudence," but the majority bounced the case back to the Appellate Division judges with orders that they look at it again; and, in light of the new standard applied by the higher court, the Appellate Division reversed its own reversal and declared that Alice Crimmins was indeed guilty of manslaughter. On May 16, 1975, she was returned to prison to continue serving out her five- to twenty-year term; and in December the Court of Appeals ruled that she could not appeal any further. It took a succession of district attorneys, a flock of underlings, thousands of police man-hours, three grand juries, two trials, a reinterpretation of appellate law, and ten years, but at last Alice Crimmins was put away.

> <

Perhaps Alice Crimmins was guilty. Perhaps not. Certainly the fragmentary evidence did not prove her guilt beyond a reasonable doubt; but she was granted no presumption of innocence. It is not that anyone deliberately set out to convict an innocent woman, but that so many people—beginning with Detective Piering—almost immediately assumed she was guilty because she was "like that."

DISCUSSION QUESTIONS

1. Does the essay argue that Alice Crimmins was innocent of the charges brought against her? What does it argue?

2. What do each of the following contribute to the conclusion that Alice Crimmins was guilty?

   > her free life-style
   > her response to seeing Missy's body
   > Joseph Rorech's evidence
   > Sophie Earomirski's evidence
   > her angry composure on the witness stand
   > that the Appellate Division reversed her first conviction
   > Vincent Colabella's evidence
   > Marvin Weinstein's evidence
   > Anthony King's statement
   > Dr. Halpern's testimony
   > the Appellate Division's second overturning of the convictions
   > The State Court of Appeals' reversal of the decision of the Appellate
   >   Division

3. What do each of these contribute to the argument that Alice Crimmins was convicted for being "like that"?

   > Detective Piering's attitude
   > police harassment
   > sensational stories in the press
   > the view of the Queens housewife quoted by Lacey Fosburgh
   > the opinion of "one of the jurors"
   > Sophie Earomirski's attitude
   > the fact that one jury was all graying, middle-aged males
   > the fact that the jury was never sequestered
   > all the appeals and reversals that followed the verdict in the original
   >   trial
   > the final reinterpretation of appellate law

4. Consider the stereotypes in this essay. What can you reasonably assume about an ex-cocktail waitress, a Catholic father of six, a high-rolling contractor who is rapidly going bankrupt, a woman who attempted suicide, and a graying middle-aged male?

5. " 'If she were my wife,' said Detective Piering, 'I'd kill her.' Instead, on September 13, 1967, he arrested Alice Crimmins for the murder of her daughter." How are these two sentences connected?

Why Haven't Marijuana Smokers Been Told These Facts?

From New York, N.Y. comes the most shocking and frightening collection of facts, research and medical findings about the dangers of smoking marijuana ever put together. An easy-to-read, eye-opening, absolutely fascinating digest of doctors' findings, medical journal reports, government studies, etc. all so startling and devastating ... so absolutely convincing ... that they are unconditionally guaranteed to make anyone you love **stop smoking marijuana**—and never touch it again.

A FATHER'S CONCERN

An East Coast father, convinced that his children were damaging themselves by smoking marijuana, and unable to answer their arguments that "marijuana is no worse than cigarettes or alcohol," determined to assemble the facts which would **prove** to them how harmful marijuana really is. He read every book on the subject he could find ... every doctor's report ... every governmental study ... every police report ... every magazine article ... every report from ancient times right up to the present. And everywhere he found a devastating case against marijuana. **The more he read, the more overwhelming the case against marijuana became.**

THE REAL MARIJUANA DANGER

He read of marijuana causing memory loss, lethargy, **actual physical brain damage.** He read of how doctors have documented that marijuana causes damage to the liver, brain, lungs and respiratory tract. He read of how marijuana can cause **damage to pregnant women and their unborn children.** Of marijuana leading to decreased sexual

Source: Advertisement for *With Love, From Dad.* Sold by Book Distributors, Inc., Smithtown, NY 11787 (1981). The ad is not edited. All ellipsis marks are those of the author.

enjoyment—or even impotence. He read of lives being ruined because of the way marijuana undermines a person's drive, dissipates energy . . . leaves users without ambition, without the will to succeed— passive, lazy, disoriented, unable to make decisions. He read of how fatal car accidents can be caused by marijuana . . . how depth perception changes and how a car that looks far away to a marijuana user can actually be only a few feet away. He even read findings that marijuana is linked to cancer.

And this is just the beginning! In all he discovered that there is a frightening, overwhelming case against marijuana . . . and the damage it can inflict on his children. But he was faced with one big problem. How to get his children to read this massive and lengthy evidence which had taken literally years of work to assemble.

758 EYE-OPENING DIGESTS!

He decided to **digest** all the frightening facts he had collected. He took all the reports, studies, medical findings, etc. by doctors, hospitals, clinics and government agencies and compressed each into 758 fascinating, easy-to-read and fact-filled digests that can be read in as **little as 15 seconds each.** And on top of each short digest he put a compelling and dramatic headline. Then he gave the result of his years of work to his children with **absolutely no "sales talk" of any kind!** An amazing thing happened! Suddenly those children who "knew it all" and who had heard so often that marijuana is "no worse than cigarettes or alcohol" were confronted with the OTHER SIDE of the story.

RENOWNED AUTHORITIES

For the first time they learned from doctors, medical experts, researchers, even former users themselves, about the harm marijuana can **really** do. For the first time they read that marijuana can actually damage the brain, the lungs, the liver. For the first time they learned how marijuana can cause death by completely distorting a driver's depth perception leading to terrible automobile accidents. For the first time they understood why so many people's lives are being destroyed because marijuana leaves users without energy, without drive, without ambition . . . without the will to succeed . . . and often **without them realizing that it is happening!** For the first time they read about marijuana causing impotence . . . even cancer.

And they read all this and much more without any "Sales Talk" of any kind. No preaching. Nothing but the facts in fascinating, easy-to-read digest form. They didn't even have to start at the beginning! No matter where they opened the father's startling report, they saw 3, 4, or 5 fascinating headlines followed by short digests they could read in as little as 15 seconds. And the more they read, the more shocked they became, just as their father had in his years of work. Yes! **For the first time they learned that anyone who smokes marijuana has to be out of his mind!**

WHAT THIS MEANS TO YOU

And now do you realize what this father's report can mean to you? It means that you can at least "reach" young people with the facts they cannot argue against. You can finally convince them once and for all that marijuana is dangerous.

WITH LOVE, FROM DAD

This remarkable and documented Father's Report is called "With Love, From Dad." It contains 758 digests and headlines and is the result of four years of work by a father who cares. If you care about the health and welfare of **your** children, we urge you to send for **your** copy today. The potency of the marijuana being smoked today is three to ten times stronger than the marijuana available just two years ago. **Never** has it been more important for your children to know the truth about marijuana. And it is up to you to give them the facts they **need** to know.

"With Love, From Dad" is not available in stores. The only way to get your copy is to follow these easy instructions. Simply put your name and address on a piece of paper with the words "With Love, From Dad" and mail it with $9.95 cash, check or money order to: Book Distributors, Inc., Department 41, 155 East Main Street, Smithtown, N.Y. 11787. Your copy will be mailed with the guarantee that you must agree it is the most important gift you ever gave your children or your purchase price will be refunded without question.

DISCUSSION QUESTIONS

1. The author ("Dad") claims that smoking marijuana causes brain damage, liver dysfunction, harm to pregnant women and their unborn children, lung damage, decreased sexual enjoyment, impotence, impaired depth perception leading to fatal accidents, cancer, and loss of the will to succeed. He asks, "Why haven't marijuana smokers been told these facts?" Can you think of an answer?
2. Are all these effects equally subject to scientific scrutiny?
3. The author's sources are "every book on the subject he could find, every

doctor's report, every governmental study, every police report, every magazine article, every report from ancient times right up to the present.'' What sources is he referring to? Do they sound equally valid as scientific documents?

4. Did he encounter no pro-marijuana literature at all?
5. ''Dad'' got his information from the works of ''doctors, medical experts, researchers, even former users themselves.'' Who are these people?
6. Who is ''Dad''? Why didn't the ad give his name?
7. Is there any evidence that ''Dad'' had other motives besides saving young people from the horrible effects of marijuana?

WILSON BRYAN KEY

Subliminal Seduction in Advertising

The full-page, four-color Calvert whiskey advertisement in the October 1971 *Playboy* appears to have ushered in a new trend in subliminal manipulative technique that might well have originated in medieval witchcraft—which, of course, all of us know was pure nonsense, based upon sheer ignorance and superstition (see Figure 1).

Before proceeding, study carefully the Calvert ad for several minutes while relaxed. Try to understand how the ad makes you feel. Then briefly write out these feelings so you can check back later on how you reacted before the analysis.

The bottom of the glass contains a cone-shaped volcano from which the whiskey and ice appear to have erupted. The volcano is an ancient symbol of fertility, in that volcanic earth is the world's most fertile soil. However, the volcano and its destructive fire are also linked with the idea of evil, symbolic not only of nature's primary force (creation), but of the fire of life (destruction). The volcano represents the passions which control our energies, a sudden and frightening eruption (orgasm) preceded by an extended time of internal, enclosed, intensifying pressure.

And, what has erupted from the Calvert volcano? Life, of course, symbolized in the golden richness of Calvert Extra Blended Whiskey. Gold— the symbol of divine intelligence, all that is superior, spiritual determination, hidden or elusive treasures, and supreme insight and wisdom—would naturally be the color of Calvert.

Just to the left of the volcano's erupting crater is a fish, swimming in the golden sea of Calvert whiskey. The fish has been symbolically known as the mystic ship of life, phallically penetrating the water as it swims, spiritually symbolic of the relationship between heaven and earth, the life force surging upward, and the spiritual world that lies beneath the illusionary visual world. Christ was often symbolized as a fish.

A mouse, however, appears to be riding the fish, its eyes and

Source: Reprinted from *Subliminal Seduction* by Wilson Bryan Key (Englewood Cliffs, N.J.: Prentice-Hall, 1973), pp. 100–106.

Soft Whiskey à la mode.

The hardest thing about it is the rocks.

nose facing the rear of the fish, its tail curved up over its back across the large right ear. The large ear suggests a mouse rather than a rat. The mouse in medieval symbolism was often associated with the devil. Symbolically, the devil is looking back upon where the fish or life force has swum. To the left and above the mouse's head, in the bottom left-hand corner of the ice cube, is the sun, its rays shining down, penetrating the golden Calvert sea of life and its inhabitants.

In the cold, dead world above Calvert's ocean of life, however, is another story. Just to the left of the sun appears a skull, the brain case marked with wavy lines, the jaws open and foreboding. The skull, of course, is symbolic of man's mortality, that which survives his being once his life and body have disappeared.

To the right, frozen into the ice cube above the golden liquid, are scorpions. The scorpion for thousands of years has symbolized the period of man's existence in which he is threatened by death. In medieval Christian art the scorpion was utilized as a symbol for treachery.

Three wolf faces appear above the scorpions. One face is to the left of the bell-shaped white space at the top of the ice cube. The nose points down at a 45 degree angle toward the bottom right corner of the cube face; the two eyes—teardrop shaped—point up and out toward the animal's ears. Behind or above and to the left of the wolf is another wolf face supported by a long neck. The second wolf appears to be biting the ear or neck of the wolf in front. To the right of the white space is the third wolf's head, the two eyes staring forward on each side of a triangular nose pointing down.

The wolf has appeared in Western culture for centuries as symbolic of evil, often a power enclosed in the bowels of the earth which at the end of the world would break free and devour the sun. The wolf myth has been related to the final annihilation of the world by fire and water.

Just to the left of the top left corner of the scorpion cube is the head of a rat, its head turned sideways, the nose pointing to the right, two ears and eyes to the left of the pointed nose. Only the head is visible, suggesting the rat may be swimming in the gray fluid symbolic of the life force which fills the ice cube and is draining out from the bottom corner of the cube on top of the skull. Gray, the color of volcanic ashes, or perhaps amniotic fluid, is symbolic of the earth and vegetation, depression, inertia, and indifference which is leaking out of the ice cube onto the surface of life.

Along the glass rim, to the right of the gray cube, is a lizard. The lizard often symbolizes distrust when it appears in dreams and often typifies one who is cold-blooded, groveling, and morally contemptible. In Japanese legends the lizard has symbolized a revengeful spirit with supernatural powers.

The top ice cube in the foreground, on the left, holds a mythological menagerie. If the cube is turned upside down—remember, the unconscious can read upside down, even mirror images—the head of a shark appears, with eyes and tooth-jagged jaws pointing to the left. Symbolic of danger, death, and evil, the shark as an archetype has been around since long before man; it is one of the earth's oldest creatures.

Just below the upside-down shark, a white bird appears in the ice cube, its head pointing down at the lower left corner of the cube. Birds have frequently symbolized human souls and carriers of the dead to paradise. In particular, the white bird is an archetypal symbol for the soul of the righteous. The white bird is upside down, or dead, in the Calvert ice cube.

To the right of the dead white bird, under the upside-down shark, appears a white mask which is an ancient symbol of deception, hypocrisy, and—in dreams—betrayal and lies. In Chinese drama a white mask represents a cunning and treacherous person.

Another mask, this one a full-face mask with a grotesque expression, appears below and to the right of the white mask, in the upper corner of the ice cube side panel facing down and to the right. The upper portion, eyes and nose, are colored brown. The lower portion of the face is white.

In the upper ice cube at the rear is another fish—the head facing left in the upper left corner—which seems to have an angry expression on its face. Beneath the fish is a form that eight out of ten test subjects identified as a white bird in flight; the head faces left, with a long neck extending to the body. A curved white line across the top of the body represents a wing in flight. The bird could be a swan. A flying bird archetypally symbolizes the flight of the soul to heaven.

Just below the swan's neck appear two dark areas, almost like eyes. Below these eyes is a small white knob that could be a nose. The white area seen above as a bird now becomes the top of a head—the bird's head becoming the left ear, the beginning of the bird's wing the right ear. The mouth of what has been unanimously identified by test subjects as a grinning white cat is partially hidden behind the distorted rim of the glass as it appears through the ice cube. The white cat is an ancient Christian symbol of laziness, lust, cruelty, egoism, flattery, treachery, and witchcraft.

It appears that Calvert Extra Blended Whiskey has a greater kick in it than anyone ever suspected. The fine details in the advertisement, including dozens of embedded SEXes in a mosaic, must have required hundreds of hours of labor by the artist. Embedding technique will be discussed in the next chapter, after which the reader should carefully review the Calvert—as well as the other ads—in this chapter. The painting, if accomplished outside the advertising frame of reference, might even be considered a masterpiece. Only the painting's major symbolic devices have been commented on here. There are many more, however, which readers may discover for themselves.

In all fairness, symbol analysis is a tricky business. Jung and many other experienced analysts continuously warned sternly against glib symbolic interpretations. Symbols have highly individual meanings in specific contexts. The object of advertising is sales, however, not psychotherapy. Advertising artists must apply symbolism likely to have wide similar meanings throughout their target markets. The interpretations of Calvert's ad were reviewed for variations in meaning with a panel of individuals and general consensus obtained on meanings before any single interpretation was accepted. This, of course, represents only a reasonable conscious interpretation of meaning. We can only speculate on the interpretations at the unconscious level. This does not mean, in any respect, that each reader would attribute precisely identical meaning or significance to these complex symbols—fish, scorpion, wolf, lizard, etc.

The interpretations presented here were reviewed against several major authoritative sources on symbolic meanings. Should any reader have a more lively, or more deeply involving conscious interpretation for any of the symbolism discussed in this book, he is urged to utilize his own meaning hypothesis for an explanation of the ad's effectiveness.

In the Calvert ad, it is absolutely certain that not more than one percent, if that many, of the over 20 million people who saw the ad consciously recognized the symbolic content. Indeed, one percent is a very high estimate for conscious cognition for any ad's symbolism. A medieval mentality would probably have recognized, at the conscious level, most of the symbolism instantly. Modern man, however, has been subjected to a very long, intensive socialization process during which he has learned to repress his conscious response to symbolic content. The Calvert ad symbolism, nevertheless, will register instantly within the unconscious of virtually everyone who perceives the ad anywhere in the Western culture—and very likely in Eastern cultures as well.

In attempting to penetrate meaning parameters in any symbolic media, the first step is to recognize the individual symbols and their meanings in the specific context. The second step is to synthesize the individual meanings into a whole to obtain a thematic meaning.

When the individual symbols are lumped together into one composite message, the Calvert ad communicated a fascinating concept into the unconscious psyches of many millions of readers—young and old, rich and poor, drinkers and nondrinkers. The thematic meaning of the Calvert ad is birth, life, and death—birth from the volcano, life in the golden sea of Calvert whiskey, and death through betrayal and degradation within the hard frozen ice cubes. Earlier a theory was developed that symbols are organized around the two polarities of human existence—the *origin* and the *end* of life. Most advertising focuses upon the origin of life, love, or—in the vulgar *Playboy* fantasy—sex. The Calvert ad covers the entire symbolic spectrum and, apparently, has successfully merchandised the product. The ad was published numerous times in several national media, including *Life* magazine with 7.5 million copies and 21 million readers.

That this advertisement was successful in selling whiskey is beyond question. The four-color page space rate in *Playboy* alone is nearly $40,000. No one fools around indiscriminately with $40,000, except possibly people in government. No businessman could tolerate unsuccessful advertising expenditures for a moment.

One question, then, remains to be considered in relation to the successful Calvert advertisement. *What does the ad do to the psyches of the over 40 million people who presumably perceived the colorful menagerie of death just in* Playboy *and* Life *magazines—especially those readers who have not yet taken a drink?*

Though directed only at the 4.5 percent of all adult men who consume four or more drinks of blended whiskey a week (heavy users), who account for 71.8 percent of all blended whiskey consumed by men, the ad was also perceived by millions of other people who do not drink, or at least did not drink until then. The Calvert Distilling Company has, one can be quite certain, pretest data on the advertisements. Perhaps a congressional investigating committee should ask for all the data it has collected on the social effects of such advertising.

According to the theory, either sex or death symbolism should work as a device by which to circumvent consciously discriminating perception. Throughout his history, man's major preoccupation has been with death, not sex. True, the population increase might be at least partially attributable to sex symbolism. However, man has worshipped death in his steady and brilliant development of weapons, elaborate rituals, and magnificent religious institutions, in the names of a hundred gods—burial temples from Egyptian pyramids to Hollywood's Forest Lawn Cemetery. Death has certainly provided mankind with a major preoccupation through thousands of years of history, during which he worked diligently to find ways in which his fear of death could be repressed, suppressed, or at least hidden temporarily from his constant conscious awareness.

New research now going on in the advertising industry is investigating the subliminal manipulability of man through death symbolism. So far, relatively few death-oriented ads have appeared in

American media. Sex has worked well for a very long time, but may be approaching a saturation point where its effectiveness has begun to decrease. Many research directors feel the SEX embeds may be losing their sell.

DISCUSSION QUESTIONS

1. In the Calvert ad, the author sees any number of images: a volcano, the sea, a fish, a mouse riding on the fish, a skull, scorpions, wolf faces, the head of a rat, a lizard, a shark's head, a white bird, a white mask, a full-face mask, an angry fish, a swan, a grinning white cat, and many embeddings of the word "SEX." How many of these can you see?
2. If you can't see all of these, will you grant that a person with more time, a richer imagination, and perhaps a better reproduction of the advertisement might find them?
3. Can you see a few images that the author didn't mention? If so, does it suggest the author was careless and overlooked a few pictures? What does it suggest?
4. The author asks you to view the ad from many angles. He says, "remember— the unconscious can read upside down, even mirror images." Is this true? Is the idea subject to proof?
5. The author interprets the images: for example, the volcano is orgasm; the sea is life; the fish can be a phallus or the life force or Christ; the mouse is the devil; the skull is human mortality; scorpions indicate treachery; wolves symbolize the end of the world; a lizard is vengeance; the shark is danger; a bird is the soul; the mask is hypocrisy; the swan is salvation; and the cat is laziness, lust, flattery, and witchcraft. How meaningful are these interpretations individually? Collectively?
6. Relating this commentary to Calvert whiskey, the author asks, "What does the ad do to the psyches of the over 40 million people who presumably perceived the colorful menagerie of death just in *Playboy* and *Life* magazines, especially those readers who have not yet taken a drink?" Comment.
7. The author speaks of "the subliminal manipulability of man through death symbolism." Does this make sense? Why or why not?

DISCUSSION QUESTIONS

1. Of what value is a poll on the creation-versus-evolution issue? Is this a question on which all opinions have equal weight?
2. Is there any evidence of bias in the phrasing of the poll questions?
3. What is the effect of offering to send the person who mails in his ballot a book "that gives overwhelming evidence in favor of creation"?
4. "Your vote urgently needed!" For what purpose might Dr. Falwell need these ballots?

Cast Your Vote for
☒ CREATION
or
☒ EVOLUTION

Where do you stand in this vital debate?

Jerry Falwell
Old-Time Gospel Hour

1. Do you agree with the "theories" of evolution that DENY the Biblical account of creation?
☐ YES ☐ NO

2. Do you agree that public school teachers should be permitted to teach our children as fact that they descended from APES?
☐ YES ☐ NO

3. Do you agree with the evolutionists who are attempting to PREVENT the Biblical account of creation from also being taught in public schools?
☐ YES ☐ NO

Answer and return today—Your vote urgently needed!

In return for your vote, I'll send you a FREE copy of "THE REMARKABLE BIRTH of PLANET EARTH"—a 111-page book that gives overwhelming evidence in favor of creation.

FREE BOOK!

Dr. Jerry Falwell
The Old-Time Gospel Hour
Lynchburg, Va. 24514

Name _____

Address _____

City _____ State _____ Zip _____

Any contribution to this campaign is tax deductible and deeply appreciated!

CEE

Please return this Entire Ballot

Deduction

All men are Socrates.

WOODY ALLEN

Deduction is the opposite of induction. Where induction moves from specific facts to a general conclusion, deduction moves from a general truth to a specific application. Because there are many kinds of deduction—some quite complicated—this discussion aims to be little more than a useful oversimplification.

The vehicle of deduction is the syllogism. The syllogism is an argument that takes two existing truths and puts them together to produce a new truth. Here is the classical example:

> MAJOR PREMISE: *All men are mortal.*
> MINOR PREMISE: *Socrates is a man.*
> CONCLUSION: *Socrates is mortal.*

In everyday affairs you meet many examples of deductive thinking. The syllogism is often abbreviated, however, with one of the parts implied rather than stated:

> *You haven't registered, so you can't vote. (IMPLICIT MAJOR*
> * PREMISE: Anyone who does not register cannot vote.)*
> *No man lives forever. Even old Rex Thompson will die*
> * someday. (IMPLICIT MINOR PREMISE: Rex Thompson is a man.)*
> *Anyone can make a mistake. After all, Roger is only human.*
> * (IMPLICIT CONCLUSION: Roger can make a mistake.)*

Many informal arguments can easily be resolved into syllogistic form. You do this so that you can judge their reliability more systematically.

A deductive argument is considered reliable if it fulfills three conditions: (1) the premise must be true; (2) the terms must be unambiguous, and (3) the syllogistic form must be valid. These requirements will be considered in turn.

ARE THE PREMISES TRUE?

First, the premises must be true. Because the major premise of a syllogism is usually derived by induction (i.e., it is a general statement drawn from specific facts), you can judge its reliability by asking whether the facts that produced it are known to be sufficient and representative. Here is a vulnerable example:

> *Gentlemen prefer blondes.*
> *George Bush is a gentleman.*
> *George Bush prefers blondes.*

This syllogism reaches an unreliable conclusion because the major premise is doubtful. The generalization about blondes exists only as a cliché (and as a title by Anita Loos); it is induced from no known sample. Political partisans regularly use dubious major premises (a war hero would make a good president; a divorced man would make a poor one; etc.) to produce desired conclusions.

IS THE LANGUAGE UNAMBIGUOUS?

The terms of deductive argument must be clear and consistent. If definitions change within a syllogism, arguments can be amusingly fallacious:

> *All cats chase mice.*
> *My wife is a cat.*
> *Therefore . . .*

> *All men are created equal.*
> *Women are not men.*
> *Therefore . . .*

But sometimes they can be genuinely misleading. The advertisement "See *King Kong*—the Academy Award Winner" was based on this syllogism:

> *The Academy Award winning movie is worth seeing.*
> *King Kong is this year's Academy Award winning movie.*
> *King Kong is worth seeing.*

Here the phrase "Academy Award winning movie" is ambiguous. In the major premise it refers to the movie chosen the best of the year; in the minor premise, to a movie winning one of the dozens of minor awards given annually. *King Kong* won its award for "Special Effects."

Ambiguous examples are not always frivolous. A major argument of our time involves these syllogisms:

Killing an innocent human being is murder.
Abortion kills an innocent human being.
Abortion is murder.

A medical procedure that preserves life and health should be
legal.
Abortion preserves life and health that would be endangered in
a clandestine operation.
Abortion should be legal.

Not all ambiguities are easily resolved.

IS THE SYLLOGISM VALID?

A reliable syllogism must have a valid form. This requirement introduces a complex area because there are many types of syllogisms, each with its own test for validity. Commonly, "valid form" means that the general subject or condition of the major premise must appear in the minor premise as well. It is easy to see that this argument is false:

All murderers have ears.
All Methodists have ears.
All murderers are Methodist.

What makes the argument unreliable syllogistically is the fact that the term "murderers" does not recur in the minor premise. A major premise about "all murderers" can only lead to a conclusion about murderers. Similarly, the premises "If Taylor loses his job, his wife will leave him" and "Taylor does not lose his job" produce no necessary conclusion. The condition "lose his job" does not occur in the minor premise.

When an invalid syllogism appears as argument, it usually maintains that things with one quality in common have a kind of identity. Such argument takes interesting forms:

The father of Miss Smith's baby has blood type O.
Charles Harwell has blood type O.
Therefore . . .

The American Communist party opposes resumption of the
draft.
Gene Schroeder opposes resumption of the draft.
Therefore . . .

Abraham Lincoln was a much-attacked president.
Jimmy Carter was a much-attacked president.
Therefore . . .

Because the crucial term does not appear in both premises of these syllogisms, any conclusion would be no more valid than the claim that all murders are Methodist.

These three tests, then, permit you to judge the reliability of a deductive argument.

INDUCTION OR DEDUCTION?

Because most syllogisms begin with an induced major premise, certain arguments can be analyzed as either induction or deduction. Here is an example: "Cecil Crow doesn't drink; he'll make some girl a fine husband." You can read this as a syllogism and attack the implicit major premise "Anyone who doesn't drink will make a fine husband." Or you can treat it as induction and argue that the sample (the fact that Cecil Crow doesn't drink) is insufficient to sustain a conclusion about his prospects as a husband. With such arguments, it is best not to quibble over terms; either approach is satisfactory.

When you evaluate a syllogism, it is best to judge it as reliable or unreliable, not as true or false. An unreliable conclusion, it must be remembered, may nevertheless be true. From the doubtful major premise ("Anyone who does not drink . . .") you cannot reasonably deduce that Cecil Crow will make a fine husband. But he might, in fact, make a very fine husband. In rejecting the syllogism as unreliable, you simply say that the fact is not proved by this argument.

You can recognize the distinction between truth and a reasonable conclusion by recalling a passage from Eugene Ionesco's *Rhinoceros.* In it the logician argues, "All cats die. Socrates is dead. Therefore Socrates is a cat." And his student responds, "That's true. I've got a cat named Socrates."

> <

Recognizing the syllogistic form of an argument will help you to analyze its reliability. It will also help you to structure an argumentative essay. Commonly, in deductive writing the first paragraph offers the major premise and the last paragraph, the conclusion. The body of the theme tries to demonstrate the minor premise. (This is, for example, the structure of the Declaration of Independence.)

EXERCISES

How reliable are these deductive arguments?

1. Of course Sylvia is a poor driver. She's a woman, isn't she?
2. How can you say you don't believe in miracles? The sunrise that occurs every day is a miracle.

3. Professor Costello's new book on marriage should be pretty informed. After all, he's been married four times.

4. Genuinely oppressed people (like the blacks) have lower academic scores and shorter life spans. Women do not have these. Women are not oppressed.

5. All lemons are yellow. My girl friend's brother is a lemon. My girl friend's brother is yellow.

6. The Roman Catholic Church should follow the example of Jesus. Jesus chose only men to preach his gospel. The Church should never permit women to be priests.

7. I'm from Milwaukee and I ought to know. Blatz is Milwaukee's finest beer.

8. My condition is beyond the help of medical science. Fortunately, Dr. Harris is a quack.

9. Both Catholics and Protestants are Christians. No one can be both Catholic and Protestant. Therefore no one can be a Christian.

10. The Easter Island statues could not have been carved, moved, and erected by mere humans. Because they were carved, moved, and erected, the work must have been done by superhuman agents.

11. The Easter Island statues were carved, moved, and erected by superhuman agents. Space travelers who could visit Earth must be superhuman agents. So the Easter Island statues must be the work of space travelers.

12. I love you; therefore I am a lover. All the world loves a lover. You are all the world to me. Therefore you love me.

ESSAY ASSIGNMENTS

Write an essay either affirming or opposing one of these statements.
The arguments you encounter in your background reading will probably
be deductive, and so will your essay.

1. Evolution is a foolish theory.
2. Marriage has a bleak future.
3. The Easter Island statues must have been erected by beings from outer space.
4. America needs stronger libel laws.
5. U.S. schools should not teach standard English exclusively.
6. The miracles of Jesus prove he was God.
7. X is a disease; it should not be punished but cured. (Fill in the X.)

Outlaw Lie-Detector Tests?

PRO AND CON

INTERVIEW WITH SENATOR BIRCH BAYH
Democrat, of Indiana

Q. Senator Bayh, why do you favor prohibiting the use of lie detectors—or polygraph tests—by private industry and the U.S. Government?

A. It just seems to me to be contrary to our basic ideas of freedom and individual rights in this country to say that, before you can get a job, you have to take a lie-detector test—and that, to keep a job, you have to be subjected periodically to that kind of intimidation. It's a kind of police-state treatment contrary to a free society. It was Richard Nixon in one of the Watergate tapes who said: "I don't know whether they're accurate or not, but that doesn't make any difference. Test them all. It'll scare the hell out of them."

Q. How is a lie-detector test any greater an infringement on a person's rights than an airline search, for example, or the blood test police give suspected drunken drivers?

A. The biggest difference is accuracy. We have a number of tests that citizens, either specifically or by implied consent, submit to: alcohol content in the blood while driving, the airline search. But those two tests can really be proved right beyond a scientific doubt. In an airline search, for example, if you get a suspicion, you find out quickly whether the machine is reacting to a set of house keys or a gun. And the test is justified, because there is the risk of imminent physical danger to many people.

Q. Doesn't the lie detector supply quick answers, too?

A. It is simply not reliable. A lie detector, you know, only measures stress—whatever the stress may be.

The fact is, the test does not necessarily prove that a person is telling the truth or that he is lying. A lot depends on the art or judg-

Source: Reprinted from *U.S. News & World Report.* Copyright 1978, U.S. News & World Report, Inc.

ment of the person who is running the test. It is not an exact science and is easily subject to misinterpretation.

Q. Do you mean lie detectors sometimes indicate a person is lying when he is, in fact, telling the truth?

A. The best research I know of indicates they're about 70 per cent accurate. Polygraph results can be highly misleading. They depend on the mind of the beholder. They are very subjective. For example, if someone is asked, "Have you ever stolen anything?" a response might be triggered if the person had taken cookies out of his grandmother's basket when he was 8 years old. Maybe the person is embarrassed about it and answers "No," and this shows up in his response.

Q. But aren't follow-up questions asked?

A. Oh, yes. They say: "Mr. Jones, there's a little shakiness in your answer about whether you've ever stolen anything. Is there anything in your background that could cause this machine to act up this way?" Operators pry and push and cajole to get people to sort of cleanse their souls. The polygraph-industry representative told me that with 90 per cent of the people they recommend not hiring, the reason is because of something the person has told them—not because of what the machine says.

The trouble is that it becomes a fishing expedition. And the more general the questions are, the less reliable the test is. A lot of people regurgitate private, personal things about themselves in an effort to prove the darn machine wrong. And the examiner makes a judgment to hire or fire. I think a good personnel man or manager is better equipped to make that decision.

Q. Just what would your bill ban?

A. What it says, in effect, is that when employers screen people for possible employment, or when they screen employes periodically to see if they've done anything wrong on the job, they cannot administer a lie-detector test. The same prohibition would apply to all agencies of the U.S. Government except two. The bill doesn't touch regular law-enforcement agencies' efforts in any way.

We have exempted the CIA and the National Security Agency, which are the only two agencies now using them. We felt the tests were justified there because they are only a very small part of a total investigative process, to which an applicant has consented. There is no meaningful consent for the usual job applicant or employe. It's take the test or lose the job!

Q. Wouldn't such a ban make it harder for businesses to detect thefts by employes?

A. According to the figures I have, about 20 per cent of employers use polygraphs. This means 80 per cent don't use them.

Take massive retail organizations like J. C. Penney or Sears. You would think that if this was the panacea for theft that some hold it out to be, these big retailers would be saying, "Let's put them to the lie-detector test." But they don't use them.

The lie detector is just a lazy person's way of trying to keep a "bad apple" from getting in his shop. I sympathize with the problem of theft that business has. But there are a lot more reliable ways to fight it. When you consider hiring somebody, you can make a background check, talk to past employers, look at employment records. You can certainly find out if the person has been convicted of crimes.

As for the loss of merchandise, the answer is better management, tighter security controls and inventory controls—not lie-detector tests.

Q. Some have proposed an alternative to a ban on lie detectors: U.S. Government licensing to insure that lie-detector operators are fully qualified. Would there be any merit in this?

A. No. There are some 15 States that now have controls on the use of lie detectors to some degree. Some States certify polygraph operators. But federal licensing, I am afraid, would lead to greater use, because people would feel that licensing meant the tests are credible. The fact is, in most courts of law, lie-detector findings are not considered reliable enough to be introduced as evidence. Also, operator error is only one side of the problem. There is also the feeling of intimidation in the mind of the person who is wired up and interrogated. There's no way that licensing can take care of that.

INTERVIEW WITH TY KELLEY Vice President, Government Affairs, National Association of Chain Drug Stores

Q. Mr. Kelley, why do you oppose legislation that would ban the use of lie detectors by private industry and the Federal Government?

A. At present, business and retailing are fighting an all-out war against crime and employe theft. A ban on lie detectors would make it more difficult for businesses to weed out job applicants who have a crime-related background, or a background of drug abuse. Since our members are in the drug-distribution business, we do not want individuals who have a history of drug abuse working in our warehousing and drugstore facilities.

Q. Just how widespread is the use of lie detectors by private business?

A. It varies among our membership. Certain members use them extensively for pre-employment screening. Other members use them periodically. At least once a year, they'll screen everyone—from the top executives all the way down to store personnel. Polygraphs are a strong deterrent to discourage someone from reaching into the till. In industry, generally, the statistics we have seen indicate that there are about 300,000 polygraph tests given each year.

Q. Why can't business fight theft in the same ways it did before the lie detector was invented?

A. Business wishes it could. Unfortunately, crime and employe theft have been increasing steadily for several decades. No matter what you do—beef up security, install expensive equipment, build cages to protect your merchandise, check employes as they leave the premises—the problem is escalating.

The loss figure that's estimated for the business community as a whole is 30 billion dollars a year. In retailing, it's over 7 billion dollars annually—and it's jumping 2 billion, 3 billion dollars at a clip each 12-month period. In the drugstore industry, the loss from crime in 1976 exceeded 700 million dollars. In this regard, we feel the polygraph is needed to protect businesses against increasing internal theft.

58

Q. But isn't a lie-detector test an invasion of privacy?

A. That argument has been presented, but we feel there must be some sort of balance maintained between an individual's right to privacy and an employer's right to protect his property. The National Association of Chain Drug Stores does not condone prying into a person's life style, and we believe the questions asked during a polygraph examination should be geared to the work situation. But as far as a person's use of drugs is concerned, we have to ask that question because of the nature of our business.

Q. Isn't there considerable doubt about the reliability of polygraph examinations?

A. The accuracy, reliability and validity question comes up time and again. However, most statistics and literature that we have on file indicate that the polygraph examination has a strong 85 to 93 per cent accuracy rate.

It is our position that the polygraph alone should not be the determining factor in whether or not a person is hired or fired. The polygraph should be used along with a host of other screening procedures to determine if a person is suitable for employment, or if a major shortage has occurred.

Q. Do you mean that a person might not be fired, even though the machine indicated that he gave a false answer to a key question?

A. That's correct. For example, an examiner might ask the question, "Have you stolen anything?" The individual says "No," and there's a reaction on the polygraph. Maybe the person is remembering that he took home a note pad and some pens from the company, and he knows this is stealing, even though it's only a minor offense. This is obviously not the kind of offense employers are after. The polygraph operator would zero in on the problem area and try to get a clarification.

Q. Haven't computer data banks and credit-reporting services made it easier than ever for an employer to find out about a job applicant's background without resorting to a lie-detector examination?

A. Not necessarily. You will run into roadblocks. You may send out a letter to a former employer and never receive a response. You may not be able to get conviction or arrest records.

And as far as personal-reference checks, how does the employer actually know that the person he's talking to is leveling with him and shooting straight from the hip?

Now, if you can't ask a person to take a polygraph test, what will be the next restriction? You won't be able to ask a person to take a simple test to determine his writing and mathematical skills; you won't be able to inquire into a person's medical background, because that's an invasion of privacy. It could go on and on.

There have to be some tools available to the employer so that he can be sure he's hiring not only a competent person but an honest person.

Q. Critics say that skills vary widely among polygraph operators, and that the examinations given by a poor operator are especially unreliable—

A. The polygraph profession admits that there are some "bad apples" out there giving tests, and they are doing their utmost to correct this situation. All of the test administrators working with our membership have met all the requirements in the States where they are operating. They are certified wherever States have that requirement.

We believe, however, that federal standards—a minimum level of education and training—would be appropriate, as it would help to upgrade the profession.

DISCUSSION QUESTIONS

1. Senator Bayh offers two syllogisms:

   Police-state intimidation should not be permitted in a free society.
   Requiring lie-detector tests for job applicants/job holders is a form of police-state intimidation.
   Requiring lie-detector tests for job applicants/job holders should not be permitted in a free society.

   No one should be kept from a job because of inaccurate information learned about him.
   Lie-detector tests (which are often administered by unskilled operators and which only measure stress) provide inaccurate information.
   No one should be kept from a job because of lie-detector tests.

   How would Mr. Kelley answer these objections?
2. Mr. Kelley offers a syllogism:

   Businesses need all the help they can get in stopping the massive losses caused by employee theft.
   Lie-detector testing helps stop such losses.
   Businesses need to use lie-detector testing.

   How would Senator Bayh attack this argument?
3. Senator Bayh says the tests are 70 percent accurate; Mr. Kelley says they have "a strong 85 to 93 percent accuracy rate." How can you account for this statistical difference?

4. Is Senator Bayh weakening his case by admitting the tests are 70 percent accurate?
5. Is Mr. Kelley weakening his cause by insisting that the polygraph alone should not be the determining factor in hiring–firing decisions?
6. Is the accuracy of the tests central to either man's case?

JUSTICE POTTER STEWART

Are Statutory Rape Laws Sexist?

Section 261.5, on its face, classifies on the basis of sex. A male who engages in sexual intercourse with an underage female who is not his wife violates the statute; a female who engages in sexual intercourse with an underage male who is not her husband does not.[1] The petitioner contends that this state law, which punishes only males for the conduct in question, violates his Fourteenth Amendment right to the equal protection of the law. The Court today correctly rejects that contention.

A

At the outset, it should be noted that the statutory discrimination, when viewed as part of the wider scheme of California law, is not as clearcut as might at first appear. Females are not freed from criminal liability in California for engaging in sexual activity that may be harmful. It is unlawful, for example, for any person, of either sex, to molest, annoy, or contribute to the delinquency of anyone under 18 years of age.[1] All persons are prohibited from committing "any lewd or lascivious act," including[2] consensual intercourse, with a child under 14.[3] And members of both sexes may be convicted for engaging in deviant sexual acts with anyone under 18.[4] Finally, females may be brought within the proscription of § 261.5 itself, since a female may be charged with aiding and abetting its violation.[5]

Section 261.5 is thus but one part of a broad statutory scheme that protects all minors from the problems and risks attendant upon adolescent sexual activity. To be sure, § 261.5 creates an additional measure of punishment for males who engage in sexual intercourse with females between the ages of 14 and 17.[6] The question then is whether the Constitution prohibits a state legislature from imposing this *additional* sanction on a gender-specific basis.

B

The Constitution is violated when government, state or federal, invidiously classifies similarly situated people on the basis of the immutable characteristics with which they were born. Thus, detrimental ra-

Source: Reprinted from Supreme Court Document: *Michael M., Petitioner* v. *Superior Court of Sonoma County, California* (March 23, 1981).

cial classifications by government always violate the Constitution, for the simple reason that, so far as the Constitution is concerned, people of different races are always similarly situated. See *Fullilove* v. *Klutznick,*—U.S.—,—(dissenting opinion); *McLaughlin* v. *Florida,* 379 U. S. 184, 198 (concurring opinion); *Brown* v. *Board of Educ.,* 347 U. S. 483; *Plessy* v. *Ferguson,* 163 U. S. 537, 552 (dissenting opinion). By contrast, while detrimental gender classifications by government often violate the Constitution, they do not always do so, for the reason that there are differences between males and females that the Constitution necessarily recognizes. In this case we deal with the most basic of these differences: females can become pregnant as the result of sexual intercourse; males cannot.

As was recognized in *Parham* v. *Hughes,* 441 U.S. 347, 354, "a State is not free to make overbroad generalizations based on sex which are entirely unrelated to any differences between men and women or which demean the ability or social status of the protected class." Gender-based classifications may not be based upon administrative convenience, or upon archaic assumptions about the proper roles of the sexes. *Craig* v. *Brown,* 429 U.S. 190; *Frontiero* v. *Richardson,* 411 U. S. 677; *Reed* v. *Reed,* 404 U. S. 71. But we have recognized that in certain narrow circumstances men and women are *not* similarly situated, and in these circumstances a gender classification based on clear differences between the sexes is not invidious, and a legislative classification realistically based upon those differences is not unconstitutional. See *Parham* v. *Hughes, supra; Califano* v. *Webster,* 430 U. S. 313, 316–317; *Schleshinger* v. *Ballard,* 419 U. S. 498; cf. *San Antonio School Dist.* v. *Rodriguez,* 411 U. S. 1, 59 (concurring opinion) "[G]ender-based classifications are not invariably invalid. When men and women are not in fact similarly situated in the area covered by the legislation in question, the Equal Protection Clause is not violated." *Cahan* v. *Mohammed,* 441 U. S. 380, 398 (dissenting opinion).

Applying these principles to the classification enacted by the California Legislature, it is readily apparent that § 261.5 does not violate the Equal Protection Clause. Young women and men are not similarly situated with respect to the problems and risks associated with intercourse and pregnancy, and the statute is realistically related to the legitimate state purpose of reducing those problems and risks.

C

As the California Supreme Court's catalogue shows, the pregnant unmarried female confronts problems more numerous and more severe than any faced by her male partner.[7] She alone endures the medical risks of pregnancy or abortion.[8] She suffers disproportionately the social, educational, and emotional consequences of pregnancy.[9] Recognizing this disproportion, California has attempted to protect teenage females by prohibiting males from participating in the act necessary for conception.[10]

The fact that males and females are not similarly situated with respect to the risks of sexual intercourse applies with the same force to males under 18 as it does to older males. The risk of pregnancy is a significant deterrent for unwed young females that is not shared by unmarried males, regardless of their age. Experienced observation confirms the common-sense notion that adolescent males disregard the possibility of pregnancy far more than do adolescent females.[11] And to the extent that § 261.5 may punish males for intercourse with prepubescent females, that punishment is justifiable because of the substantial physical risks for prepubescent females that are not shared by their male counterparts.[12]

D

The petitioner argues that the California Legislature could have drafted the statute differently, so that its purpose would be accomplished more precisely. "But the issue, of course, is not whether the statute could have been drafted more wisely, but whether the lines chosen by the . . . [l]egislature are within constitutional limitations." *Kahn* v. *Sherin,* 416 U. S. 351, 356, n. 10. That other States may have decided to attack the same problems more broadly, with gender-neutral statutes, does not mean that every State is constitutionally compelled to do so.[13]

E

In short, the Equal Protection Clause does not mean that the physiological differences between men and women must be disregarded. While those differences must never be permitted to become a pretext for invidious discrimination, no such discrimination is presented by this case. The Constitution surely does not require a State to pretend that demonstrable differences between men and women do not really exist.

NOTES

[1]But see n. 5 and accompanying text, *infra.*
[2]See Cal. Penal Code §§ 272, 647 (a) (West Supp. 1979 and 1980).
[3]Cal. Penal Code § 288 (West Supp. 1979). See *People* v. *Dontanville,* 10 Cal. App. 3d 783, 796, 89 Cal. Rptr. 172, 180 (2d Dist.).
[4]See Cal. Penal Code §§ 286 (b) (1), 288 (b)(1).
[5]See Cal. Penal Code § 31 (West 1970 and Supp. 1980); *People* v. *Haywood,* 131 Cal. App. 259, 280 P. 2d 180 (2d Dist.); *People* v. *Lewis,* 113 Cal. App. 2d 468, 248 P. 2d 461 (1st Dist.). According to statistics maintained by the California Department of Justice Bureau of Criminal Statistics, approximately 14% of the juveniles arrested for participation in acts made unlawful by § 261.5 be-

tween 1975 and 1979 were females. Moreover, an underage female who is as culpable as her male partner, or more culpable, may be prosecuted as a juvenile delinquent. Cal. Welfare and Inst. Code § 602 (West 1972 and Supp. 1980); *In re Gladys R.,* 1 Cal. 3d 855, 867–869, 464 P. 2d 127, 136–138, 83 Cal. Rptr. 671, 680–682.

[6]Males and females are equally prohibited by § 288 from sexual intercourse with minors under 14. Compare Cal. Penal Code § 288 (West Supp. 1979) with Cal. Penal Code §§ 264, 18 (West Supp. 1979).

[7]The court noted that from 1971 through 1976, 83.6% of the 4,860 children born to girls under 15 in California were illegitimate, as were 51% of those born to girls 15 to 17. The court also observed that while accounting for only 21% of California pregnancies in 1976, teenagers accounted for 34.7% of legal abortions. See *ante,* at 5, n. 3.

[8]There is also empirical evidence that sexual abuse of young females is a more serious problem than sexual abuse of young males. For example, a review of five studies found that 88% of sexually abused minors were female. Jaffe, Dynneson & ten Bensel, Sexual Abuse of Children, 129 Amer. J. of Diseases of Children, 689, 690 (1975). Another study, involving admissions to a hospital emergency room over a three-year period, reported that 86 of 100 children examined for sexual abuse were girls. Orr and Prieto, Emergency Management of Sexually Abused Children, 133 Ameri. J. of Diseased Children, 630 (1979). See also *State* v. *Craig,* 169 Mont. 150,—, 545 P. 2d 649, 653; Sarafino, An Estimate of Nationwide Incidence of Sexual Offenses Against Children, LVIII Child Welfare 127, 131 (1979).

[9]Most teenage mothers do not finish high school and are disadvantaged economically thereafter. See Moore, Teenage Childbirth and Welfare Dependency, 10 Family Planning Perspectives 233–235 (1978). The suicide rate for teenage mothers is seven times greater than that for teenage girls without children. F. Nye, School-Age Parenthood (Wash. State U. Ext. Bull. No. 667) 8 (1977). And 60% of adolescent mothers aged 15 to 17 are on welfare within two to five years of the birth of their children. Teenage Pregnancy, Everybody's Problem, DHEW Publications (HSA) No. 77-5619, at 3–4.

[10]Despite the increased availability of contraceptives and sex education, the pregnancy rates for young women are increasing. The Alan Guttmacher Institute, 11 Million Teenagers 12 (1976). See generally C. Chilman, Adolescent Sexuality in a Changing American Society (NIH Pub. No. 89-1426) (1980).

The petitioner contends that the statute is overinclusive because it does not allow a defense that contraceptives were used, or that procreation was for some other reason impossible. The petitioner does not allege, however, that he used a contraceptive, or that pregnancy could not have resulted from the conduct with which he was charged. But even assuming the petitioner's standing to raise the claim of overbreadth, it is clear that a statute recognizing the defenses he suggests would encounter difficult if not impossible problems of proof.

[11]See, *e. g.,* Phipps-Yonas, Teenage Pregnancy and Motherhood, 50 Am. J. of Orthopsychiatry 403, 412 (1980). See also *State* v. *Rundlett,* 391 A, 2d 815, 819, n. 13, 822 (Me.); *Rundlett* v. *Oliver,* 607 F. 2d 495, 502 (CA1).

[12]See *Barnes* v. *State,* 244 Ga. 302, 260 S. E. 2d 40; see generally Orr & Prieto, *supra;* Jaffe, Dynneson & ten Bensel, *supra;* Coilman, *supra.*

[13]The fact is that a gender-neutral statute would not necessarily lead to a closer fit with the aim of reducing the problems associated with teenage pregnancy. If both parties were equally liable to prosecution, a female would be far less likely to complain; the very complaint would be self-incriminating. Accordingly, it is possible that a gender-neutral statute would result in fewer prosecutions than the one before us.

In any event, a state legislature is free to address itself to what it believes to be the most serious aspect of a broader problem. "[T]he Equal Protection Clause does not require that a State must choose between attacking every aspect of a problem or not attacking the problem at all." *Dandridge* v. *Williams*, 397 U. S. 471, 486–487; see also *Williamson* v. *Lee Optical Co.*, 348 U. S. 483.

DISCUSSION

Any court decision expresses a syllogism: The major premise is the law; the minor premise, the facts of the case.

Here, Michael M., a 17-year-old male, was convicted under Section 261.5, California's statutory rape law. He had sexual relations with a 16-year-old girl, legally classified as a minor. (At 17, he also was a minor.)

The defendant challenged the law with this syllogism:

> The Fourteenth Amendment (right to equal protection under the law) is violated when a person is discriminated against on the basis of race or gender.

> The defendant (a minor male who took part in a consensual sex act with a minor female, and who was prosecuted for the act while she was not) suffered discrimination on the basis of gender.

> The conviction violated his rights under the Fourteenth Amendment.

The Supreme Court rejected this argument in a 5 to 4 decision. How did Justice Stewart attack the syllogism?

MAURICE McCRACKEN
Opposition to the Draft

In 1951, I fell within the age range of those required to register for the draft. I registered under protest. If I were of draft age now, I would not register. The only valid protest is resistance and complete non-cooperation with what we believe to be wrong.

The draft is evil. It is a vehicle of oppression. A year ago Jimmy Carter's Selective Service director wrote a long report which said that peace-time registration was unnecessary. There are 2 million persons on active military duty and over a million more in the reserves. Should war come, there will be no conventional military combat with soldiers fighting it out in the trenches. This is the age of first-strike nuclear combat. Between Russia and the United States there are enough nuclear warheads to kill every human being on the planet—over and over again.

Draft registration is moving the U.S. a long step closer to being a police state. A tactic of a police state is to threaten more and more people with arrest and imprisonment if they do not conform to its will. Such a law threatens anyone who advises a young man not to register for the draft with the same penalty as the non-registrant—a possible prison sentence of five years and a possible fine of $5,000. In the draft registration resistance movement, I find that considerable time is spent on how to counsel young men about registration so it will not appear that we are actually advising them not to register. Why this hesitancy and timidity?

I not only advise young men of draft age not to register, I *urge* them not to register. Is the church, are parents, teachers, and others who have had a strong positive influence in shaping the characters of these young men, now going to abandon them? We have taught them that we are all members of one human family, whatever our race, whatever our creed, whatever our nationality.

If a young man comes to his parents, to his teacher, to his minister, or to some other trusted friend, and says, "I'm a member of a gang and I've been offered $500 to bump off a leader of a rival gang.

Source: Reprinted from *The Churchman* (March 1981), p. 14.

What do you think I should do?" We would quickly enough tell him that murder is wrong and that he should refuse to commit this crime.

Or, if a youth comes and tells us that he's been offered a sum of money to set fire to a building so its owners can collect the insurance, we would not lay before him various alternatives. We would say, "Arson is wrong and you should not engage in it no matter how much you are being paid."

War is the supreme evil. It not only engages in murder and arson, but in torture, rape, and every other social evil and on a massive scale. We are betraying them if we do not tell our youth that we believe they should not register for the draft. We are betraying them if we do not give them this kind of moral support and guidance at this time when they need it most.

Let us never forget that we may be a party to turning these peace-loving, life-affirming young men into killers who themselves may be among the dead.

The U.S. government has a stranglehold around the throat of the American people. One hand that is doing the strangling is the Internal Revenue Service. The other hand is the draft.

A military budget of $140 billion has been set for 1981. Estimating that this budget will increase $30 billion each year for the next four years, we will have spent one trillion dollars on the military. This is *mad*—spelled M-A-D—and it stands for Mutual Assured Destruction.

DISCUSSION QUESTIONS

1. The author marshals a number of syllogisms to oppose registration for the draft.

> *In an age of first-strike nuclear combat when we already have 3 million persons in the active or reserve military, it is unnecessary to add more people to our military forces.*
> *The proposed draft would add more people to our military forces.*
> *The proposed draft is unnecessary.*
> > <
> *Americans should resist attempts to make America a police state.*
> *The draft uses police-state tactics (threats of fines and imprisonment) for those who do not register.*
> *Americans should resist the draft.*
> > <
> *Responsible advisors should urge young people not to commit murder or arson.*
> *The draft could involve young people in wartime combat, which is really murder and arson.*
> *Responsible advisors should urge young people not to respond to the draft.*

> <
Responsible adults should warn young people against activities that might kill them.

The draft would involve young people in wartime combat, which could kill them.

Responsible advisors should warn young people against the draft.

How might a pro-draft advocate answer these arguments?

2. The author complains of two strangleholds that the government has on the American people: the draft and the Internal Revenue Service. Why does he bring up the IRS? Does it help his case to add a complaint about taxes?

Reprinted from the *National Catholic Reporter* (July 17, 1981), p. 14.

DISCUSSION QUESTIONS

1. The cartoonist is arguing that the Moral Majority is not a Christian organization. Construct the syllogism that would express this argument.
2. How might a member of the Moral Majority attack the syllogism?

Argument by Authority

Never go to a doctor whose office plants have died.
ERMA BOMBECK

Much of what you believe—or are asked to believe—must be accepted simply on the authority of an expert. Your doctor says you have glaucoma. Your mechanic says the car needs a valve job. Your newspaper reviews *Heaven's Gate* and calls it awful. Scientific authorities say the universe is expanding. In such instances, you are asked to accept a view on the basis of someone's testimony.

It is reasonable to credit such testimony if it fulfills two conditions: (1) The speaker must be a genuine expert on the subject at hand. (2) There must exist no reasonable probability of bias. When Zsa Zsa Gabor, for example, turns from her acting career to praise the effects of acupuncture, you can justly question her expertise in the area. Also, when Robert Young appears on television praising the richness of Sanka Coffee, you know he is being paid for the advertisement and suspect a degree of bias.

Remember, however, that these unreliable arguments are not necessarily false. Zsa Zsa Gabor may be expressing an important truth about acupuncture, and Robert Young may be giving his honest opinion about Sanka Coffee. Nevertheless, it would be unreasonable to accept an argument—or to build a persuasive essay—*solely* on the authority of such speakers. You should relate their views to other evidence and to the word of other authorities.

EXPERT TESTIMONY

Many arguments raise the question of genuine expertise. The authority may be unnamed. (Advertisements for health products often print testimony from "Brazilian researchers" or from "Dr. Jonah B.") He may be unfamiliar. (*"Promise of Saccharine* is a provocative book—readable and profoundly informed."—Col. Winston X. Montgomery) He may be known largely by his degrees. (A Kansas medico, in recommending goat-gland surgery to restore vitality, signed himself "John R. Brinkley, M.D., C.M., Dr. P.H., Sc.D. . . .") And he may appear with magnified credentials. (A temperance circular quoting William Gladstone's condemnation of alcohol described him as "the greatest Prime Minister in English history.")

Sometimes speakers of unquestioned authority express themselves in areas outside their competence. You hear actress Brooke Shields warning of the medical effects of smoking, and evangelist Jerry Falwell discussing the weaknesses in evolutionary theory. One advertisement describes a star third baseman, then adds, "His good judgment on the ball field holds true with his selection of wearing apparel. That's why he picks Munsingwear all the way." A religious newspaper headlines an article by L. Nelson Bell, M.D., "A Physician Looks at the Virgin Birth," then prints his biblical argument based on a reading of Isaiah, Matthew, and Luke. Dr. Bell offers no medical opinion at all. Such "authorities" must be judged on the quality of their evidence, not on their word as experts.

Religious Authority

Equally questionable as authorities are "God" and "everyone." Because the claim is not subject to hard evidence, one can affirm almost any opinion by saying it conforms to the divine will. A correspondent to the *Mobile Press* in 1975 assured readers that earthquakes on the West Coast were punishment for California's sinful life-style. A later correspondent declared it would violate "Christ's plan for the world" if the United States gave up its holdings in Panama. And during the 1980 election, the Moral Majority (and similar organizations) made it clear that Ronald Reagan was God's choice for President of the United States.

Christian authors routinely quote passages from the Bible to declare the will of God, and thus open up a rich area of argument. As mentioned earlier, religious questions often do not lend themselves to meaningful discussion because people cannot agree on necessary definitions. Clearly, an argument involving biblical authority can be persuasive only when addressed to someone who already accepts the validity of scripture and who interprets it in the same sense as the speaker. (Large differences exist, for example, among those who claim the Bible *is* the word of God, those who say it *contains* the word of God, those who enjoy it as an anthology of great literature, and those who reject it altogether.)

Even when preliminary agreement exists, problems remain. Because the biblical texts were written over some 1300 years and represent a wide variety of authors, occasions, opinions, literary types, and translations, a person can find a passage or two to support any argument he or she chooses to make. (Bishop James Pike illustrated this by asking ironically, "How many persons have been reborn from meditating on the last line of Psalm 137: 'Blessed shall he be that taketh and dasheth the little ones against the stones'?") Consequently, facing a scriptural argument, you should take time to trace the references. You will find that authors often quote passages out of context (they might be championing the superficial counsel of Job's friends) and that, not uncommonly, they quote from inaccurate memory and refer to lines scarcely related to the issue at hand. ("Only God can save America now. See Chronicles 7:14.")

Mass Authority

The authority of "everyone" is claimed in statements beginning, "They say," "Everyone knows," or "All fair-minded people agree." Such argument can be convincing in instances where "they" (some notable majority) have demonstrably committed themselves on a matter they are competent to judge. Arguments announcing "More women choose Simplicity than any other pattern" and "Budweiser—Largest Selling Beer in the World" are genuinely impressive because, in these areas, the opinion of a mass audience is superior to that of any particular expert. (What renowned epicure is qualified to assure you that Pabst Light is America's best-tasting beer?)

It is important to remember that America's democratic procedures and its jury system both rely on the expertness of "everyone."

Mass authority, however, can be distorted in a number of ways. It can be claimed arbitrarily: ("Everyone knows that Jimmy Carter stole the 1976 election.") It can be coupled with ambiguous language. ("More men get more pleasure out of Roi-Tan than any other cigar at its price.") And it can be invoked in areas that call for technical expertise. (A 1976 Gallup Poll reported that 41 percent of Americans believe that cigarette smoking is a cause of birth defects.) In such instances, "everyone" is a dubious authority.

When you're having severe chest pains, it is no time to take a poll.

Still, mass opinion is worth listening to, especially when it becomes more or less unanimous. Remember the famous counsel: "If you can keep your head when all about you are losing theirs, probably you haven't grasped the situation."

Divided Authority

The word of a genuine expert will not, of course, settle all disputes. Alexander Pope put the question best:

Who shall decide when Doctors disagree,
And soundest Casuists doubt, like you and me?

The plain fact is that many issues are complex and that, in these areas, experts hold opposing views. Legal authorities disagree whether certain evidence-gathering measures violate constitutional safeguards. (Were the ABSCAM officials framed?) Eminent psychiatrists appear in court arguing the competence of particular defendants. (Was John Hinckley insane?) Medical scientists do not agree whether a month-old fetus is human. (Is abortion murder?) Whose opinion should you accept?

In such cases, it is probably wise to credit the larger body of expert opinion or to withhold judgment and await further pronouncements in the area.

Critical Authorities

You should recognize that some authorities have more established reputations than others. Many periodicals carry reviews of books, plays, and movies, for example, but those of the major New York newspapers, the *Christian Science Monitor,* and national magazines such as *Time, Newsweek, Harper's, Atlantic, Saturday Review,* and *New York Magazine,* are generally thought most critically reliable.

If a book, movie, or play wins praise from these critics, the reviews may be quoted in magazine advertisements or on book jackets. If an advertisement quotes reviews from other sources, it strongly suggests the work was not praised by the major critics. An advertisement for Ian Fleming's *On Her Majesty's Secret Service,* for example, boasted these reviews:

> *"Packed with danger, mystery, crime, and wild pursuit . . . I can recommend it with confidence to readers who sat up late nights to finish the preceding 10."—Vincent Starret,* Chicago Tribune

> *"Hair raiser."*—Boston Herald

> *"Astonishing . . . ingenious."*—Diners Club Magazine

> *"The hottest sleuth in the suspense field, James Bond, really tops himself in this new Ian Fleming thriller."*—St. Paul Dispatch

> *"More fun that Tarzan and Superman combined."*—Denver Post

> *"Taut, instructive and artfully told."*—Chicago Daily News

> *"You can't argue with success."—Anthony Boucher,* New York Times Book Review

> *"A fine surge of adrenalin in our veins."*—Columbus Dispatch

> *"Solid Fleming."*—New York Herald Tribune Books

Although it appears at first glance that authorities were unanimous in acclaiming this novel, such is scarcely the case. Only two of the reviews were from major critics, and these were notably less enthusiastic than the others. The *New York Times* declared it would not argue with general taste. And the *New York Herald Tribune* said the novel was a good example of the kind Fleming writes.

This is not to suggest that you should not enjoy Ian Fleming novels.

You should, however, recognize the varying standards of critical authorities and not misread such advertisements as expressions of universal acclaim. You should be less than impressed, for example, when you see the paperback edition of Nancy Freeman's *Joshua Son of None* boasting rave reviews from the *El Paso Times,* the *San Gabriel Valley Tribune,* the *Macon Georgian,* and the *Oceanside Blade-Tribune.*

You should recognize these distinctions when writing a critical essay. If the book or movie you're championing is praised by the major critics, quote the reviews. If it found favor only with lesser authorities, probably you should not mention the reviews at all.

BIASED TESTIMONY

Even when speakers are admitted experts in the field under discussion, an argument should be examined for the possibility of bias. An argument is said to have a probable bias if the authority profits from the view expressed or if it reflects the predictable loyalty or routine antagonism of a group. To dismiss the testimony of such persons is not to call them liars or even to say that they are wrong; it means a condition exists that makes it unreasonable to accept the conclusion *solely* on their authority.

You don't ask a barber whether you need a hair cut.

Rewarded Opinions

Experts profit from making an argument when it brings them money or prestige. The financial incentive is easy to recognize when Joe DiMaggio recommends Mr. Coffee products, when Sybil Leek makes lecture tours proclaiming she is a witch, and when owners of outdoor movies protest the unnaturalness of daylight savings time.

Today many people earn a living by convincing you of preposterous "facts." Tabloid advertisers boast incredible systems that will let readers grow new hair, develop a larger bustline, win at the racetrack, lose weight in selected areas, and grow rich by practicing witchcraft. Papers like the *Star* and the *National Enquirer* routinely carry stories of reincarnated housewives, cancer cures, and outer space creatures that appeared on Earth. Recent bestselling books reveal that Errol Flynn was a Nazi spy, that Marilyn Monroe was murdered, that the Mafia killed President Kennedy, and that the kidnapped Lindbergh baby is still alive. Such stories are fun to read, and there may even be splinters of truth in some of them. But you can give no special belief to the authors of such tales. They are making money peddling these extravagant claims.

The effect of prestige is clear when individuals discuss their incomes, their reading habits, and their sex lives. In these areas, ego is threatened—and people lie.

The impact of money and prestige on an expert is sometimes difficult to establish. Few scientific authorities have affirmed the existence of the Loch Ness monster or the abominable snowman, for example; but these few have won a level of recognition—along with television appearances, speaking engagements, and book contracts—that they could never win voicing more orthodox opinions. These experts may be expressing their honest judgments, but you should remember all that acclaim when evaluating their testimony.

Predictable Judgments

Argument by authority is presumed biased if it is totally predictable—that is, when it reflects the traditional loyalty or antagonism of a particular group. The definitive example occurred in 1977 when Alabama's football team was ranked second in the final AP and UPI national polls. Thereupon the Alabama state legislature issued its own poll, and the Crimson Tide moved up to No. 1. Equally predictable are pamphlets on smoking and health distributed by the Tobacco Institute, articles on gun control and crime appearing in the *American Rifleman,* and the publicized study of pain relievers produced by the Bayer Company.

This presumption of bias appears most notably in political argument. When *any* Democrat is nominated for president, the man and his platform will be praised in liberal periodicals (*Washington Post, St. Louis Post Dispatch, Commonweal, The Progressive,* and so on) and condemned in conservative publications (*Chicago Tribune, U. S. News & World Report, Los Angeles Times, National Review,* and so on). When *any* president finishes his State of the Union message, opposition speakers will call his program inadequate, wrongheaded, and potentially dangerous. You must judge these claims on specific evidence; such predictable views carry little authority.

DISTORTING QUOTATIONS

Besides a doubtful expert and a biased opinion, other misleading features attend argument by authority. Statements are sometimes abridged. (The advertisement for Kyle Onstott's *Mandingo* quotes a review from the *Dallas News:* ". . . like no other book ever written about the South. . . .") Claims may be irrelevant to the issue at hand. (The paperback edition of *Nightmare in Pink* prints Richard Condon's opinion that "John D. MacDonald is the great American story-teller.") Quotations can appear without source. (See *Hand in Hand*—"The Most Widely Praised Picture of Them All!") And undated quotations can be impressive. (In the 1980 presidential campaign, opponents printed statements Ronald Reagan made years before when he was a Democrat.)

Exact quotations can be presented in a distorting context. Under the heading "How L.B.J. Would Remake America," *Common Sense* printed a sentence from President Johnson's 1964 State of the Union message: "We are going to try to take all the money that we think is unnecessarily being spent and take it from the 'haves' and give it to the 'have nots' that need it so much." As the context of the speech made clear, the President did not advocate taking from the rich to give to the poor; he proposed taking money from the more heavily funded federal programs and putting it in those with smaller appropriations.

In the same way, temperance advocates like to strengthen their argument by quoting lines from Chaucer ("Character and shame depart when wine comes in") and Shakespeare ("O thou invisible spirit of wine, if thou hast no name to be known by, let us call thee devil!"). The lines, of course, are not direct expressions of these authors; they come from literary characters who are speaking in a dramatic context.

Audio/Video Taped Evidence

With the advent of the tape and video recorder, one can produce new kinds of distorted testimony. In the 1972 campaign in Alabama, opponents spliced together separate parts of a taped interview and broadcast Senator John Sparkman's voice saying, "Will the cause of desegregation be served? If so, the busing is all right." During his administration President Richard Nixon recorded his phone calls and office conversations and produced the tapes that eventually implicated him. Noting that the President made totally contradictory statements on the tapes, Congressman Tip O'Neill speculated about Nixon's intention:

> *Now that tells you what he was going to do with those tapes. He was going to take them with him when he left and spend years editing them, and then he could string together a record of his own which would show he was the greatest man ever to live. He'd be able to prove it with the tapes. You never would have known about any of the other tapes. That would have been thrown away. They would have only given you all these tapes with him making a hero of himself.*

In the early 1980s, the FBI convicted the ABSCAM officials with videotapes showing them taking money and making incriminating promises to an agent posing as an Arab monarch who sought favors. Here it is important to remember that the FBI agents had complete control of the situation. They could introduce topics, guide the conversation, stop it when convenient, tape some episodes, not tape others, and then choose which tapes they wanted to show in court. The ABSCAM defendants may not have been faultless, but it is hard to imagine St. Francis of Assisi surviving such a test.

One must take great care in analyzing audio and video evidence. There is much to be considered besides the words and pictures presented.

Lies

Expert testimony can lend itself to bald misstatement of fact on the part of authorities or of those who quote them. A national columnist accused author Quentin Reynolds of being a Communist and a war profiteer. A U.S. senator called newsman Drew Pearson a child-molester. Many have circulated the story that three Pennsylvania students on LSD became blind from staring at the sun for several hours and that a Michigan schoolteacher took off all her clothes to demonstrate female anatomy to her coed sex-education class. All these sensational claims were lies.

Fictional quotations appear as evidence. For many years the statement "We shall force the United States to spend itself to destruction" has been attributed to Nikolai Lenin and used to ground conservative political argument. Lenin never said that or anything like it. More recently, liberal sources circulated a paragraph protesting the Communist threat and concluding, "We need law and order"; they ascribed this to Adolf Hitler. The quotation is pure fiction. Several years ago a tabloid newspaper headlined the news that marijuana may cure cancer. The story quoted Dr. James H. Kostinger, director of research for the Pittsburgh Academy of Forensic Medicine, who had been conducting studies in this area for four years. Investigation later revealed that the academy did not exist and that no medical school in Pittsburgh had ever heard of Dr. Kostinger.

> <

Although expert testimony can be misused by dishonest writers and speakers, it remains a forceful element of legitimate argument. When genuine authorities agree with you, quote them in your writing. Your case will be more persuasive.

EXERCISES

How reliable are these arguments from authority?

1. Fluoridation causes gum disease. Many eminent authorities, such as Dr. H. K. Box, University of Toronto, and Dr. G. C. Geiger, Florida State Dental Health officer, have observed a marked increase in periodontal (gum) disease where small amounts of fluoride occur naturally in water.
2. *Shakespeare of London* by Marchette Chute. "The best biography of Shakespeare."—Bernadine Kielty, *Book-of-the-Month Club News.*
3. The Mont Blanc Diplomat—"Many pen experts here and abroad consider the Diplomat to be the finest pen ever designed. It's Europe's most prized pen, unmatched in writing ease."
4. "I might possibly be the Lindbergh child."—Harold Olson.
5. "If a man also lie with mankind, as he lieth with a woman, both of them have committed an abomination: They shall surely be put to death."—Leviticus 20:13.
6. Recent report shows Anacin's pain reliever is *Doctors #1 Choice.*

7. Dr. Philip Handler, board chairman of the National Science Foundation, bluntly told a House subcommittee investigating drug laws, "It is our puritan ethics . . . rather than science" that say we should not smoke marijuana.
8. In 1968, Pope Paul VI said that bones found beneath St. Peter's Basilica 18 years earlier had been identified "in a manner we think of as convincing" as those of the apostle St. Peter.
9. Baron Philippe de Rothschild's Mouton-Cadet—"Enjoyed more by discerning people than any other Bordeaux wine in the world."

ESSAY ASSIGNMENTS

Write an essay either affirming or opposing one of these statements. The arguments you encounter in your background reading will include expert testimony, and so should your essay.

1. Marijuana smoking should be legalized.
2. Vitamin C pills are necessary for good health.
3. Speaking in tongues is a genuine spiritual gift.
4. Flying saucers are here.
5. Fluoridation of drinking water is dangerous.
6. A faith healer can help you.
7. To remain healthy, one should avoid X. (Fill in the X.)

DAVID AVERY[1]

The Case for "Shock" Therapy

Jack Nicholson in the film *One Flew Over the Cuckoo's Nest* is punished with electroconvulsive therapy (ECT) for his high-spirited capers in a mental hospital. The scene demonstrates a popular misconception of ECT as a medieval torture inflicted on helpless or nonconforming mental patients. A group called the Network Against Psychiatric Assault has asked for a total ban on ECT, describing it as a "bogus, barbaric and destructive technological weapon." Some states have passed laws restricting ECT treatment in favor, as one California legislator said, of "more creative, positive treatments." Professionals who oppose it speak of its risks and dangers. Dr. John Friedberg argues (*Psychology Today,* August 1975) that it "obliterates memory," "damages the brain," and "has caused more suicides than it has prevented."

Yet, if we take a second look at "shock treatment," we find that the opponents such as Dr. Friedberg rely on opinion and anecdote and ignore the scores of controlled studies done in recent years to attest to its safety and effectiveness. Most importantly, the movement to abolish ECT disregards the thousands of patients for whom the treatments offer the only rescue from deep and often suicidal depression.

Four controlled studies involving over 1,000 depressed patients show a lower suicide rate with ECT compared with other treatments. ECT is particularly effective in the treatment of clinical depression, which, unlike situational sadness, is associated with a very high death rate from suicide, malnutrition, heart attack, and exhaustion. Data from 15 studies involving over 4,500 depressed persons indicate that the overall death rate is significantly lower with ECT than with psychotherapy. Although antidepressant medications are also effective in less severe cases, studies demonstrate that drugs take longer than ECT to act and may prolong the agony of depression.

[1]The author is a fellow in psychopharmacology at the Stanford University School of Medicine and the Palo Alto Veterans Administration Hospital.
Source: Reprinted from *Psychology Today Magazine.* Copyright © 1977 Ziff-Davis Publishing Company.

INTROJECTED ANGER

We don't know why ECT works, but we do know that the punishment theory is mistaken. A popular opinion is that depression represents "introjected anger." According to this theory, the fright and pain from ECT satisfies the person's need for self-punishment, and recovery takes place. Yet, ECT is painless. The patient receives an anesthetic and is unconscious during the one or two minutes of treatment.

Controlled studies were devised to test the punishment theory. Some depressed people unknowingly received a sham treatment (a subconvulsive dose of electrical current) and did no better than the controls, while those who received a dose high enough to induce a seizure experienced marked improvement. These studies prove that a seizure is necessary for the treatment to be effective, not a painful experience that "shocks" a person back to health.

Why is seizure a *sine qua non?* Evidence suggests deficiencies of two neurotransmitters in the central nervous systems of depressed persons, norepinephrine and serotonin. Even though some animal studies show increased production of these substances during seizures, it is too early to formulate a mechanism to explain how ECT works. We don't know how aspirin works either, but that doesn't diminish the empirical evidence for its efficacy.

ECT has been proven an effective treatment for depression, but is it safe? Much is made of the risk of death during ECT use, but one survey done in Denmark reveals that only one person died out of a total of the 3,438 who were treated over a one-year period. Moreover, critics who emphasize the death risk do not mention that the risk of death within the year for a depressed person *not* receiving ECT is 300 times greater. The deaths and brain damage that *have* been attributed to ECT are nearly always complicated by significant life-threatening problems. In his *Psychology Today* article, for example, Dr. Friedberg cited the case, in 1942, of a 57-year-old man who died after ECT and attributed the brain damage found at the autopsy to the ECT. Dr. Friedberg neglected to mention that the man had a history of severe heart damage, and that neuropathologists found the cause of death to be a heart attack. Heart damage, not ECT, is a well-documented cause of brain cell death.

A recent review by neuropathologists concludes that neuronal damage due to ECT in a physically healthy person is unlikely. At least six studies show that animals given ECT have no destruction of neurons. In addition, since 1972, two animal studies using the most sensitive microscopic techniques revealed that seizure activity comparable to ECT caused no change in the ultrastructure of the brain.

LOSS OF MEMORY

The question of whether ECT causes significant loss of memory is complicated by the memory problems associated with depression itself. Half of the depressed patients who have not received ECT complain of memory problems and often have such difficulty concentrating that they do poorly on objective memory tests. ECT does cause a few minutes of confusion on awakening and a transient memory disturbance. People are occasionally unable to remember events that happened during the few weeks of treatment. However, they are able to recall as well as ever events from the more distant past and are able to learn and retain new information as well as, or better than, before. A recent study showed progressive *improvement* in short-term memory in depressed patients receiving ECT. In 1975, a study done six months after treatment showed that on six objective memory tests, ECT patients performed as well as recovered depressed people who did not receive ECT.

Sylvia Plath's *The Bell Jar,* Robert Pirsig's brilliantly reconstructed account of his past, *Zen and the Art of Motorcycle Maintenance,* and Mark Vonnegut's *The Eden Express* are hardly the products of damaged, enfeebled minds, even though the authors all received ECT *before* the books were written.

The ECT controversy reflects a tendency to see a natural antagonism between science and humanism. Many critics reject the treatment because they wish to see the mind as separate from the brain—free from the biological whims that affect every other organ of the body. Yet, much can be learned from both the recent biological data and the insights of humanism.

DISCUSSION QUESTIONS

1. How effective are these entities in an argument by authority: (a) David Avery, (b) fellow in psychopharmacology, (c) Stanford University, (d) School of Medicine, (e) Palo Alto VA Hospital, and (f) *Psychology Today.*
2. The author refers to a number of studies that support the use of shock therapy:

   "scores of controlled studies" showing the safety and effectiveness of ECT

   "four controlled studies" indicating a reduced suicide rate with ECT

   "data from 15 studies" showing a lower death rate with ECT than with psychotherapy

   "controlled studies" devised to test the punishment theory

   "evidence" suggesting depression involves deficiencies of norepinephrine and serotonin.

   "some animal studies" showing increased production of norepinephrine and serotonin during seizures

> *"one survey done in Denmark"* indicating a minimal death rate
>   following ECT
> *"a recent review by neuropathologists"* reporting that neuronal
>   damage from ECT is unlikely
> *"six studies"* showing animals have no neuronal destruction during ECT
> *"two animal studies"* showing no change in the ultrastructure of the
>   brain following ECT
> *"a recent study"* showing progressive improvement in short-term
>   memory following ECT
> *"a study"* indicating ECT patients score well on objective memory tests
>   six months later

Are these references impressive as argument? Are they all equally impressive?
3. Why didn't the author spell out some of the facts relating to his studies in
   more detail?
4. Consider the evidence in the essay that indicates there is another side to the
   ECT issue. Was the author wise to write the first paragraph the way he did?

GEORGE J. KOELZER

ABSCAM: In Defense of Senator Williams

Let me reintroduce myself. My name is George J. Koelzer. I am an attorney practicing in Manhattan, also in New Jersey, and I am here today to speak before you now, because it's my honor and my privilege to represent Harrison Williams who is to be tried before you over the next several weeks.

My purpose in addressing you now is to tell you briefly— although perhaps not as briefly as you may like, because it's a rather long and complex case, but I ask your patience and indulgence now and throughout the case. To address you as briefly as I can, consistent with my responsibilities as attorney for Harrison A. Williams, Jr., about the facts that will be proven in this case.

Let me tell you straight away, if the facts were as Mr. McDonald just described to you, I would hardly be here taking up your time. They are not.

How are they different?

Before I begin to take up your time and have you listen over the next several weeks to this case—and I appreciate your promise to well and truly try the case and your promise to be patient as Judge

Opening statement of the lawyer defending Harrison Williams, the U.S. senator (New Jersey) charged with bribery and conspiracy in the ABSCAM investigation. In the prosecution's opening statement, Edward McDonald charged that the FBI had videotapes showing the senator urging an Arab shiek (actually a disguised FBI agent) to invest in a Virginia titanium mine by promising to use his influence to get federal contracts to buy the output of the mine; for this, he was to receive a concealed 18 percent share of the enterprise. (It was also alleged that Senator Williams promised to arrange legal matters so the Shiek could settle in the United States.) Indicted with Senator Williams were Alexander Feinberg, George Katz, and Angelo J. Errichetti (the mayor of Camden, New Jersey). Henry A. (Sandy) Williams was involved but chose to testify for the prosecution in order to avoid indictment. The ABSCAM program was masterminded by Melvin Weinberg, a long-time confidence man and convicted swindler; it was directed by FBI agent Anthony Amoroso. The trial occurred in April 1981.

This speech is abridged, with the approval of the author.

83

Pratt said yesterday. For the first function or job of a juror is patience, and it will be taxed.

Let me mention a few things that Mr. McDonald conveniently omitted. Mr. McDonald said there are over 300 tapes. I could be wrong, don't hold me to it. I think there are more like four or five hundred. It doesn't matter when you get up to that number.

In accordance with the rules of the Court and the direction of the Court before the trial began, the Government—the prosecution in this case—told us that they were going to play parts of 25 tapes, some video, some audio.

We in turn said, because we were obligated to, that we might play as many as 125 tapes. Please don't be alarmed. Please don't be alarmed. I will not try to belabor it. I know your time is valuable.

Think of the implication of that for a moment. We didn't make those recordings. Indeed, as I will elaborate for a moment, my client, the others there, and Mr. Feinberg, and the other names that you heard, Mr. Katz and Mr. Errichetti, never knew that they were being recorded. The prosecution made each and every one of those recordings, whether audio or video.

> <

Let me say, before I go on much further, a few words about my client.

Senator Williams sits in this courtroom at the table from which I just arose. He is a man who, as Mr. McDonald just said, is a United States Senator. He is a human being who sits here charged in this case. You are to be his judges. You are the judges of the facts. You are not judges of the law, as Judge Pratt is; you are judges of the facts. No one else could tell you what the facts are, not I, for I am an advocate, not my opponent, not even Judge Pratt.

Senator Williams looks upon you as judges as to what is to happen in this case. You are to look back over the events of 13 months, surreptitiously recorded by the prosecution in this case. Senator Williams is a man 61 years of age. You will learn more about him and his background and his personality, and the facts in evidence will show you this: He was born on December 10, 1919, raised in a town in New Jersey known as Plainfield, went to school. World War II came, and he served with distinction throughout World War II—served on a mine sweeper, was a flight instructor, had a distinguished career in the United States Navy during the Second World War.

Thereafter, both before and after the war, he attended a college out in Ohio known as Oberlin, a fine institution, obtained his degree from that school, came back and attended a very, very fine law school here in New York, Columbia University School of Law up on

Morningside Heights. He obtained his degree from there and eventually began the practice of law as a young man in the state of New Jersey.

He became interested in public affairs and politics. He became active in his town and ran, I believe, for the council. In any event, originally met with a lack of success.

In 1953 at the age of 38, he was elected to Congress as a Congressman, an off-year election, as they say; it was in mid-term. There was a vacancy that arose, and he was re-elected in 1954, served in Congress again from '54 to '56. But in '56 when he ran for a third time, he was defeated.

You might recall—some of us are a little older—it was the year known as the Eisenhower landslide. He was defeated.

In 1958 the opportunity arose, and he ran for and was elected to the U.S. Senate where he has served ever since. He has had a distinguished career in the U.S. Senate, and I expect that you will hear proof about that.

You are entitled to know the nature of the person that you are to judge. You are entitled to know his background. What he stands for, what his character is. He is not a man who is corrupt in any way or sense of the word.

I tell you and I tell you now—I will tell you again during this opening, and I will tell you in summation—the best evidence of Senator Williams' being not guilty of the charges the prosecution has brought against him, the best evidence you will hear—and I will produce witnesses I feel certain, I will produce documents I feel certain—but nevertheless, the best evidence you will hear will be the very tapes which the prosecution itself prepared. I will discuss them very briefly with you this morning.

My client, Senator Williams, has enjoyed an impeccable reputation, highly respected. Ask yourselves this: Does it make sense? Is it human experience that after sixty years one's personality and way of life suddenly changes? The answer is, "No, of course not." We all know that.

Senator Williams happens to be a Democrat and served in Congress as a member of the Democratic Party. Therefore, in the course of things, he had occasion to meet with Errichetti. He was by no means an associate or could even be described as a friend of Errichetti's. Little was known at that point in time by Senator Williams or indeed by virtually anybody that we have been able to find about Errichetti. You will find a great number of tapes—many of them will be played by us—of things said by this fellow, Angelo Errichetti. I tell you right now, for you may recall yesterday morning downstairs in the Ceremonial Courtroom, Judge Pratt mentioned that there will be some very foul language. I can tell you I have listened to all the tapes, and to the best of my recollection—and I am pretty darn certain about it—you will never once hear that from Senator Williams. You will hear language from Mr. Errichetti, but not in the presence of Senator Williams. As I recall always in the presence of the likes of Weinberg, language that would make longshoremen over on Third Avenue blush. I'm a grown man. I have seen a lot. I have done a lot. I have heard a lot. I must tell you that I was amazed listening to it, and you will be too. We will have to endure that together as we investigate these facts of this case and determine where justice lies.

> <

I have mentioned briefly this fellow "Weinberg." Melvin Weinberg, we are told, is a fellow that got in trouble with the law, and was prosecuted, and agreed to help out the FBI. As a result his sentence was reduced, and here we are today.

Well, as so much is the case with Mr. McDonald's opening and the prosecution's case, it is not that simple.

Weinberg had a long and checkered career. I will not belabor it. Essentially, he has been a criminal since he reached the age of about eight or nine. He has been perpetually in trouble. The point to bear in mind, when you hear him testify—and most of all when you watch him on the tapes—is that he has said and indeed has testified, has boasted, has bragged, that he is the greatest con man. I wouldn't at all argue with that assertion.

If it turns out at the end of the case, that my client, Senator Williams was conned, so be it because he is like you or me, a human being. He is not infallible. He is not without some fault or flaw, but he is not—I repeat—not a criminal. Above all, he is not corrupt. He was fooled by a Weinberg, so be it. I have a strong suspicion the proof will show you that not only did Weinberg fool Senator Williams and others—Weinberg did a pretty good job fooling the prosecution throughout this as well. Weinberg has had a long and checkered career with the law. He has been picked up from time to time, and he has had these problems, and what does he do whenever he gets into a problem? He becomes what the FBI calls an "informant."

In the early '70's he was an informant and, all the time he is helping out the FBI, being a wonderful citizen who has seen the light and the errors of his ways, what is he doing? He is running his deals on the side.

A time comes after this last escapade of Weinberg, and there are varying versions—whether in Pittsburgh or here in New York—but he is in and out of scraps all the time. He strikes up a deal with these fellows in the FBI, and off he goes. A man who has lived by his wits utterly, totally, who is completely immoral, disgusting; and he goes off.

You will find the evidence will show you that once this system, scheme, scam as the prosecution refers to it, began rolling, there were tremendous financial incentives to one Mel Weinberg, to keep it going. What did he do? He was getting—and don't hold me to the exact figures at this time—thousands of dollars a month. Three thousand dollars a month, five thousand dollars, sixty thousand dollars a year. That is not bad money. A little added bonus, and the testimony will be, that the FBI said, "You don't have to pay taxes on it." At this time he is making more than the Chief Justice of the United States Supreme Court, the Director of the Federal Bureau of Investigation, and the Vice President of the United States as well. Why shouldn't he keep it going?

He has a great thing going. These FBI fellows supposedly running this whole operation (using this reformed sinner, Melvin Weinberg, who is making a handsome living out of this), they also have a great incentive to keep it going. They're career men in law enforcement, and why not? The bigger the name you catch, the better off you are; the better the chances are for promotion and raise and so on and so forth. That is human nature. We have seen it all our lives. Weinberg made the bulk of the recordings of the audio tapes that stand before you in that cabinet and some of which you will hear. Enough to give you the evidence. I promise you if I overdo it, if I play too many, forgive me, but it is necessary.

I am sure that I need not say to you that this is a most important matter to my client, to myself, to the prosecution as well, and I suggest a most important matter to each of you. Because you're being called upon—those of you who have sat on juries before are aware of it, and those of you who have not may not be aware—you are called upon to sit as judges of the facts, to sit in judgment of your fellow man. Nothing you will do in your lives will rise to that dignity as to sit in judgment of your fellow man. It becomes almost biblical when you think about it. We lawyers are in Courts all the time, whereas you are here for a brief visit, a few weeks out of your lives. We do this all the time. We think about the majesty of your role, the importance of your role. But on to Weinberg.

Weinberg is a highly paid Government employee. He is given the right, the power, the authority to decide what he shall record and what he shall not record. Nobody disputes this. He is given the authority to decide what he can erase and what he won't erase, when to turn the switch on, when to turn the switch off.

> <

Now, what about the video tapes? You will see video tapes. We expect to produce video tapes that the Government itself won't produce. And think about that for a moment. We have designated them and we fully expect to show them. They haven't said that they will show them. Why? Because we want to have you hear the case and decide it on all the evidence, not what the prosecution only wants you to hear, but *all* the evidence.

I have a problem with that though. It is a problem that I will have to live with throughout this case. When you have a Weinberg controlling the switch on the machine, when you have a Weinberg deciding when you record and when you won't record, when you have a Weinberg deciding when you will erase and when you won't erase, when you have a Weinberg sitting in a room with a video camera going (and there are little gaps, but I will not make much out of it because we really don't know) and controlling the situation, directing the conversation—the net result of all that is that you the jury, the judges of the facts in this case, will see and hear only those tapes, those things on the tapes that the Weinbergs and his pals, the Amorosos, want you to hear.

Think about this at every instance of every minute that you sit and listen to or watch a video tape. At every point, at every one of those meetings, one or two people are present, depending upon the circumstances—be it Weinberg, sometimes Weinberg and Amoroso— knowing that everything that they say and everything that they do is being recorded. And they know why it is being recorded: because someday down the road there will be 16 citizens such as you who will hear it. Why do you do that? The answer is obvious. They want to convict. One hardly goes to all this exercise, all this running around, all these meetings, all that expense, all that manpower, if it is just a matter, "Well, maybe we will or maybe we won't. Let's see what sort of things happen." That is not the way it works. I appeal to your common sense.

Again on every tape that you will hear, on every tape that you will see, there will be others other than the two gentlemen charged here in this case—others whom you have heard about, Katz, Errichetti, Sandy Williams—who haven't the slightest idea that they are being recorded.

Now, does that mean that they are saying things or doing things that they wouldn't otherwise say or do? I don't know. But I've thought a little about it. You have all perhaps seen the show *Candid Camera*. It is humorous. It is interesting. I do not know if it is still on TV or not. People get a little embarrassed. Nobody did anything wrong. But it would be a little embarrassing afterward when they went into a store or whatever. Why? A very simple reason. Consider. I stand before you now in a courtroom. I do this, for this is my profession; this is my occupation—I try cases. I have done that for the last what, fifteen, sixteen years. I know that everything I say in this courtroom is being taken down by that gentleman. It will eventually be typed up. I obviously—any lawyer does, Mr. McDonald did—obviously thought about what he was going to say and chose his words accordingly because it's of record as we say.

Now, if I or some other lawyer or some other person stops at a local bar on the way home for a glass of beer, or sits in his den watching a football game, or plays in the backyard with his son or daughter—do you act the same as if everything you say and do is recorded? The answer is, of course not. There, in a relaxed, private atmosphere, which is conducive to an easy-going conversation—not a false one, not an inaccurate one, just as I would not talk to my son in my backyard playing ball as I would to the Court of Appeals (he would not know what I was talking about)—you act differently.

More than that, the Weinbergs and the Amorosos can guide, control and steer the conversation. They can use magic words—buzz words, as somebody once described them. Words like "influence," "contracts," "immigration," "legislation." We'll call them "buzz words."

Mark my words—and I will describe the facts in a little more detail, and again I beg your patience—mark my words, every tape we have ever seen, every tape that exists, every single solitary one, will establish this for you. There is no question—to my recollection—the first time government contracts are brought up, they are brought up by Melvin Weinberg. The idea, the insistence, the demand, the condition that stock certificates be in someone else's name, hidden or whatever, is not of anyone on trial in this case. It's that of Mel Weinberg. Every time anything happens that the government throws up to you and says, "Look, this is evidence of corruption, this is evidence of guilt," it is in every sense, in every instance, the product of the malignant imagination of Mel Weinberg and his cohorts.

> <

In June there is a meeting, June 7th; tape recorded is a telephone conversation between Melvin Weinberg and Alexander Feinberg. Feinberg says he's just spoken to Senator Williams—this is about the stock—and Senator Williams says to put it in his name—this is Feinberg's expression of Senator Williams—"The hell with it, I am going to report it."

Weinberg says he can't do that. They're liable to foul up Weinberg's steady income. That is why you can't do it.

You will see tapes, you will see conversations that are so obviously manipulated, so obviously controlled, so obviously directed by Weinberg, the master con man, that you wonder how this can come to be. Human nature is all I can say. But throughout, Senator Williams, Mr. Feinberg, the others, what do they talk about? Paying taxes. Hiring competent accountants. You are not going to do that if you are trying to conceal something. That is nonsense. Why even bother?

You heard about a discussion on June 28th with the Sheik, which you will see, and you will see what the Senator says. And you will also hear Mr. Weinberg and the Senator downstairs just before he goes upstairs to the room in the Marriott, down in Arlington, Virginia. I believe Room 1104, but I am not positive—we'll find out.

Weinberg meets him downstairs and says, "You got to impress the Sheik. Don't worry."

Williams says, "What is this about? It's a loan—strictly a legitimate loan."

Weinberg says, "Go upstairs and talk to the Sheik."

With Weinberg and the Senator, we then meet the Sheik. Weinberg leaves as soon as he introduces him. Then this fellow Errichetti, barely known to Senator Williams. Errichetti, who has a mouth that you will not believe. Errichetti had said, when they were waiting for the Senator to show up, "I'll get a pin and stick it into him if he doesn't say the right things. I'll use a baseball bat on him."

On and on and on. The Senator says he knows certain people. He is drawn out, and it is true he knows them and talks about titanium. Not about the titanium mine down in Virginia, because everyone knows the Government has stock piles. They're busy talking to these paint companies. If it makes this fellow Weinberg happy that Sandy should talk about contracts, let him talk about contracts or whatever.

It is very important, and you will see with your own eyes and hear with your own ears the proof. As Mr. McDonald eloquently put it, "You can't cross examine tape." True—and they can't cross examine their own tapes. But this is what they will have to do. If this is a conspiracy, revolving around the United States Senator to get government contracts—and it's ludicrous when you see the whole scenario played out—no one other than Weinberg can take it seriously.

And I doubt that Weinberg did. If this were a conspiracy to obtain government contracts, you will see time and time again Errichetti saying, "Get rid of the Senator. We don't need him. I can go to this guy. I can go to that guy. And in the White House I can do this." Oh, you can bet Weinberg wasn't about to do that.

Why? Because he had a meal ticket here from the Government, from the prosecution, from the FBI. He's making a couple of thousand, a tax break, and he winds up getting a bonus, extra payments. He's getting everything under the sun. As one lawyer in the Government put it in one proceeding, he has a bonus depending upon the number and the status of the people who are charged. Some system of government!

When you see these things, you weigh these things. You consider these things. Ask yourselves throughout, who orchestrated this? Who controlled it? Who? Why would he? Why did he? Was this a scheme by the Senator, Mr. Feinberg and Katz and the pathetic Sandy Williams to defraud or violate Federal Law? Nonsense. Rather, this is a scheme created, controlled, orchestrated, produced and directed by Weinberg, and ably assisted by Amoroso, to get people to say on video tape or audio tape something that could be used before a jury in a courtroom somewhere. As Weinberg said to another person we may call to testify—we expect to call—"It doesn't matter what they do so long as they say it on tape."

Indeed, when a commotion arises—and you will hear testimony about this, about Weinberg putting words in people's mouths, such as Senator Williams—Weinberg tells Government lawyers, Federal prosecutors and FBI agents, "If I don't put words in his mouth, we will never make a case." That's the kind of case you are dealing with here. It is a fraud. It is a sham. It is a farce. And if it weren't such tragic, serious business, it would almost be laughed out of court. But you have to cry rather than laugh.

Pay close attention to the tapes. Pay close attention to the people you are dealing with. Listen carefully. Listen for the nuances. Who is it that wants to pay taxes? Who is it that wants to hire top accountants and lawyers? Who is it that wants to deal with this thing in a legitimate way? Look at the person sitting at the table where I sit in this courtroom, and look the other way at the Government witnesses.

> <

One more matter and then I will conclude. The Judge pointed out I used more than enough time.

The final matter that the Government charges is this. On January 15th, they say Senator Williams meets the Sheik because the Sheik wants to come into the country. And the Sheik meets him (and you will see the tape of this), and the Sheik says, "I understand you are going—you can introduce legislation."

Of course, this is a fake Sheik. "And I understand you can introduce legislation so that I can stay in the country."

The Senator says, "No. There is no way that can be done."

There must be facts. There has to be some merit. There are all sorts of things, procedures, administrative things and so on and so forth that you have to know.

Well, ultimately, you sort of see this conversation gets bogged down on the video tape.

And then the Sheik says, "I want to offer you some money."

And the Senator says, "No, no, no." Five, six times.

"When it comes to things that are public business, public whatever"—and he goes on to explain. All of a sudden, Amoroso comes running into the door. "Sheik, you've got a phone call." Stop everything.

You know why? Watch it. See for yourselves. They don't want that poor fellow whom they have charged and put on trial to even give an explanation that could possibly help him before a jury like you.

Not satisfied with that, later on in the conversation—the conversation goes on a little further and the Senator goes back and says, "Look, you have to understand something."

Of course, he thinks mistakenly, sadly, he's dealing with some foreign potentate of some sort.

You've got to understand something and so on and so forth. "Now, that's not the way we do things."

What do they do? They ring the phone. The FBI is sitting in the next room.

The point I am getting at is this. What you are going to see on tape and what you are going to hear on tape is only what they want you to hear. They didn't give anybody a fair chance here. They didn't. Whether or not they should put people to a morals test, that is another story for another day. But even if that's the case, what they are trying to do—I don't know. They didn't even get a fair test because if anybody wants to act in a way to exculpate, they stop it. And above all they don't want you to see what we will show you.

This machination, the extent that they went through over and over again to make sure people said not what they meant, not what was the situation, but what Weinberg wanted them to say on these tapes that they will so proudly show you—this is a sad business.

I will wind up and I will conclude—and I have taken so much of your time, I apologize—by saying listen carefully to *all* the evidence. It is not the case Mr. McDonald described to you. If it were, I wouldn't have taken your time now, much less for the next several weeks when all the evidence is in.

I will conclude by saying—as I have been trying to describe for you for the past hour—that the evidence admits of only one possible conclusion. That on the charges that I say were malignantly brought through the use of a device like a Mel Weinberg, there is but one verdict, but one verdict at all. And that would be a verdict of not guilty.

Thank you very much.

DISCUSSION QUESTIONS

1. Consider this passage:

> Before I begin to take up your time and have you listen over the next several weeks to this case—and I appreciate your promise to well and truly try the case and your promise to be patient as Judge Pratt said yesterday. For the first function of a juror is patience, and it will be taxed.

Clearly the author is addressing the jury directly and informally, with no polished text before him. Do you think his language and oral style would be effective in the courtroom?

2. What effect would these lines have on a jury?

> "I ask your patience and indulgence now and throughout the case."
>
> "I will not belabor it. I know your time is valuable."
>
> "You might recall, some of us are a little older, it was the year known as the Eisenhower landslide."
>
> "No one else could tell you what the facts are, not I, for I am an advocate, not my opponent, not even Judge Pratt."
>
> "Nothing you will do in your lives will rise to that dignity as you sit in judgment of your fellow man."
>
> "I would not talk to my son in my backyard playing ball as I would to the Court of Appeals (he would not know what I was talking about)".

3. How does the author work to establish Senator Williams as a reliable authority, as a person to be believed?
4. How does he try to discredit Melvin Weinberg as an authority?
5. Does the case simply pit one man's word against another's?
6. The author argues that the audio-and videotapes are unrepresentative because Weinberg and the FBI could control the conversation and control the taping machines. Is this a reasonable argument?
7. "Whether or not they should put people to a morals test, that is another story for another day." Do you think the FBI (or anybody) has the right to put people to a morals test?

RUTH ADAMS
FRANK MURRAY

Vitamin E in the Hands of Creative Physicians

Of all the substances in the medical researcher's pharmacopoeia, perhaps the most maligned, neglected and ignored is vitamin E. In spite of this apparent ostracism in the United States, however, some of the world's leading medical authorities are using alpha tocopherol—more commonly known as vitamin E—to successfully treat and cure a host of mankind's most notorious scourges.

For those medical researchers who are at work trying to treat and prevent heart attacks—our No. 1 killer—and to help many more thousands who are dying of related circulatory disorders, vitamin E is playing a major role. And for many athletes, vitamin E (in the form of wheat germ oil, specially formulated oils for stamina and endurance, vitamin E capsules and perles, etc.) has long been as indispensable as calisthenics.

"There are over 570,000 deaths from heart attacks each year," says a publication of the American Heart Association, "many thousands of them among people in the prime of life—and growing indications that heart disease may be a disease of prosperity."

In scientific minds, vitamin E may be related to fertility and reproduction, said an article in *Medical World News* for April 18, 1969. But a famous ball player, Bobby Bolin of the San Francisco Giants, credits the vitamin with keeping his pitching arm in condition. He developed a sore shoulder in 1966, resulting in a poor pitching season for two years. He began to take vitamin E. The article said that he expected to be a "regular starter" at the beginning of the 1969 season, and that vitamin E was responsible for the good news.

It isn't surprising that many athletes have discovered the benefits of taking vitamin E regularly. The vitamin is in short supply in most of our diets. Vitamin E is an essential part of the whole circulatory mechanism of the body, since it affects our use of oxygen. When

Source: Reprinted from *Vitamin E, Wonder Worker of the '70's?* (New York: Larchmont Books, 1972), pp. 17–26, 31–32.

you have plenty of vitamin E on hand, your cells can get along on less oxygen. This is surely an advantage for an athlete, who expends large quantities of oxygen. And, according to recent research at the Battelle Memorial Institute, which we will discuss in greater detail in a later section of this book, vitamin E, along with vitamin A, is important to anyone who lives in the midst of constant air pollution.

From *The Summary,* a scientific journal published by the Shute Institute in Canada, a publication we will frequently refer to, we learn additional facts about vitamin E. Dr. Evan Shute, who heads the clinic, and Dr. Wilfrid E. Shute, his brother, have pioneered in work with vitamin E for more than 20 years. *The Summary* condenses and abstracts for doctors and medical researchers some of the material on relevant subjects that has appeared in medical journals throughout the world.

For instance, a Hungarian doctor reports on the encouraging effects of vitamin E in children born with certain defects. Of all vitamin deficiencies, she believes that vitamin E is the most important in preventing such occurrences. She has given the vitamin with good results in quite large doses to children who would otherwise be almost incapacitated. Mothers, too.

She tells the story of a woman who had three deficient children, two of them with Down's Syndrome or mongolism. When she was pregnant for the fourth time, the physician sent her away for a rest—"tired, aging, torpid" as she was, with "a diet rich in proteins, liver, vegetables and fruit with large doses of vitamins, especially vitamin E, and thyroid hormone." She returned in six weeks to give birth to a perfectly healthy baby!

As for another insidious disorder—chronic phlebitis—Dr. Evan Shute says that most doctors have no idea of how common this condition is. It should be looked for in everyone, he says, certainly every adult woman. After describing the symptoms—a warm swollen foot and an ache in the leg or foot which is relieved by raising the feet higher than the head—he tells his physician readers, "Look for chronic phlebitis and you will be astounded how common it is. Treat it with vitamin E and you will be deluged with grateful patients who never found help before."

Describing a symposium on the subject of vitamins E, A and K, Dr. Shute tells us that speakers presented evidence that vitamin E is valuable in doses of 400 milligrams daily for treating claudication—a circulatory condition of the feet and legs—and that a similar dosage helps one kind of ulcer.

High dosage of vitamin E improves survival time of persons with hardening of the arteries and should always be given to such patients, according to Dr. Shute. He adds that there are some 21 articles in medical literature, aside from the many he himself has written showing that vitamin E dilates blood vessels and develops collateral vessels—thus permitting more blood to go through, even though the vessel is narrowed by deposits on its walls.

An article that appeared in *Postgraduate Medicine* in 1968 by Dr. Alton Ochsner, a world-famous lung surgeon, states that he has used vitamin E on every surgical patient over the past 15 years and none has developed damaging or fatal blood clots.

Dr. Shute goes on to say that, at the Shute Clinic, all surgery patients are routinely given vitamin E both as a preventive and as a curative measure.

He quotes an article in *Annals of Internal Medicine,* saying that thrombosis or clot formation "has become the prime health hazard of the adult population of the Western world." Dr. Shute adds these comments: "Here is a real tragedy. Twenty years after we introduced a simple and safe clotting agent, alpha tocopherol, to the medical world, everything else is tried, including dangerous drugs and the anti-coagulants, and with all these the results are extremely unsatisfactory. When will the medical profession use vitamin E as it should be used for this condition?"

He quotes a statement from the *Journal of the American Medical Association* showing that the average teenage girl or housewife gets only about half the amount of iron she should have from her diet in the United States. Then Dr. Shute says, "Another nutritional defect in the best fed people on earth! In one issue the *JAMA* shows the average American is often deficient in iron and vitamin A. Now what about Vitamin E?" He, of course, has pointed out many times that this vitamin is almost bound to be lacking in the average diet. As we mention elsewhere, up to 90% of the vitamin E content of various grains is lost during the flaking, shredding, puffing processes that are used to make breakfast cereals.

Dr. Shute then quotes a newsletter on the U.S. Department of Agriculture survey revealing that only half of all American diets could be called "good." He comments thusly, "One continually reads claptrap by nutritionists contending that the wealthiest country in the world feeds everybody well. This obviously isn't true. It is no wonder that deficiency of vitamin E is so common when even the diet recommended by the National Research Council of the U.S.A. contains something like 6 milligrams of vitamin E per day before it is cooked!"

In another issue of *The Summary,* we learn how two Brazilian researchers are working on heart studies done on rats that were made deficient in vitamin E. Of 26 rats, only six normal ones were found. All the rest showed some heart damage when they were tested with electrocardiograms and other devices.

Two German researchers report on the action of an emulsified vitamin E solution on the heart tissues of guinea pigs. They found that the vitamin protects the heart from damage by medication, and helps to prevent heart insufficiency. Dr. Shute adds that this paper indicates that vitamin E should be investigated further in hospital clinics.

Animals deficient in vitamin E produced young with gross and microscopic defects of the skeleton, muscles and nervous system. They had harelips, abdominal hernias, badly curved backs and many more defects. This was reported in *The Journal of Animal Science,* Volume 22, page 848, 1963.

Two American obstetricians report in the *American Journal of Obstetrics and Gynecology* that they know of no way to prevent serious damage and death for many premature infants. Dr. Shute comments, "These authors apparently have not seen our reports on the use of vitamin E in the prevention of prematurity." He goes on to say, "No comparable results have been reported."

A report in the journal, *Fertility and Sterility,* indicates that in six percent of patients studied, the cause of abortion and miscarriage lay in the father's deficient sperm, not in any deficit of the mother's. The authors studied carefully the medical histories of many couples who had been married several times. Dr. Shute comments, "We have long advocated alpha tocopherol for poor sperm samples, especially in habitual abortion couples."

A Romanian farm journal reports that extremely large amounts of vitamin E, plus vitamin A, were given to 77 sterile cows. Within one to one-and-a-half months, their sexual cycles were restored and 70 percent of them conceived.

A German veterinarian reports in a 1960 issue of *Tierarztliche Umschau* that he uses vitamin E for treating animals with heart conditions. A one-year-old poodle with heart trouble regained complete health after 14 days on vitamin E. A three-year-old thoroughbred horse with acute heart failure was treated with vitamin E for two weeks, after which time its electrocardiogram showed only trivial changes even after exercise. The vet uses, he says, large doses of the vitamin.

And an Argentinian physician reports in *Semana Med.* that vitamin C is helpful in administering vitamin E. It works with the vitamin to retain it in body tissues. Dr. A. Del Guidice uses the two vitamins together in cases of cataracts, strabismus and myopias. He also noted that patients with convulsive diseases are much helped by vitamin E—massive doses of it—so that their doses of tranquilizers and sedatives can be lessened.

A letter from Dr. Del Guidice to Dr. Shute tells of his success in treating mongolism in children with vitamin E. For good results, he says, it must be given in large doses from the age of one month on. He continues his treatment for years sometimes, and claims that spectacular results can be achieved in this tragic disease.

Two Japanese scientists report in the *Journal of Vitaminology* that hair grew back faster on the shaven backs of rabbits when they applied vitamin E locally for 10 to 13 weeks.

And again from Argentina comes word of vitamin E given to 20 mentally defective children in large doses. In 75 percent, the intelligence quota was raised from 12 to 25 points, "with improved conduct and scholarly ability. Less attention fatigue was noted in 80 percent, and 90 percent had improved memory." A short experience with neurotic adults showed that vitamin E brought a definite reduction in phobias, tic, obsessions and other neurotic symptoms.

In one issue of *The Summary,* Dr. Shute prints a letter of his to the editor of the *British Medical Journal* (July 1966) urging this distinguished man to consider vitamin E as a treatment for pulmonary embolism. He says, "I have used nothing else for years and no longer even think of embolism (that is, blood clots) in my patients, even in those with records of previous phlebitis. Dosage is 800 International Units a day." He adds a PS to readers of *The Summary:* "The Editor could not find space for this letter unfortunately."

A *British Medical Journal* editorial comments on our present methods of treatment for blood clots in leg veins. Raising the foot off the bed, bandaging the legs and getting the patient on his feet doesn't seem to be very helpful, says the editor. Using anticoagulants seem to help some, but we should speedily develop some new methods of treatment. Dr. Shute comments that one would think that vitamin E has a clear field, since nothing else is very effective. It is easy to use, he goes on, safe and effective.

Each issue of *The Summary* contains many articles that have appeared in world medical literature on vitamin E and related subjects. In other countries, vitamin E is treated quite seriously in medical research, is routinely used in hospitals and clinics. In our country, such use is rare.

These are just a few of the case histories that Dr. Shute reports, at his own expense, in *The Summary.* The book is not available for nonmedical people, since it is written in highly technical terms. However, we suggest that you recommend these publications to your doctor, if you or someone you know is suffering from a disorder that

might be treated successfully with vitamin E. The address is: Dr.
Evan Shute, Shute Foundation for Medical Research, London, Ontario,
Canada.

DISCUSSION QUESTIONS

1. The case for vitamin E is supported by reference to a range of authorities:

    a. a publication of the American Heart Association
    b. an article in *Medical World News*
    c. Bobby Bolin of the San Francisco Giants
    d. many athletes
    e. recent research at the Battelle Memorial Institute
    f. *The Summary*
    g. The Shute Institute in Canada
    h. Dr. Evan Shute
    i. Dr. Wilfred E. Shute
    j. a Hungarian doctor
    k. speakers at a symposium on the subject of vitamin E
    l. 21 articles in medical literature
    m. an article in *Postgraduate Medicine*
    n. Dr. Alton Oschner
    o. an article in *Annals of Internal Medicine*
    p. a statement in the *Journal of the American Medical Association*
    q. a U.S. Department of Agriculture survey
    r. the National Research Council of the United States
    s. two Brazilian researchers
    t. two German researchers
    u. *the Journal of Animal Science*
    v. two American obstetricians
    w. the *American Journal of Obstetrics and Gynecology*
    x. a Romanian farm journal
    y. a German veterinarian
    z. *Tierarztliche Umschau*
    aa. an Argentinian physician
    bb. *Semana Med.*
    cc. Dr. A. Del Guidice
    dd. two Japanese scientists
    ee. the *Journal of Vitaminology*
    ff. an editorial in the *British Medical Journal*

   Evaluate the relative authority of these.

2. A number of consecutive paragraphs give quotations from respected medical journals along with Dr. Shute's commentary. Do these usually say the same thing?
3. The authors begin by noting that vitamin E has been "maligned, neglected, and ignored" by American doctors. How can this occur if the vitamin has been so successful in tests and studies?

4. Studies do show that animals and humans deficient in vitamin E improved significantly when given the vitamin. Does this prove that vitamin E should be added to most people's diet?
5. Who publishes *The Summary?*
6. How successful was Bobby Bolin as a pitcher in 1969?
7. Make a list of the maladies that vitamin E is said to cure. Do these wide-ranging claims for the vitamin make the case for it more persuasive?

Dr. James Durant, Professor of Psychology at Millburn University, demonstrates to a companion his celebrated powers of psychokinesis. The photograph was taken at the Faculty Club before a dozen professors. The event was supervised by Dr. Xavier Crosert, dean of the College of Arts and Sciences. (Redstone Wire Service photo)

DISCUSSION QUESTIONS

1. To establish the credibility of this argument, you must consider the photograph itself as well as the many references and sources involved. How reliable as authorities are the following?

    a. Dr. James Durant
    b. Professor of Psychology
    c. Millburn University
    d. a dozen professors at the Faculty Club
    e. Dr. Xavier Crosert

    f. Dean
    g. College of Arts and Sciences
    h. Redstone Wire Service
    i. *The Language of Argument*
    j. Daniel McDonald
    k. University of South Alabama
    l. Harper & Row, Publishers

2. If your investigation found all these sources to be reliable, might you still have reason to doubt the existence of psychokinesis?

Semantic Argument

Never eat at a place called Mom's.
—NELSON ALGREN, "What Every Young Man Should Know"

Semantic argument tries to make a persuasive point by using impressive language rather than by presenting or arranging evidence. It should convince no one.

Semantic argument always sounds good. Its effectiveness derives from the nature of words. A word can have two levels of meaning: a denotative meaning—that is, some specific thing or condition to which it refers ("mailman," "swim," "beige")—and a connotative meaning—that is, certain emotional responses that it arouses. Connotations can be negative ("politician," "deal," "filibuster") or affirmative ("statesman," "negotiation," "right of unlimited debate"). Semantic argument uses connotative words to characterize an issue or to enhance the tone of a discussion.

SNARL WORDS AND PURR WORDS

Connotative words (sometimes called "purr words" and "snarl words") do not prove anything; they simply label a thing as good or bad. American politicians of both parties regularly run for office, for example, on a program favoring *obedience to God, family, and country; adherence to law and order; separation of powers; fiscal responsibility; personal integrity; economic progress without inflation;* and *faith in the American dream.* They oppose *absenteeism, wasteful spending, communism, anarchy, economic floundering,* and *stagnation.* The essence of such argument is its vagueness—and its usefulness. When asked for an opinion on a controversial issue like busing, for example, a candidate can resort to language:

> *I'm glad you asked that question because I share your concern in this matter. My record shows I have always fought for the cause of education and for our children, who are the hope of this great nation. I recognize the profound complexities in this area and the honest differences presently existing between good men. I assure you I will work for a positive, fair, and democratic solution. Trust me.*

What is the speaker's view on busing? You can't even guess.

This kind of argument can praise any entity—a party platform, a current novel, a union demand—as *authentic, just, reasonable, natural,* and *realistic* or condemn it as *irresponsible, asinine, phony, dangerous,* and *superficial.* It can praise one citizen as a *Samaritan,* a *patriot,* and an *independent thinker* and reject another as a *do-gooder,* a *reactionary,* and a *pseudo-intellectual.* (One person's academic freedom is another person's brainwashing.) Such terms have little specific meaning. A rich collection highlighted the 1978 Alabama elections. There Fob James, a little-known candidate, won the governorship with a campaign that affirmed the *politics of compassion* and a *renaissance of common sense.*

Semantic language depends on its emotional associations. An automobile is more appealing when called an *Eagle SX/4;* a bill, when called a *right-to-work law;* and a military settlement, when termed *peace with honor.* In successful argument, much depends on establishing the right words. It is easy to champion *baseball, hot dogs, apple pie, and Chevrolet;* and it is hard to attack a position bulwarked with powerful language. (How can one oppose *fair trade* laws, the *right-to-life* movement, or a *clean air* act?)

Advertisers have called up an impressive range of associations to offer *Blue Cross, Lemon-fresh Joy, Cashmere Bouquet, Old Grand-Dad,* and *Lincoln Continental Mark VI*—plus *Barclay, Hustler, 280-ZX, Triumph Spitfire, English Leather,* and *Brut 33 by Fabergé.* Such names often make the difference. Millions of dollars have been earned and lost as *Carnation Slender* won the market from *Metrecal,* as *DieHard* outsold the *J. C. Penney battery,* as *Taster's Choice* defeated *Maxim* instant coffee. Today the largest selling perfume in the world is called *Charlie.*

Advertising executives Al Ries and Jack Trout (*Positioning,* 1981) argue that the second largest-selling mouthwash would have done better with a different name: *"Scope?* It sounds like a board game from Parker Brothers."

NAMES

Even names of people carry meaningful associations. In comic fiction, you know immediately that Mary Worth is good and that Snidely Whiplash is bad. Also, real-life examples demonstrate American rejection of vague or aristocratic names. Hollywood hired an actor named Leroy Scherer and starred him as Rock Hudson. (An actress named Doris von Kappelhoff became his co-star, Doris Day.) Household Finance Corporation has loan officers across the country who are presented to the public as "friendly Bob Adams."

Names are important in politics. John Varick Tunney had always been called Varick until he chose to run for office. After Opinion Research of California polled citizen response to the name *Varick,* he reverted to his unused first name and became Senator John Tunney. It is notable that the serious candidates for the presidency in 1976 (Senators Udall and Jackson, President Ford, Governors Reagan and Carter) were introduced as *Mo, Scoop, Jerry, Ron,* and *Jimmy.* In the 1980 race, the candidates were *Jimmy, Ted, Ron, George, Bob, John,* and *Big John.* Only Senator Baker *(Howard)* had a name that needed work.

INDIRECT STATEMENT

Semantic argument can also work indirectly; that is, in particular contexts, a purr word expressed is also a snarl word implied. To advertise "Oil Heat is SAFE," for example, is to imply that gas and electric heat are dangerous. To describe a movie as "not recommended for immature audiences" is to boast that it is impressively sexual or violent. When Tampax was advertised as a "natural cotton" product, it was reminding readers of the sponge tampons that had been associated with toxic-shock syndrome and several deaths.

Such argument was evident in the 1980 presidential campaign. When Senator Ted Kennedy challenged the President for the Democratic nomination, administration spokesmen were too civilized to mention the Chappaquiddick accident, but they regularly described President Carter as solid and responsible, the kind of person who would never panic in an emergency situation. During the general election, the Democrats broadcast a 5-minute television spot showing President Carter bustling through a hectic day and working late into the night. The implicit message was that candidate Ronald Reagan was nearly 70 years old and might not be able to handle the demanding pressures of office. In such instances, you are expected to recognize the implications of the surface argument.

Often, however, semantic claims are not meant to be penetrated. This is especially true when impressive language is used to mask a negative admission. For example, when government economists announce that the inflation rate is "slowing down," they wish to communicate optimistic reassurance rather than what the words really say, that prices are still high and are still climbing. When manufacturers label a garment "shrink-resistant," they want to suggest that it will not shrink, not what the term literally says, that the garment will resist shrinking and thus that shrinking will certainly occur. Advertisers for an inexpensive portable radio wish to imply that it is powerful and can pull in signals from distant stations, but what they say is, "You can take it anywhere."

PERSUASIVE STYLE

The attempt to communicate more than is literally said occurs also when a persuader uses impressive language to add character to an argument. Couching their views in religious allusions, folksy talk, or esoteric jargon, the advocates argue more with style than with facts. In a letter to *Saturday Review,* for example, Gelett Burgess maintained that Shakespeare of Stratford did not write the plays attributed to him. The language was intellectual:

> *Sir:*
>> *My recent communication relative to Oxford-is-Shakespeare elicited responses which evince and hypostatize the bigoted renitency usual in orthodox addicts. For the Stratfordian mythology has engendered a strange nympholepsy like a fanatical religion which is not amenable to reason or logic and abrogates all scientific method.*

As a contrast, consider the tone of this fund-raising letter sent out by Senator Jesse Helms during the 1980 campaign:

> *Dear Friend:*
>> *Will you do me a personal favor and place the enclosed bumper sticker on your car today?*
>> *And, will you use the enclosed form to let me know if I can send you a Reagan for President button to wear?*
>> *I'll be deeply gratified if I could hear from you immediately. . . .*
>>
>> *Won't you please, please dig down deep and give as you have never given before?*
>> *Whether Ronald Reagan wins or loses is up to folks like you and me.*
>> *The decision rests in our hands.*
>> *I pray that you will answer this call for help. God bless you.*

The author tries to make his message more persuasive by speaking as a Christian southern gentleman.

You should, of course, judge an argument solely on the evidence brought forward to support a conclusion, not on the effect of connotative language. Similarly, in writing argument, fight the temptation to overuse snarl and purr words. Avoid pedantic language and high-sounding phrases. Your reader will think, perhaps rightly, that you are compensating for weaknesses in your case.

> <

Connotative language defies meaningful analysis. Is it true that "Education without God produces a nation without freedom," that Nike running shoes are "faster than the fastest feet," that Fleischmann's Gin is "Clean . . . Clean . . . Clean"? Who can say? Until the claims are clarified and documented, such vague language can produce only empty and repetitive argument. Fleischmann advertisements, it should be noted, once offered to explain "What do they mean CLEAN . . . CLEAN . . . CLEAN?" The answer: "They mean the crispest, brightest drinks under the sun are made with clean-tasting Fleischmann's Gin." This is about as meaningful as semantic argument gets.

EXERCISES

How effective are these semantic arguments?

1. Look morning-lovely all day long. Use Revlon "Love-Pat."
2. Advertisement for *Valley of the Dolls:* "Any similarity between any person living or dead and the characters portrayed in this film is purely coincidental."
3. The Russian purges of the 1930s have been too emotionally depicted. What really occurred was a transfer of population, a rectification of frontiers, and an elimination of unreliable elements.
4. Every dogma has its day, and the dogma *du jour* is that women are oppressed. This notion seems to elicit favorable noises from the least likely people, including some feminist bogeypersons as Pope Paul and Hugh Hefner.
5. I can't decide what brand to smoke. I'm choosing between Barclay, Benson & Hedges, Carlton, Cambridge, Kent, Parliament, Tareyton, and Winston.
6. The human organism is a homeostatic mechanism; that is, all behavior is an attempt to preserve organismic integrity by homeostatic restoration of equilibrium, as that equilibrium is disturbed by biologically significant organizations of energies in the external or internal environments of the organism.
7. For a great light beer, try Anheuser-Busch Natural Light. Just ask for "a Natural."
8. When a correspondent wrote *Personality Parade* asking whether Elvis Presley had learned to act, columnist Walter Scott responded, "Mr. Presley has always been good to his mother."
9. I can't decide which car to buy. I'm choosing among a Dodge St. Regis, an Olds Cutlass Salon, a Caprice Silver Classic, and a Chevelle Malibu Classic Estate.
10. When the U.S. Senate "denounced" him for "reprehensible behavior," Senator Herman Talmadge declared this was a personal victory. The Senate had chosen not to "censure" him.
11. Rololfo Valentino—"The Shoes for Lovers"

ESSAY ASSIGNMENTS

Write an essay either affirming or opposing one of these statements. The material you encounter in your background reading will include a good deal of semantic argument, and so may your essay.

1. Abortion is murder.
2. Feminist organizations want to destroy American family life.

3. Who needs poetry?
4. Capital punishment is necessary.
5. The publishers of *Hustler* and *Penthouse* should be sent to jail.
6. America needs some old-fashioned patriotism.
7. X should be abolished. (Fill in the X.)

TEX CAMPBELL

Do Motorcyclists Have a Death-Wish?

"Death On Wheels" is one of the most blatantly ignorant, poorly rea-
soned, and clumsily written pieces of overt anti-biker propaganda that
it has ever been my displeasure to read. Its thesis—that motorcycles
are insanely dangerous and that bikers are obsessed with death—is
patently false to anyone with any experience of riding or any knowledge of bikers. Unfortunately, the average citizen is about as uninformed as Art Chenoweth, the Portland writer who calls upon cliches
and hackneyed stereotypes to make his simple-minded case against
street motorcycles and their riders.

If it weren't for the fact that most of his readers know little
about bikers, I would ignore Chenoweth and "Death On Wheels,"
treating them both with the contempt they deserve. But this ragged
exercise in anti-biker hysteria appeared in "Northwest Magazine," a
Sunday supplement to Portland's newspaper, *The Oregonian.* Because
it appeared in a respected newspaper, this article will convince many
naive readers, who will recirculate the same drivel elsewhere. Unfortunately, the damage has been done—few readers of *The Oregonian*
will see this reply to Chenoweth's rubbish, and the biker readership
of *Easyriders* knows the truth already. What's really scary is that
some dumbass car jockey may really buy this death wish baloney and
decide to assist some scooter tramp into the next world—grant his
wish by centerpunching him with the family bus. It's too late to undo
all the harm of this dangerous, irresponsible essay, but just for the record, let's examine the alleged biker romance with death.

For the most part, Chenoweth plays on his reader's preconcep-
tions and stereotypes about bikers, but even when he attempts to be
factual, he winds up with egg on his face. Finding the zero-percent
increase in Portland motorcycle fatalities between 1978 and 1979 embarrassing to the clumsy case he attempts to rig against bikers, the
writer points to a nine-percent increase in all types of motorcycle accidents during the same period. Presumably (since it's virtually the

Source: Reprinted from *Easyriders* (August 1981), pp. 111–115.

only actual statistic we're provided in the entire article), this figure justifies his later assertion. "Well, if they're [motorcyclists] really smart, they won't ride bikes on the street. Statistics should persuade them of that, just as statistics have persuaded so many people to stop smoking."

You don't have to be an actuary to spot the writer's statistical trick here, conveniently failing to provide the reader the figures for automobile and motorcycle registrations during the period in question. Were there more or fewer bikes on the street in 1979 than in 1978? More or fewer cars? If, in point of fact, there were more bikes on the streets of Portland in 1979 than in 1978, that nine percent jump may, for example, be nothing more than an expected reflection of those other increases. Moreover, if, as Chenoweth suggests, those statistics should convince the motorcycle rider to stay off the street, they should do the same for automobile drivers and pedestrians, since the yearly accident rate for each climbs more often than not. Even casually examined, then, his statistics reveal little about the dangers of riding bikes on the streets, nor do they warrant the alarmist tone of his conclusions.

The questionable "factual" evidence thus disposed of, we can turn our attention to the more philosophical aspects of this article. But first, a word about Art Chenoweth's rhetoric. In case you needed any proof that this essay stacked the deck against bikers, take a look at the language employed. Notice, for example, that while giving us Portland's motorcycle death statistics for 1978, the writer tosses in the incidental, if not irrelevant, fact that two pedestrians had been "mowed down" by bikes. Not "struck," mind you, or "knocked down" or even "flattened." No, "mowed down," an emotionally colored phrase implying that these weren't accidents, a phrase that suggests defenseless victims intentionally slaughtered in cold blood, conjuring up images of the St. Valentine's Day massacre. By contrast, Chenoweth later speaks of the "gang biker who gets smeared over the Sunset Highway" with the same matter-of-fact indifference you'd use to describe a squashed possum on the Interstate, and with the same assumption that it was the victim's own stupidity that brought about his death. The essay is peppered with words like "rotten" and "sleaziness" and "raunchy" to describe the "dirty leather world of the biker clubs." But none of this, obviously, has much to do with bikers and death wishes.

Unfortunately, many unsophisticated or uninformed readers won't be aware that their emotions are being manipulated by the writer and their stereotypes being reinforced by his biased presentation. That's why articles like "Death On Wheels" harm the cause of motorcycle safety and serve to deepen the mutual mistrust between bikers and citizen car drivers. The same uninformed reader will fall for Chenoweth's reportorial pose of knowledgeable objectivity. ("The article was in the newspaper, wasn't it? Then it must be true.") Yet this same writer knows so little about the world of bikes and bikers that he refers to the magazine you're reading as *Easyrider.*

Finally, a few words about mortality. "Death On Wheels" attempts to make the case that bikers have a death wish because death appears as a prominent motif of their lifestyle and culture. It's certainly true that death and its symbols (skulls and the like) appear in the life and literature of scooter people. But it is equally untrue that this constitutes a morbid preoccupation with the Grim Reaper. Today's society wants to pretend death doesn't exist, so it herds its old and sick and dying off to "homes" and hospitals, it embalms its corpses so that decomposition can't occur, it calls on a cosmetician to restore the "natural" blush of life to the face of a cadaver, and it hides the reality of death behind euphemisms like "passing away," robbing all of us—the mourners and the mourned—of the simple dignity of dying. So you tell me which attitude is more natural and healthy: the biker's sober recognition of this most basic fact of life, or society's attempt to sanitize death right out of our awareness?

Ultimately, death is what gives life meaning. The knowledge that our life will end gives personal significance to our actions. We make those choices that determine how we will spend our lives in the full knowledge that we won't have the chance again. Just as we couldn't appreciate the light of day unless we had experienced the darkness of night, only by an acceptance of death can we fully savor life. If bikers party heartier and run it to the redline more than the average Joe, it's due in part to their having a more mature perception of the ubiquity of death and the brevity of life.

Motorcycles are not, obviously, the safest form of transportation available. When a bike tangles with a car (usually driven by someone who's never ridden a motorcycle even once), the scoot and its rider generally come out on the losing end. And some of these encounters are terminal for the biker. All this is simple fact. But does it then follow that bikers have a death wish? No, on the contrary, they have a life wish. Speaking personally, I've never known a friendlier, more alive, more exuberant bunch than scooter people. They're in love with life, with the endlessly varied experiences it can offer, with the manifold diversity of life's possibilities. Death wish? Bullshit. While millions of miserable straights wither in the nine-to-five confinements of their deadly routines and responsibilities, bikers are out in the wind, packing more life into one day than most citizens will experience in a year.

If none of us risked our safety at least a little, what a dreary world we'd be plodding along in. Only by pushing it toward the edge now and then can we enjoy the security away from that edge. We're all going to croak, that's for sure. But in a very real sense, a lot of people are already dead even though they walk and talk. These neo-zombies are the victims of fear and conventionality and superstition and lies and their own meagre spirits.

I hope and expect to live a long time, but what makes today's experiences special is the knowledge that I might up and die right here at the typewriter before I finish this sentence you're reading. When I die, I hope I'm on my feet and giving it my best shot. Bikers know what I mean, and they won't trade the candyass security of death on the installment plan for the righteous risks of real life.

"When a man dies," wrote Charles Peguy, "he dies not from the disease alone. He dies from his whole life." Bikers die like everybody does. But they live like nobody else.

DISCUSSION QUESTIONS

1. The author responds to Art Chenoweth's essay charging "that motorcycles are insanely dangerous and that bikers are obsessed with death." Is this an accurate restatement of what Chenoweth said?
2. He objects to Chenoweth's language, to his calling the bikers "rotten" and "raunchy," to references to the "sleaziness" of the "dirty leather world of the biker clubs," to the description of two pedestrians being "mowed down" or of the "gang biker who gets smeared over the Sunset Highway." Is this a reasonable objection?
3. The author also objects to the language of the safe, middle-class world that puts old people in "homes," until they "pass away," whereafter it hires a cosmetician to restore the "natural" blush of life to the face of a cadaver. Is this a reasonable objection?
4. Consider the author's own language. How denotatively and connotatively meaningful are these lines:

> blatantly ignorant
> poorly reasoned
> clumsily written
> overt antibiker propaganda
> clichés and hackneyed stereotypes
> simple-minded case
> ragged exercise in antibiker hysteria
> dumbass car jockey
> death wish baloney

winds up with egg on his face
dangerous irresponsible essay

5. "These neo-zombies are the victims of fear and conventionality and superstition and lies and their own meagre spirits." Would this sentiment be more effective if presented in more denotative language?
6. What evidence is offered to support the claim that bikers live harder because they have "a more mature perception of the ubiquity of death and the brevity of life"?
7. "Bikers know what I mean, and they won't trade the candyass security of death on the installment plan for the righteous risks of real life." Does this line refute Chenoweth's claim that bikers have a death wish?

JAMES COUNCIL

THANK YOU FOR NOT SMOKING OR ANYTHING

My name is Jim Council. Fifty years ago I was a little boy, but now I'm all grown up. I smoke cigarettes. And I have had it with all the public-spirited grannies and nannies who keep telling me why I shouldn't smoke, where I shouldn't smoke, and how to live a richer, healthier life. To the Surgeon-General, the Cancer Society, the Lung Association, the memorable Joe Califano, and all you champions of public-smoking laws—I extend my curse.

There's only one anti-smoking organization I have any respect for, and that's one called SMASH (the Society for Mortification and Smoker Humiliation). This was established three years ago by a man named Rick Bennett in Washington state, and its essential mission is to beat up smokers. Any member who clobbers a smoker (known in the literature as "the smashee") earns a Hero Medallion and is eligible for membership in the SMASH Hall of Fame. The organization issues a guerilla manual spelling out DAMN (Drastic and Mortifyingly Nasty) countermeasures to be used against smokers lighting up in any area other than "the closets where they belong." The SMASH motto reflects the refined sensibilities of the membership:

> He Who Ignores a Request to Stomp One Butt
> Gets Two Butts Stomped.

Now I can't really object to these people. There's something complete and satisfying about their approach to things. The Smasher is a bullying psycho, of course, but he has a set of beliefs, a clear goal, and a program. I can handle him. If he threatens to beat me up, I can respond: I can beat *him* up; I can threaten him with my dog or my lawyer; I can hire a longshoreman to break his thumbs. It may get messy, but it will all be straight-forward and aboveboard.

I have less respect for all the people working to pass public-smoking laws. They want to restrict my smoking to my bedroom and one corner of a night-club and the back of an airplane. (SMASH

Source: Reprinted from *Alabama Sun* (October/November 1980), pp. 7–8.

members would let me smoke on the wing of the plane.) The smoking-law advocates want to separate me from my nonsmoking friends and give none of us any say in the matter. They want to make restaurants give half their space to a nonsmoking section and put up large signs over the area and small signs on the tables declaring "SMOKING PROHIBITED BY LAW." Printing on the small signs—in the proposed California and Dade County laws—must be "not less than ⅜ of an inch in height."

Much of this nonsense comes from nice people (like Carol Burnett) who fret about public health, and much comes from bureaucratic types who need nit-picking jobs and like to measure rooms and the print on little signs and issue non-compliance citations. Either way it reflects a mindless do-goodism which lacks the kind of fervor which makes SMASH and Carry Nation interesting. (Carry Nation, God bless her, insisted that President McKinley died of nicotine poisoning, a condition which was notably aggravated by two bullets in his stomach.)

But I'm not much worried about these anti-smokers either. (I still love Carol Burnett.) They can't bother me unless they get a law passed, and that's hard to do. I can marshal my forces in the democratic system and debate and lobby and mock and write letters and vote. I can handle these people.

What I really can't stand are the surrogate parents who treat me like a child and put up little signs saying "Thank You for Not Smoking." These mothers have me hemmed in. Oh, I could chain-smoke in their area. I could rip down the signs. I could write in comments, suggesting colorful acts I'd thank local people for performing. But these are demeaning responses. They make me look like a teenager or a slob or some kind of crazy zealot. So I can't do much of anything.

These stupid signs are popping up all over, and they defeat me. All I can do is fume and write this essay.

> <

OK, let's start at the beginning. Let's look at the whole tobacco scene. Why do all these people want me to stop smoking. I see three reasons—none of which amount to much.

CLAIM #1: Smoking Cigarettes Is Bad for Me

Tell me about it. I know what you're going to say. I've read the reports saying tobacco smoke contains nicotine and carcinogens and carbon monoxide and that inhaling it increases my chances of getting lung cancer and heart disease and all those other things. (I may be the only person in the South who read the Surgeon-

General's 1200-page report most of the way through.) I'm not impressed.

Does cigarette smoke contain carcinogens? Sure it does. And so do bleaching detergents, diet drinks, peanut butter, chlorine-treated water, coffee, bacon, urban air, the paint on my walls, and—now—beer. (This fall, the FDA warned us all that beer contains nitrosamines.) So where does that leave me? I can live a few years longer (maybe) if I forgo coffee, cigarettes, clean clothes, beer, peanut-butter sandwiches, big cities, and bacon-and-eggs. That's real living. And if I give up all this, what do I get? I'll have a better chance of living to be 80 years old so I can sit on a porch in Florida and look at my knuckles. Big deal!

The fact, Mr. Surgeon-General, is that living is hazardous to my health. And I'm the one who should define what I mean by "living."

Also, I'm not convinced that smoking causes any illness, not without some tricky redefinition of "cause." It's a plain fact that 95/96/97 percent of lifetime smokers don't get lung cancer and that a lot of nonsmokers do. Where's cause in that?

The Surgeon-General's Report illustrates the chanciness of all the cause-effect claims by offering a rich collection of language:

> Smoking "is causally related to" A.
> It "contributes to" B.
> It "acts synergistically to enhance the risk of developing" C.
> It "is related to" D.
> "An association" to E "has been reported."

Now I'm not blind to all this. I don't pretend that smoking may not increase my risk of getting A, B, C, D, and E. But these are not inevitable horrors; they're remote and unlikely threats to a life I'm going to lose anyway. While I've got it, baby, it's *my* life. I'm the one who decides what to do with it.

Let me say the unsayable: *Cigarette smoking is a rich and pleasurable experience.* (Read that again!) Smoking adds a happy dimension to my work, my social life, and my solitude. It helps me write. (As I fuss with this paragraph, a Viceroy burns in the ashtray on my left.) It helps keep my weight down. It eases introductions to new friends. It reflects my style. It tastes good. I'm not about to give this up.

I don't need the government or the medical establishment or private agencies or officious little signs to tell me what to do. I know the facts, I see the risk, and I choose to smoke. All you people, get off my back. I know what's good for *me*.

CLAIM #2: Smoking Cigarettes Is Bad for the People Around Me

Let me begin by saying that I don't smoke in elevators or doctors' offices. I don't light up in any place where I think someone might be bothered by my smoking—unless, of course, that someone puts up one of those nasty "thank you" signs. Then I'm smoking on principle.

Having said that, I hasten to add that I don't think my cigarette smoke hurts much of anybody. The Surgeon-General's Report said it found "little or no physiologic response to smoke" in healthy nonsmokers. OSHA has established 50 parts-per-million as a safe carbon monoxide limit for workers over an eight-hour day. Tobacco smoke, under realistic conditions, rarely exceeds 10 parts-per-million. Those are the facts.

The anti-smoking zealots don't want to talk about facts, however, or realistic conditions. They like to report high levels of carbon monoxide in the air around smokers. In one experiment they put four people—two smokers and two nonsmokers—in a closed, Volkswagen-size car in a closed garage and had the smokers smoke ten cigarettes in a one-hour period. Then the researchers reported an offensively high level of carbon monoxide afflicting the nonsmokers. Man, that's heavy science! The only conclusion you can draw from this study is that a prudent nonsmoker shouldn't accept an invitation to sit with smokers in a small car in a closed garage. (I have my doubts about those guys anyhow.)

The arguments get even weirder. Follow this one. The anti-smokers like to talk about the large numbers of Americans who suffer from conditions which are aggravated by tobacco smoke. They have emphysema, sinusitis, bronchitis, asthma, etc. To protect their health, cigarette smokers should be segregated away from them. This seems reasonable enough. The flaw in the argument is that these suffering souls are the same individuals who—in the anti-smokers' other literature—got those throat and lung diseases *because they were cigarette smokers.* The same people are reported as offensive smokers in one study and as offended nonsmokers in another. This leaves the critics in a curious position. They are working to protect large numbers of Americans from the effect of their own cigarette smoke. They are arguing they should be segregated—from themselves. (Welcome, Alice, welcome to Wonderland.)

Now I don't mind interesting craziness. I have some myself. (I think Coca-Cola gives me cold sores. I kind of believe in talking in tongues. I think Jimmy Carter has been a good President.) I'm willing to let anti-smokers count the parts-per-million of carbon monoxide in some garage. They can calculate the "social cost" of smoking. They can compute all those "excess deaths." ("Excess deaths"—think about that.) But I do mind being pushed around by these numbers. Just because they have some imaginative statistics doesn't mean I should have to hide in a closet to light up.

Besides, anyone who wants to segregate smokers is working from a principle which can reasonably be applied to rambunctious children, crippled old people (especially those with walkers who slow up a line), epileptics, and citizens who eat bermuda onions or wear strong perfume. This, friends, is a thoroughly crappy principle.

In a pluralistic society I have a right to do a lot of things which may offend somebody. I can eat snails, be homosexual, own a gun, have loud parties, cheer the Ayatollah, litter my front lawn, weigh 300 pounds, and vote for Jerry Brown. If I'm not demonstrably harming someone (besides myself), government should leave me alone. That's what individual freedom is.

Let's get on.

CLAIM #3: Smoking Cigarettes Is Bad

In my copy of his Report, the Surgeon-General twice refers to mortality ratios as "morality ratios." That's not even a Freudian slip. I think that's what he means.

One reason lots of people are so up-tight about my smoking is that they see tobacco as a neatly defined evil, which they are permitted to hate. And they have to hate something.

This is, I suppose, a fairly natural response to the frustrations and complexity of our world. A man lives in a society where inflation eats up his savings and minorities riot and he can't get gas for his car and his friends get sick and die and the Bomb may fall at any time. He can't understand any of this. If he tries to study to find real answers, he runs up against Keynesian economics, Islamic morality, the DNA molecule, process theology, and SALT-2—and he can't understand that either. So lots of people give up and embrace the easy answers they need to get along. They insist everything will be fine if we just get rid of communism or cane sugar or nuclear reactors or "demon" rum. They believe everything will be resolved if we accept Jesus or vitamin E or transformational grammar or solar energy. Nuke the P.L.O.!

Many of the people who identify cigarettes as the cause of cancer also champion laetrile as the cure. It figures. The true-believer lives in a comfortable world. I just don't want him messing up mine.

> <

Having discussed the whole tobacco argument, I'm back where I started. What can I do about all those "Thank You for Not Smoking" signs?

I think I'll put up some signs of my own.

The right language would mock the self-satisfied quality of the thank-you-for-doing-it-my-way signs. It would scorn that smug, we-all-know-I'm-better-than-you-are attitude. Hell, it could even strike a blow for human individuality and social variety! How about these for openers?

> THANK YOU FOR NOT BEING JEWISH.

> THANK YOU FOR NOT SPEAKING IN TONGUES.

> THANK YOU FOR NOT READING *PLAYBOY.*

> THANK YOU FOR NOT HAVING A DIALECT.

> THANK YOU FOR NOT VOTING
> FOR THIRD-PARTY CANDIDATES.

> THANK YOU FOR NOT HAVING AN ABORTION.

> THANK YOU FOR NOT BEING OLD.

That's enough, I think. I must have made my point by now.

> <

Thank you for letting me get all this off my chest.

DISCUSSION QUESTIONS

1. Go through the essay and do a profile of the speaker. He is a writer; he read the Surgeon-General's Report; he dissects facile argument; he can beat up SMASH members; he defends minorities; he champions beer, peanut butter, clean clothes, big cities; and so on. How does all this affect his argument in favor of smoking?
2. What evidence do you have that the person who wrote the essay is at all like this speaker?

3. Consider the entities the speaker rejects:

> *SMASH*
> *any member who clobbers a smoker*
> *a bullying psycho*
> *champions of public smoking laws*
> *bureaucratic types who need nit-picking jobs*
> *the "mothers" who put up "Thank You for Not Smoking" signs*
> *Carry Nation*
> *the Surgeon-General*
> *four people smoking in a closed garage*
> *segregationists who object to children, old people, and epileptics*
> *true believers offering simplistic solutions*
> *people who object to Jews, tongues-speaking Christians,* Playboy
> *readers, and foreigners.*

Is this a representative list of people who oppose smoking?

4. Does it help his case to add the "I still love Carol Burnett" line? Does it hurt him to include "Thank You for Not Having an Abortion" among the signs he wants to put up?

5. Some lines are effective in establishing a tone. What do these lines add to his argument:

> *"While I've got it, baby, it's my life."*
> *"All you people, get off my back."*
> *"This, friends, is a thoroughly crappy principle."*
> *"I think Coca-Cola gives me cold sores."*

6. How does the speaker respond to the statistical evidence relating cigarette smoking to increased incidence of lung cancer and heart disease?

S. L. VARNADO

"Hi, God!" — The Cult of Liturgical Informality

One afternoon my youngest son came home from Catholic school and informed me that his class had learned a new song for the Children's Mass next day, and that I probably would not like the new song, and did I want to hear it. Such an adroit introduction—calculated to whet my sense of righteous indignation as well as my curiosity—was irresistible, and I told my son to proceed. In a thin monotone he sang as follows:

> *Hi, God! How do you feel today?*
> *Can you hear us, God?*
> *There's a lot we'd like to say!*

Songs of this kind, I suppose, are what the good nuns at the school mean by making religion "relevant," but to me they make religion irrelevant and even archaic. Asking God how he "feels today" and inquiring about his hearing may have been all right for Neanderthal Man, but such an approach seems a bit eccentric for parochial school kids who learn, in their science classes, about black holes, DNA, and evolution (my son and I grapple with these concepts in his homework).

But the anthropomorphic conception of God was not my chief objection to the song. My chief objection was to the sense of unabashed egalitarianism shown toward the Deity—an attitude at once chatty, patronizing, and informal. Hi God, indeed! Do we really want children—or anybody else for that matter—addressing the Almighty in such a cavalier fashion?

This is a small incident, to be sure, but it is not without symbolic overtones. The attitude expressed in the song—the trivializing of the sacred—is a common phenomenon in Catholic worship these days. It is the outgrowth of a sort of unofficial movement or cult that arose in the Church shortly after Vatican II and that has been gaining momentum since. For the sake of simplicity it might be termed the Cult of Liturgical Informality. Its advocates—progressive bishops, rogue priests, fidgety nuns, dissatisfied intellectuals, and many rather bewildered lay people—are united by a vague impulse to make the liturgy livelier and more in keeping with modern times. To achieve this end they will try anything, no matter how exhibitionist, gauche, or just plain silly. Liturgical tradition counts for nothing, and they gleefully sacrifice the *mysterium tremendum* in favor of "relevancy, creativity, innovation."

For example, I witnessed a Mass celebrated by a dignified and highly educated priest of about 65. He entered the church with an air of grave decorum, and it was not until he was halfway to the altar that I noticed the bunch of multicolored, helium-filled balloons that he carried in his hand. These he proceeded to pop—one by one—throughout the service, with an expression of growing ecstasy on his face. I was appalled, but I am an optimist and I clung to the desperate hope that he would at least try to relate the balloons, in some symbolic fashion, to what was happening in the Mass. I thought perhaps that one of the biblical readings might possibly be the story of creation from Genesis, and that the bursting balloons might be intended to illustrate the big bang theory that the astronomers are full of these days. But I was wrong. It was detonation for detonation's sake.

Once set upon such a course, the disciples of the Cult of Liturgical Informality find unlimited possibilities opening before them; and one must admit that they have overworked their parochial imaginations to achieve new effects—"consciousness raising," I believe it is called. Thus, one priest makes a point of carrying on a running commentary during Mass, like a sports announcer: "Okay. Now we're about to begin the Liturgy of the Eucharist—where the action is, so to speak—so let's all hang loose and really try to get with it." Another goes in for sartorial innovation, including blue jeans, T-shirt, sandals, and no Roman collar. At a Mass I attended, the celebrant stopped the service *in medias res* to sing "Happy Birthday" to a venerable octogenarian in the congregation who probably did not know what was going on and who would have loathed it if she had. And then there was jolly old Father X who, according to one of my juvenile informants, performed the Children's Mass in a clown costume.

Children, in fact, are the special targets of the innovators. At a Mass in one of our local churches on Palm Sunday, a group of little girls clad as cheer leaders came in carrying large cardboard letters that spelled out "Jerusalem." This was a sight, I admit, to make the very stones cry out. On another occasion there was a Velveteen Rabbit

Mass for the kiddies, a delightful romp in which the children lay their stuffed animals upon the altar in a gesture of infantile sacrifice.

The idea of entertainment looms large in the minds of the disciples of liturgical informality, who seem to feel that the public will only attend church if there is a good show to be seen. Several years ago, I read of a Mass celebrated in Washington, D.C., at which a group of acrobats performed on the high wire. This, I thought at the time, would have been a fit occasion for the choir to sing "Nearer My God to Thee." Stranger still was an account carried by *Time* of an "outdoor Mass" celebrated in a rural area, the *pièce de résistance* of which was the arrival of the priest in a forklift truck. I never allowed myself to speculate on the possibility of this device being used during the Elevation.

Various kinds of popular music, including rock, disco, and folk, have long been staples at some of these performances, and recently there has been a tendency toward "liturgical dancing." A column in the Catholic press by a certain Fr. Joseph M. Champlain (a notable expert in such matters) describes one such experiment. To the pious strains of "Day By Day" two junior high ballet students, it seems, performed what Fr. Champlain calls "a liturgical expression of thanksgiving after Communion. . . . The congregation was absolutely still. I also detected tears here and there from persons moved by the event." (Fr. Champlain failed to note whether the "stillness" of the congregation was the result of shock, and whether the tears were of joy or of sheer rage, but I suppose that is a small point amidst such relevancy.)

The perpetrators of this sort of folly are, so far as I can tell, well-intentioned people who labor under the simplistic belief that merely by combining religion with worldly interests they can interest the worldly. The theory contains a modicum of truth. St. Paul tried it, with limited success, on the Greek intellectuals at Mars Hill. Likewise, the Catholic Church has always attempted to assimilate into her liturgy the best elements from many cultures. But the operative word is *best.* The process requires skill, prudence, and plenty of time— perhaps centuries. Like marriage, it is "not to be entered into lightly." But the Cult of Liturgical Informality represents the wholesale misapplication of the theory. These benighted, if well-meaning folk, have attempted to weld the spirit of the International Rotary Club, the Boy Scouts, the Pink Ladies, and a Barnum and Bailey circus upon the ancient rite. This is like substituting a Dale Carnegie course for the Spiritual Exercises of St. Ignatius Loyola, or transporting the Grand Ole Opry to the Sistine Chapel.

In recent months, the atmosphere at some of these charivaris has become so overripe that Rome has been forced to protest. On Holy Thursday of this year, Pope John Paul II issued an Apostolic Letter (*Dominicae Cenae*) aimed at some of the abuses; and some months ago the Congregation for the Sacraments and Divine Worship followed up with a letter setting forth specifics (*Inaestimabile Donum*).

In his Letter, the Pope takes issue with what he calls the modern urge to "desacralize everything," and with "a tendency to do away with the distinction between 'sacred' and 'profane.' " He speaks of the need for reverence, simplicity, and dignity in the performance of the Liturgy, and glances obliquely at "cases of a deplorable lack of respect toward the Eucharistic species." The minister, he says, "cannot consider himself a 'proprietor' who can make free use of the liturgical text and of the sacred rite as if it were his own property, in such a way as to stamp it with his own arbitrary personal style."

This gets at the heart of the matter. The Liturgy is not a "personal event"—it is, in a sense, public property. It belongs to the whole Church. By injecting personal whims, crochets, and eccentricities into the celebration, the innovators are commandeering something that is not theirs. In the process, they trivialize the great event. The mysterious and awesome feeling that the Protestant theologian Rudolf Otto termed the *numinous*—the *mysterium tremendum et fascinans*—will not remain long in an atmosphere replete with clowns, balloons, and rock music.

One can steadfastly hope that the Holy Father's words will have their effect in countering this new form of barbarism. If not, we may soon find that we need to alter the Third Commandment: not "Remember the Sabbath to keep it holy," but "Remember the Sabbath to keep it silly."

DISCUSSION QUESTIONS

1. The author objects to a number of features of Catholic worship:

    a children's hymn beginning "Hi God"
    liturgical "relevancy, creativity, innovation"
    a priest in blue jeans and "no Roman collar"
    a priest who sang "Happy Birthday" to an elderly parishioner
    children laying their stuffed animals on the altar in a gesture of sacrifice
    the use of disco, rock, and folk music
    liturgical dancing

    What is he affirming?

2. The essay mentions two extreme examples: the "highly educated" priest who kept popping balloons throughout mass and the commentator-priest with the

hip jargon ("the Liturgy of the Eucharist—where the action is, so to speak—so let's all hang loose and really try to get with it"). Do these examples seem real or literary?

3. The author rejects the "Velveteen Rabbit Mass" as an example of "infantile" sacrifice. Such things derive, he says, from "rogue priests," "fidgety nuns," and "dissatisfied intellectuals." Go through his essay distinguishing meaningful language from semantic argument.

4. The author says "Hi God" might have been "all right for Neanderthal Man" but that it does not belong in a modern parochial school that teaches about DNA and evolution. Taking this essay as evidence, do you feel the author himself is comfortable with the concepts of DNA and evolution?

5. Is there any evidence that simple children's hymns, up-to-date music, liturgical dancing, and so on are a post-Vatican II phenomenon rather than part of the Roman Catholic liturgy from its beginning?

DISCUSSION QUESTIONS

With the exception of the words "a" and "of" and the possible exception of the word "Bloomingdale's," every word in this advertisement has both a denotative and a connotative meaning. Distinguish these.

Fallacies

The flowers that bloom in the spring, tra la, Have nothing to do with the case.
WILLIAM S. GILBERT, *The Mikado*

Certain forms of misleading argument occur so commonly that they have been specifically labeled. Although most could be analyzed as faulty induction, deduction, and so on, they are treated separately here because the terms describing them should be familiar to you. You will meet them often; they are part of the language of argument.

FALSE ANALOGY

To argue by analogy is to compare two things known to be alike in one or more features and to suggest they will be alike in other features as well. This is reasonable argument if the compared features are genuinely similar. (Josh Woodward is an outstanding player-coach; he will make a fine manager.) It is fallacious if the features are essentially different. (You have *fruit* for breakfast; why not try *Jell-O* for breakfast?)

You test an analogy by asking whether the comparison statement (if there is one) is true and whether the elements compared in the argument are sufficiently alike. A comparison statement is particularly questionable if it is simply an adage. Reelection campaigns regularly submit, for example, that "You wouldn't change horses in the middle of the stream." But even the smallest consideration will remind you of situations in which you would be eager to change horses. Equally vulnerable are arguments insisting, "You can lead a horse to water but you can't make him drink" (meaning some people are unteachable) and "Where there's smoke, there's fire" (meaning some gossip is true). Hearing these analogies, you might want to point out that scientists can, with brain probes, make a horse drink itself sick—and that where there's smoke, there could be dry ice.

More often, you challenge an analogy by showing a fundamental difference between the things compared. A common argument insists, "We have Pure Food and Drug Laws, why can't we have comparable laws to keep movie-makers from giving us filth?" Here you must examine the definitions relating to "pure" and "filth." Food is called *impure* when the person eating

126

it gets physically sick. Because the individual who devours X-rated movies does not get sick, there is no comparable definition of pornographic *filth*. Thus the analogy fails. Similarly, facing the argument "We should no more teach communism in the schools than we should teach safe-cracking"—you can respond that knowing a thing is not practicing it and that, unlike safe-cracking, being a communist is not a crime.

Some analogies are more complex. An instance is this argument, which has appeared in many temperance campaigns: "There are 10,000 deaths from alcohol poisoning to 1 from mad-dog bites in this country. In spite of this, we license liquor but shoot the dogs." Because it is desirable to get rid of any dogs or any liquor that proves deadly, this analogy seems reasonable. The argument, however, hinges on the implicit recommendation that *all* liquor be outlawed. And this action is reasonable only if you are willing to pursue the comparison and shoot all dogs. Similarly, you should scrutinize popular arguments that compare independent nations with dominoes, and federal deficit spending with a family budget.

In writing persuasive essays, you will find analogies useful for illustrating a point or speculating on an event. But be careful. The comparison may make your subject seem trivial. (Evangelist David Noebel wrote that "Sex education without morals is like breakfast without orange juice.") Or it may add strange dimensions of meaning. (Author Jessamyn West praised the book *Four Cats Make One Pride,* saying, "It is about cats in the same way that *Huckleberry Finn* is about boys and *Madame Bovary* is about women.")

Keep your analogies simple and direct. Elaborate comparisons are rarely effective as argument.

PRESUMED CAUSE-EFFECT

Relating an event to its cause can lead to three different fallacies.

Argument in a Circle

Circular argument occurs when speakers offer a restatement of their assertion as a reason for accepting it. They make a claim, add "because," then repeat the claim in different words. ("Smoking is injurious because it harms the human body," or "One phone is not enough in the modern home because modern homes have plenty of phones.")

Sometimes the expression is more oblique, with the "because" implied rather than stated. (William Jennings Bryan once declared, "There is only one argument that can be made to one who rejects the authority of the Bible, namely, that the Bible is true.") It is pointless to argue that a thing is true because it is true. Repetition is not evidence.

Post Hoc Ergo Propter Hoc

The *post hoc* fallacy ("After this, therefore because of this") occurs when a person mentions two past events and insists that because one happened first, it necessarily caused the second. On such evidence, one can argue that Martin Luther left the Catholic priesthood in order to get married, that President Hoover caused the Depression, and that young people rioted during the 1960s because they were brought up under the permissive theories of Dr. Spock. Such logic can make much of local coincidence. *Christian Crusade* compared the statistics for two 6-week periods and headlined "Murder Rate Jumps 93 Percent in Oklahoma Following Death Penalty Ban." The cause-effect relationship was, it said, "self-evident."

Post hoc reasoning is fallacious because it ignores more complex factors that contribute to an event. A Smith-Corona advertisement proclaims that "Students Who Type Usually Receive Better Grades" and suggests that buying one's child a typewriter will improve his or her schoolwork. The fallacy here is the implication that simply owning a typewriter makes the difference. Other factors seem more likely to account for the higher grades: The parents who would buy their child a typewriter were those concerned about the youngster's education, who took pains to see that he or she studied—those who could afford to provide other cultural advantages as well. The typewriter alone gave no one higher grades.

Recognizing the post hoc fallacy will keep you from jumping to unwarranted conclusions. No one can deny, for example, that there exist people who wear copper bracelets and no longer suffer arthritis pain; heroin addicts who have been shown to have significantly fewer accidents than other drivers; patients who have been treated with L-DOPA and have experienced aphrodisiac effects; and individuals who had been related to John Kennedy's assassination (or to King Tut's tomb) who have died in a variety of ways. Nevertheless, the cases do not justify sensational cause-effect conclusions. A post hoc judgment would ignore the range of other factors involved.

Non Sequitur

Non sequitur means, "It does not follow." This fallacy occurs when a person submits that a given fact has led or must inevitably lead to a particular consequence. One can take a present fact (Governor Jerry Brown has been romantically involved with Linda Ronstadt) and project a conclusion (he would make a poor president). Or one can take an anticipated fact ("If the Equal Rights Amendment becomes law") and spell out the consequences ("American family life is doomed"). The reasonable objection, of course, is that the conclusion does not necessarily follow from the given cause.

The term non sequitur is widely used. And it lends itself to describe a multiple-cause argument ("The more you know—the more you do—the more you tax your nerves—the more important it is to relax tired nerves. Try safe, nonhabit-forming Sedquilin") or an argument so extreme that it falls outside the usual categories ("Of course the Jehovah Witnesses are communists; otherwise there wouldn't be so many of them"). But the term is of little value in defining general argument; almost any kind of fallacious reasoning is a non sequitur.

BEGGING THE QUESTION

Individuals beg the question by assuming what it is their responsibility to prove; they build their argument on an undemonstrated claim. Generally it takes the form of a question. ("Have you stopped beating your wife?" or "Is it true blondes have more fun?") It can, however, appear as a declaration. ("Busing is no more the law of the land than is any other communist doctrine.")

Another form of begging the question is to make a charge and then insist that someone else disprove it. ("How do you know that flying saucers haven't been visiting the Earth for centuries?" or "How can you explain the many miraculous cures produced by Edgar Cayce?") In all argument, the burden of proof is on the individual making the assertion. Never let yourself be put in a position where you have to disprove a claim that was never proved in the first place.

IGNORING THE QUESTION

People can ignore the question in two ways: They can leave the subject to attack their opponent, or they can leave the subject to discuss a different topic.

Argumentum ad Hominem

An *ad hominem* argument attacks the opposing arguer rather than the question at issue. ("Senator Thurmond favors resumption of the draft because he is too old to have to serve," or "District Attorney Phillips wants to become famous prosecuting my client so he can run for governor.") Here, nothing is said of the main issue; the speaker ignores the question by attacking an adversary.

It should be added, to avoid confusion, that an argument about a particular individual—a candidate, a defendant—is probably not ad hominem argument. In such a case, the person *is* the issue.

In your writing, try to avoid ad hominem argument. Attacking your opponent is almost an admission that your case is weak. If you have a substantial argument and want people to know it, a good policy is to flatter your adversary.

Extension

The fallacy of extension has the same effect. Here advocates "extend" the question until they are arguing a different subject altogether. (Invoking Senator Kennedy and Chappaquiddick, pro-Nixon bumper stickers proclaimed, "Nobody Drowned at the Watergate!") Invariably the new subject is one the speakers find easier to discuss. Regularly, opponents of gun registration begin their argument, "If guns are *outlawed*. . . ."

Either-Or

The either-or fallacy is a form of extension. Here partisans distort an issue by insisting that only two alternatives exist; their recommendation and something much worse. They will describe a temperance election as a choice between Christianity and debauchery. They will depict abortion as a choice between American family life and murder. Should you question America's involvement in an African or Latin-American war, they can challenge, "Which side are you on, anyway?"

To all such examples of ignoring the question, the reasonable response is "Let's get back to the issue."

FALLACIES IN OTHER FORMS

Most of the fallacies mentioned can be analyzed as examples of induction, deduction, semantic argument, and so on. Any false analogy, for example, is a deduction with invalid form. Any post hoc error is induction with an insufficient sample. And any kind of bad argument can be called a non sequitur. But special terms do exist for these fallacies, and it is perhaps valuable to have two ways of looking at them.

Unless you are championing a particularly weak cause, keep these fallacies out of your writing.

EXERCISES

Identify the fallacies in these arguments.

1. Major Claude Eatherly must be honored as a man of upright conscience. After partaking in the atomic raid on Hiroshima, he left the Air Force and suffered a mental breakdown.
2. All the speakers at the women's liberation rally were ugly as sin. No wonder they hate men.
3. I pay for my college education just the way I pay for my groceries in a supermarket. Why does the administration think it can tell me what courses I have to take?
4. Arguing from the principle that a person is sick "when he fails to function in his appropriate gender identification," Dr. Charles Socarides, a New York psychoanalyst, concludes that homosexuality is a form of emotional illness.

5. If evolution is true, why has it stopped?
6. No one in his right mind would give a baby a loaded machine gun to play with. Why then do so many people keep urging academic freedom on campuses?
7. I don't like the idea of abortion either, but I think it's better than having some poor woman kill herself trying to raise eleven or twelve children.
8. If capital punishment is immoral, then why did Jesus choose it as the means to save the world?
9. Register Communists; not guns.
10. I don't want to elect a divorced man as president. If a man can't run his own house, he surely can't run a whole country.
11. Gay people are essentially criminal. Look at all the homosexuality that goes on in prison.
12. Okay, if you think psychokinesis isn't possible, explain to me how Uri Geller can bend keys just by staring at them.

ESSAY ASSIGNMENTS

Write an essay either affirming or opposing one of these statements. The arguments you encounter in your background reading may well include logical fallacies. Your essay should have none, or at least none you didn't intend.

1. We should never have deserted our allies in Vietnam.
2. A massive conspiracy led to the assassination of President Kennedy.
3. Prostitution should not be considered a crime; there is no victim.
4. Daylight savings time is unnatural.
5. If I had a different name, I'd be a more successful person.
6. America's space program was a waste of money.
7. X causes crime. (Fill in the X.)

Diary of an Unborn Child

October 5

Today my life began. My parents do not know it yet, I am as small as a seed of an apple, but it is I already. And I am to be a girl. I shall have blond hair and blue eyes. Just about everything is settled though, even the fact that I shall love flowers.

October 19

Some say that I am not a real person yet, that only my mother exists. But I am a real person, just as a small crumb of bread is yet truly bread. My mother is. And I am.

October 23

My mouth is just beginning to open now. Just think, in a year or so I shall be laughing and later talking. I know what my first word will be: MAMA.

October 25

My heart began to beat today all by itself. From now on it shall gently beat for the rest of my life without ever stopping to rest! And after many years it will tire. It will stop, and then I shall die.

November 2

I am growing a bit every day. My arms and legs are beginning to take shape. But I have to wait a long time yet before those little legs will raise me to my mother's arms, before these little arms will be able to gather flowers and embrace my father.

November 12

Tiny fingers are beginning to form on my hands. Funny how small they are! I'll be able to stroke my mother's hair with them.

November 20

It wasn't until today that the doctor told mom that I am living here under her heart. Oh, how happy she must be! Are you happy, mom?

Source: Reprinted from *Mobile Press*.

November 25
My mom and dad are probably thinking about a name for me. But they don't even know that I am a little girl. I want to be called Kathy. I am getting so big already.

December 10
My hair is growing. It is smooth and bright and shiny. I wonder what kind of hair mom has.

December 13
I am just about able to see. It is dark around me. When mom brings me into the world, it will be full of sunshine and flowers. But what I want more than anything is to see my mom. How do you look, mom?

December 24
I wonder if mom hears the whispering of my heart? Some children come into the world a little sick. But my heart is strong and healthy. It beats so evenly: tup-tup, tup-tup. You'll have a healthy little daughter, mom!

December 28
Today my mother killed me.

DISCUSSION QUESTIONS

1. The argument about abortion hinges on the issue whether a fetus in early stages is a human person or a collection of cells. What evidence is offered here that the fetus is a person?
2. Consider all the things this fetus knows. It talks of sunshine, flowers, a mother, a father, a female name, death, the relative health of some fetuses, and the intellectual debate about personhood. What fallacy is illustrated here?
3. "I am a real person, just as a small crumb of bread is yet truly bread." How reasonable is this analogy?
4. Comment on the problems of definition that exist when an entity with no brain or brain cells says, "it is I already."
5. Who is saying "Today my mother killed me"?

CHRISTOPHER P. ANDERSEN
You Are What You're Named

One classes someone else when that person's name is given to him. Every Christian name has a conscious or subconscious cultural association which parades the images others form of its bearer, and has an influence on shaping the personality in a positive or negative way.

CLAUDE LÉVI-STRAUSS

Your name is the most important thing you will ever possess. What's in a name? We now know that names are so important that they figure in every human relationship. You must never enter into a business deal, fall in love, get married, have an affair, hire, fire, promote or go to work for someone else without first considering the implications of the other person's name.

What's in a name? Among other things, the difference between success or failure in the business world, or between social acceptability and an emotional, educational, even sexual handicap. Names are far more than mere identity tags. They are charged with hidden meanings and unspoken overtones that profoundly help or hinder you in your relationships and your life.

A rose by any other name may smell as sweet, but many people by another name would undoubtedly be better off. Some names trigger a positive response when we hear them; we tend to associate others with negative qualities. And if after reading this book you discover that you are a victim of your name, there *is* something you can do to make your name work for you.

Onomatology—the study of names—has been confined over the years to examining the etymology (linguistic origins) of names. But a handful of psychologists and other students of human behavior, so few that they scarcely number a dozen, have uncovered a startling new aspect to the science of onomatology. They have discovered that we are all affected in our business, family, social and sexual relationships by the connotations our names carry.

The scientific data are growing steadily. Three separate studies—among Harvard graduates in 1948, among child inmates of a New Jersey psychiatric institute and among mental patients in a Chicago institution—indicated that behavior problems occur much more frequently among those people with "peculiar" names. Not that a name need be bizarre to elicit a strong response from others. John may well inspire trust and confidence, while Benjamin is viewed with suspicion. Whatever the reactions of others, a name is unquestionably a vital part of each individual's psychological profile. For example: People with out-of-the-ordinary names are much more likely to commit crimes or suffer from some psychosis. Girls named Agatha are less popular and generally less attractive than girls named Susan. An Elmer is less likely to get good grades in school than a David. Barbaras tend to be aggressive—and successful. An Allen is generally regarded as serious, sincere and sensitive, and a Nancy as spiteful. Michaels are often perceived as winners, and Oscars as losers. People whose last names begin with the letters A through R generally live longer, healthier lives than do people in the S-Z group. The rich and the super-rich are, as we shall see, much more inclined to have strange names and use them to intimidate others. Learning about the power and influence of names can help you be a winner at—the Name Game.

In fact, you have been playing the Name Game all your life, whether you are aware of it or not. But even before you could start playing, your parents played, using you as a pawn. "There is no doubt that in many cases given names, short names and nicknames or whatever forename is bestowed or inflicted on the innocent newborn is a clear indicator of where his parents want him to go," contended psychiatrist Eric Berne, author of the bestselling *Games People Play* and originator of Transactional Analysis. "He will have to struggle against such influences, which will be continued in other forms as well, if he is to break away. This is something parents have control over and should be able to foresee." The sorry fact is that parents choose not to recognize the power that they possess. Instead, they show roughly the same degree of care in naming their children as they do in naming their pets, and sometimes less.

Soon enough, it was your turn to play the Game. As a child, you were influenced by your playmates' names, and you picked friends and enemies accordingly. In school, you either benefited or suffered from your name. Teachers viewed you, it has now been scientifically established, in a certain way in large part because of your name. These associations were to be reinforced over the years.

When you enrolled in college, or applied for your first job, you may well have used your full formal name—first, middle and last—to lend weight to your application. Before getting engaged, you almost certainly toyed with your intended's name. Perhaps you scribbled it over and over again next to yours, or tried to imagine what your first name would look like once it was wedded to his surname on a marriage license.

On the job, you have been swayed by the impressive-sounding names of your superiors. But you have also felt superior to some of your co-workers because their names conveyed the unarticulated message that they are losers. If you have ever hired someone, you avoided applications with names that for some reason made you feel uncomfortable. At the same time, you were inclined to give the nod to those whose names, carrying positive connotations, spelled out success. And when your first child arrived, you dipped into your own deep well of prejudices and came up with a name that, as Eric Berne stated, was "a clear indicator of where you want him to go."

Thus the circle closed.

YOUR NAME IS YOUR FATE

Test your familiarity with the powerful influence names have on our lives by arranging the following men's and women's names according to what you perceive to be their general desirability. Which would *you* choose to name your son, your daughter?

Arlene	*Barrett*
Maureen	*Kevin*
Jennifer	*Benjamin*
Norma	*Stephen*
Shirley	*Michael*

Studies indicate that Jennifer should rate at the top of the girls' names, followed by Shirley, then Arlene, Norma and Maureen. Michael is the most positive of the boys' names. Close behind are Stephen and Kevin—two strong, easily accepted names—while Barrett and Benjamin trail at a considerable distance. To you, the differences may have been imperceptible. But they nonetheless would have had an unparalleled impact on your child throughout his life.

The proof that we are either the victims or beneficiaries of our names is all around us. Yet despite the substantial evidence, every year names are inflicted on an estimated 3 million newborn Americans whose parents give little or no thought to the broad implications. More and more parents are consulting astrology charts and numerologists, but the overriding concern in selecting a name (aside from paying homage to a relative) is still the same: How does it sound? Phonetic balance, as name authority Evelyn Wells pointed out as early as 1946, is a legitimate concern. "Science," she wrote, "tells us of the power of sounds and words to influence the mind." But science now tells us that the cadence and the melody of a name are not nearly so significant as the associations it carries.

One who understands all too well is *New York Times* columnist Russell Baker. "At this very moment," he lamented, "it is an almost certain bet that somewhere in America a mother is naming her newborn son Kenneth and thereby freighting him with heavy psychological luggage that he will carry with him to the grave. The difficulty with being a Kenneth is that Kenneths are expected to be lean and fibrous. A Sydney or a Wallace has a perfect right to be shaped like a rail or a balloon, and the Kenneths' knowledge that they are denied this freedom of contour must surely fill them with hostility." As for those poor fellows named Irving, Baker continued with tongue firmly planted in cheek, an Irving "knows that he is consigned to the intellectual life, doomed at worst to years with Nietzsche in the library stacks, at best to writing brilliantly denunciatory letters to the editors of elite magazines."

Humorous—and quite plausible. We tend to become what others expect us to become, to conform to society's expectations. That may even extend to one's physical appearance. A person whose name implies obesity—Bertha, for example—may subconsciously try to live up to that preconception. The name Irving *does* have a certain egghead quality; hence the proliferation of Irvings on the faculties of universities. And as Harveys became increasingly incensed over their lackluster image, thousands of them (including one closet Harvey, pianist Van Cliburn) banded together in 1970 to get people to stop thinking of Harveys as bumbling boobs—and thereby lessen every Harvey's chances of becoming one.

There is ample cross-cultural evidence that this phenomenon is by no means restricted to American society. The *British Journal of Psychology* reported that the Ashantis of Ghana name their children after the day of the week on which they were born. According to the old nursery rhyme, "Monday's child is fair of face/Tuesday's child is full of grace/Wednesday's child is full of woe/Thursday's child has far to go/Friday's child is loving and giving/Saturday's child works hard for a living/But the child that is born on the Sabbath Day/Is bonny, and blithe, and good, and gay."

Monday's child, named Kwadwo, is expected to be quiet and peaceful. The grim forecast for Wednesday's child, named Kwaku, is apparently shared by the Ashanti, who look upon Wednesday's child as aggressive and temperamental—a monumental headache. In accordance with this self-fulfilling prophecy, boys born on Wednesday were found among the Ashanti to have a significantly greater frequency of juvenile court arrests than boys bearing the names of other days of the week.

As author Muriel Beadle says, "For any child a name which interferes substantially with normal interaction is a handicap. The expectations of one's society shape behavior."

DISCUSSION QUESTIONS

1. The author mentions the "science of onomatology," the "scientific data [that] are growing steadily," the "ample cross-cultural evidence," and the "proof" that is "all around us." What substantial evidence does he give to show that Susans are attractive, Barbaras aggressive, and Nancys spiteful?
2. "People whose last names begin with the letters A through R generally live longer, healthier lives than do people in the S-Z group?" What evidence supports this? What evidence *could* support it?
3. If you met a person named Cabbage Mackeral Smith and discovered he had had a difficult, frustrated life, would you assume that his name contributed to his difficulty? What besides his name was probably a significant cause?
4. What common fallacy is illustrated when one says a person's name was the cause of his personal problems?
5. Consider your own first name. According to Dr. Berne, this is a "clear indicator" of where your parents wanted you to go. Where did your parents want you to go?
6. Have you ever chosen or rejected a friend on the basis of his or her first name? Is it possible you may have done it unconsciously?
7. How creditable is Russell Baker in a scientifically persuasive essay?
8. "The name Irving *does* have a certain egghead quality; hence the proliferation of Irvings on the faculties of universities." How many Irvings teach at your school?
9. These are real names. What do you know about the named individuals? What can you reasonably speculate about them?

Lance Alworth	J. Dudley Dixon III
Sylvia Council	Mitchell Fairman

Dupont Gonzalez
Jim Bob Harris
Ima Hogg
H. Robert Huntley
Fob James
Savannah Lee Jensen
Boris Karloff
Elwood Lilly
Oscar Lipscomb
Ace Loomis

Jahala Noble
Maureen O'Mara
Rhonda Young Ready
Barefoot Sanders
Bug Scott
Denise Shumock
Donald Sniegowski
Marion Sidney Sweatt
Alesa Weiskopf

HUMPHREY ATKINS

Northern Ireland

NOT A "COLONIAL SITUATION"

First of all let me dispel a few widespread myths about Northern Ireland. It is emphatically not a "colonial situation": it is not "Britain's Vietnam." For a start it is geographically and politically part of the national territory of the United Kingdom—constitutionally just as much so as England, Scotland or Wales. It is not some far-flung outpost of imperialism struggling to free itself from the suppressive yoke of an ancient conqueror.

By air from London it takes about the same time as the shuttle from Washington to New York, and it is to London that the vast majority of the people of Northern Ireland freely look for the foundations of their way of life. Their political preoccupation—expressed in election after election—is with preserving the union with Great Britain and their attachment to the supreme authority of the British government and Parliament.

What I am saying, in short, is simply this: The idea put about in the United States and elsewhere by people emotionally committed to a united Ireland that Britain is in Northern Ireland against the wishes of the people there is demonstrably false. Anyone advancing such views is either totally ignorant of the facts or deliberately irresponsible and mischievous.

Which brings me naturally to the associated issue of "get the British army out of Northern Ireland." In the light of what I have just said, you might just as well call for the withdrawal of British troops from England, Scotland or Wales—because you are really posing the absurd proposition of removing units of the nation's armed forces from a part of the national territory. It is like arguing that the armed

A speech delivered by the North Ireland Secretary of State to the Association of American Correspondents, London, England, October 26, 1979.

Source: Reprinted from *Vital Speeches of the Day* (November 15, 1979), pp. 66–67.

forces of the United States have no right to be in California or Connecticut.

As those of you who have studied the problem will know—and those of you who haven't certainly ought to know—we are dealing with a well-orchestrated propaganda campaign which goes hand in hand with the vile and inhuman terrorist campaign of the provisional IRA. As long as Northern Ireland wishes to remain a part of the United Kingdom—and Parliament has provided for a periodic referendum to test that desire—the army will be there, as it should be for national defense purposes. It was there in garrison strength in permanent barracks before the present situation arose. And it is only there in considerably greater numbers on an active basis now because of the terrorist campaign.

Those who cynically clamour for an end to its active role in aid of the police in Northern Ireland know perfectly well that nothing would please both her majesty's government and the people of Northern Ireland more. And these same people—whether they be in Northern Ireland itself, in the Republic of Ireland, in Great Britain, or in the United States of America—also know perfectly well that the reversion of the army's role in the province to its normal garrison activity can very simply and swiftly be achieved. All it needs is for the fruitless terrorist campaign which some of these people misguidedly support, or murderously participate in, to come to an end. The ball is firmly in the IRA's court—not ours.

But until such times as these men without morals or mandate halt their campaign of carnage and destruction, the army will continue to fulfill its difficult and dangerous task of aiding the small and hard-pressed police force of the Royal Ulster Constabulary to protect the citizens of Northern Ireland from the worst excesses of the terrorists. And whatever the impression you may get from some of the headlines, they have been doing this with conspicuous success.

I venture to suggest that were a similar sustained terrorist threat to be launched in, say, Texas or Alaska, aimed at forcing the state against its democratic will to become part of a neighboring country, Washington would hardly leave it to the local civil power to cope on its own.

In saying all this I am not denying the democratic right of people in Northern Ireland or the Republic of Ireland to aspire to the peaceful unification of the whole island of Ireland by consent. Nor do I deny their right to work publicly and politically toward that end. It is an aspiration shared by the main political parties in the Republic of Ireland and by the Social Democratic and Labour Party in

Northern Ireland, which represents some 20 percent of the voters.

But all of them recognize it as a long-term goal which, if it is to be achieved at all, must be by the freely expressed democratic wish of a majority of the people in Northern Ireland. None of the elected political leaders north or south supports or condones the achievement of a united Ireland by force of arms. They realize that "unity" obtained at the expense of the maimed and the murdered would not be worth having even if it were possible—which it is certainly not. And I need hardly remind this informed audience that only a few weeks ago on his historic visits to Ireland and the United States, the Pope added his clear condemnation of terrorist violence to the many other influential voices which have been raised against it, including the President of the United States and other leading political figures there like Senator Kennedy, Speaker O'Neill, and Governor Carey.

The urgent need in Northern Ireland is for provincial political institutions to be reestablished so that the government and Parliament in London can restore to the people of Ulster more control over their own domestic affairs. But the formula must be broadly acceptable to both sections of the community in Northern Ireland, and it must involve a form of government which both sections can identify with and spontaneously support. That is the task which I have been actively engaged in with the leaders of the main political parties in Northern Ireland since taking office in May. It is one that, following my statement in the House of Commons yesterday, is about to enter a new accelerated phase.

Briefly, the government plans to have a conference of the four main political parties in Northern Ireland under my chairmanship—parties which between them account for four out of five voters in the province. The intention is that it should meet before the end of November; but before it does so, the government will publish a consultative document as a basis for its deliberations.

This document will contain—by way of illustration—a number of different "models" or possible systems of government, any one of which might in the government's view suit the special circumstances of Northern Ireland. All will be capable of adaption, and our hope is that they will be adapted at the conference in such a way that they can be accepted by representatives of both sides of the community as fair and just.

But I would delude myself and mislead you if I were to pretend the way ahead will be easy. It will require a superhuman effort on the part of all the participants and enormous goodwill and forbearance on the part of those outside Northern Ireland who will be anxious observers of our progress—notably in Great Britain, the Irish Republic and the United States. It will greatly help this process if there is more understanding at all levels in those countries of the true situation in Northern Ireland and the totally legitimate and responsible role of Her Majesty's government and armed forces in the province.

I hope that as a result of speaking to this audience today more of that awareness will be forthcoming in the United States—and that that will in turn temper the attitudes and utterances and activities of some people and groups there who in their profound ignorance of the situation only play into the hands of an outcast terrorist organization whose stated aim is to destroy the democratic structure of government in Ireland North and South and replace it with a distinctly Marxist orientated regime.

DISCUSSION QUESTIONS

1. In rejecting the notion that Northern Ireland is Britain's Vietnam, part of a "colonial situation," the author uses a number of analogies:

   > Northern Ireland is geographically and politically part of the national territory of the United Kingdom—constitutionally just as much so as England, Scotland, or Wales.
   >
   > Asking that British troops be removed from Northern Ireland is like arguing that the armed forces of the United States have no right to be in California or Connecticut.
   >
   > Were a similar sustained terrorist threat to be launched in, say, Texas or Alaska, aimed at forcing the state against its democratic will to become part of a neighboring country, Washington would hardly leave it to the local civil power to cope on its own.

   Do these seem to be reasonable comparisons?

2. In the following examples, distinguish between meaningful language and semantic argument:

   > "Anyone advancing such views is either totally ignorant of the facts or deliberately irresponsible and mischievious."
   >
   > "we are dealing with a well-orchestrated propaganda campaign which goes hand in hand with the vile and inhuman terrorist campaign of the provisional IRA."
   >
   > "All it needs is for the fruitless terrorist campaign which some of these people misguidedly support or murderously participate in to come to an end."
   >
   > "an outcast terrorist organization whose stated aim is to destroy the democratic structure of government in Ireland North and South and replace it with a distinctly Marxist orientated regime."

3. Does the author make any reference to the words "Catholic" and "Protestant" in his essay? Does this suggest there is more to the issue than he has indicated?

"It's a mistake inviting a conservative and a liberal to the same party. Bailey wants to save unborn babies and Rankin wants to save the snail darters."

© 1980 by National Review, 150 East 35th St., New York, NY 10016. Reprinted from *National Review* (November 28, 1980), p. 1456.

DISCUSSION QUESTIONS

1. Name the fallacy illustrated by this cartoon.
2. "It's a mistake inviting a conservative and a liberal to the same party. Bailey wants to_____, and Rankin wants to_____ _____." Fill in the blanks to form the same fallacy as it might be expressed by a liberal.
3. Can you express a simple, one-sentence reply to such fallacies?

Statistics

"Statistics are a highly logical and precise method for saying a half-truth inaccurately.
　　　—From a file in the NASA archives

There are a number of ways in which statistics can be used to distort argument. Persuaders can cite impressive averages, irrelevant totals, and home-made figures. They can offer a number in a context that makes it appear larger or smaller, according to their wish.

AVERAGES

A common fallacy involves the use of "average" figures: average income, average price, average audience size, and so on. It is easy to argue from such statistics because the word "average" can mean three things.

What, for example, is the average if a group of fifteen homemakers, responding to a poll question, say that they watch television 48, 40, 30, 26, 22, 18, 12, 10, 9, 8, 5, 5, 5, 1, and 0 hours a week? From this it can be said that the group watches television an average of 15.933 hours a week, or 10 hours a week, or 5 hours a week. The 15.933 figure is the *mean* (the total number of hours watched, divided by the number of viewers); the 10 figure is the *median* (the middle number in the series); and the 5 figure is the *mode* (the number that appears most frequently).

Each kind of average has its value, according to the kind of material being measured. But all three are available to the person who seeks to manipulate an argument.

QUESTIONABLE FIGURES

Vague statistics can produce impressive averages. Numbers derived from memory, guesswork, and exaggeration can be averaged with amazing precision. (In the preceding paragraph, the 15.933 average was computed after fifteen homemakers made rough guesses of their television viewing time.) Dr. Kinsey interviewed American men and reported that those without a high-

145

school education averaged 3.21 sex experiences a week. The annual FBI report *Crime in the United States,* compiling material from police departments across the country, showed that Baltimore in one year had suffered a crime increase of 71 percent. But police departments report crimes differently and with different degrees of accuracy; the sensational Baltimore figure derived from more accurate police reporting in the second year rather than from a huge increase in crime.

Similarly, amazing claims can be drawn from a small or partial sample. Some years ago a survey reported that 33-1/3 percent of all coeds at Johns Hopkins University had married faculty members. Johns Hopkins had three women students at the time. Advocates of extrasensory perception thrive on partial samples. They like to report cases where a gifted individual (Hubert Pearce, Basil Shakleton, or another) has produced laboratory results in which the odds are 10,000,000 to 1 against chance as the explanation. Commonly, it is discovered that such cases were *part* of a longer series of tests and that the results of the entire experiment were not given.

IRRELEVANT NUMBERS

An argument can be bulwarked with irrelevant statistics. Some years ago cigarette companies responded to evidence that smoking may cause cancer by counting filter traps. Viceroy boasted 20,000 filters ("twice as many as the other two largest-selling brands") until Parliament began claiming 30,000, and Hit Parade overwhelmed both with 400,000. (That was an average figure. The testing lab reported that one Hit Parade filter had 597,000 filter traps.) These are impressive figures but totally pointless. There was no evidence that *any* filter protected a person from the dangerous effects of smoking. And no one had defined "filter trap." This practice of putting large numbers to undefined elements is particularly notable in people who like to count UFO sightings.

Currently, ads for cigarettes and pain relievers offer precise numbers and irrelevant comparisons. Kent Golden Lights are celebrated for having only 8 milligrams of tar ("as low as you can go and still get good taste") in an ad pointing out that Camel Lights and Raleigh Lights have 9 milligrams of tar and Salem Lights have 10. Anacin boasts 800 milligrams of "pain reliever" and observes that Tylenol, Bayer, and Bufferin have only 650. There is no evidence that these distinctions make any real difference to the consumer.

Even when counting clearly defined entities, speakers can offer irrelevant numbers. In a period of high unemployment, they can proclaim that more Americans are working than ever before. Responding to the demonstrated statistical relationship between cigarettes and increased incidence of lung cancer, they can observe that the vast majority of smokers do not get cancer. As violent crimes increase, they can oppose gun-control legislation by computing that only 34/10,000 of 1 percent of American handguns are involved in homicides.

There is also a kind of irrelevance in statistics derived from a singular example. Hollywood Bread, for example, advertised that it had fewer calories per slice than other breads; this occurred because its slices were cut thinner. Carlton cigarettes boasts it has regularly been tested as lowest in "tar" of all filter kings; one reason is that it has a longer filter than other cigarettes of the same length and therefore contains less tobacco. Television personality Hugh Downs announced that he got 28.3 miles per gallon while driving a Mustang II from Phoenix to Los Angeles; the trip is largely downhill.

HOMEMADE STATISTICS

The preceding examples indicate that people do not have to make up statistics to create a misleading argument. But, of course, they can make up statistics if they want to. For example, the temperance advocate who built an analogy on the claim that there were 10,000 deaths from alcohol poisoning to one from mad-dog bites, was using figures that exist nowhere else.

Homemade statistics usually relate to events that have not been measured or are impossible to measure. Authorities can be suspiciously precise about events too trivial to have been counted. (Dr. Joyce Brothers reported that the "American girl kisses an average of seventy-nine men before getting married." And a Lane cedar chest advertisement warned that moths destroy $400,000,000 worth of goods each year.) They can be glibly confident about obscure facts. (A *Nation* article said that there were 9,000,000 rats in New York City; and Massachusetts Congressman Paul White, introducing a bill to make swearing illegal, announced that Americans curse 700,000 times a second.)

Imaginary numbers like these usually relate to areas in which it is impossible to get real figures. To make an impressive argument, advocates may want to specify the number of homosexuals in America today—or the number of pot smokers, or adulterous wives. They may want to report how much money was spent on pornography last year—or on welfare fraud or illegal abortions. The writers can find some information in these areas, but because final exact counts remain unavailable, they are strongly tempted to produce a statistic that supports the case they are trying to make. Many give in. Remember this the next time you see headlines that announce that a rail strike in Chicago is costing the city $60,000,000 a day.

Even in instances where a measure of scientific computation has occurred, resulting statistics often seem singularly creative. Recent news stories have announced that 17 percent of babies born to near-affluent parents are unwanted; that 5 percent of Americans dream in color; that heroin addicts in New York City steal $2 to $5 billion worth of goods a year; and that men aged 35 to 50 average one sexual thought every 25 minutes. With a little practice, you can identify homemade statistics with the naked eye.

ENHANCING A STATISTIC

By careful presentation, persuaders can make any statistic seem bigger or smaller, as their argument requires. For example, many newspapers reported the 1968 Oberlin College Poll revealing that 40 percent of the unmarried coeds had engaged in sex, that one in thirteen of these became pregnant, and that 80 percent of the pregnancies were terminated by abortion. The ''80 percent'' figure seems startling until you ask ''80 percent of what?'' Relatively modest statistics appear sensational when given as percentages of percentages of percentages.

More commonly, one changes the character of a statistic by simple comparison. The speaker relates it to a smaller number to make it seem large or to a larger number to make it seem small. The contrasting number need have no relevance aside from offering an advantageous comparison.

In presidential primaries, candidates routinely predict weak results. The speaker—George McGovern, John Anderson, or another points out that the contest is not in his strongest state, that other duties have limited his public appearances, and that, all in all, he will do well to win 8 percent of the vote. Then when he wins 11 percent, his followers announce, ''He did well. His vote exceeded expectations.'' One reverses the process to dwarf a statistic. In the early 1970s, when George Wallace—the law and order candidate—had to face the fact that Alabama had the highest murder rate of any state in the nation (11.4 per 100,000), it was explained that this figure was not nearly so high as that of Detroit, Los Angeles, and other major cities.

In a summary statement on statistical manipulation, Darrell Huff (*How to Lie with Statistics,* 1954) counseled the business community:

> *There are often many ways of expressing any figure. You can, for instance, express exactly the same fact by calling it a one percent return on sales, a fifteen percent return on investment, a ten-million-dollar profit, an increase of profits of forty percent (compared with 1935–39 average), and a decrease of sixty percent from last year. The method is to choose which one sounds best for the purpose at hand and trust that few who read it will recognize how imperfectly it reflects the situation.*

In a society subject to political controversy, social argument, and Madison Avenue rhetoric, such argument is common.

> <

You should recognize examples of distorted statistics and, of course, avoid them as much as possible in your writing.

Even when numbers favor your case, do not use them too extensively. A mass audience is rarely persuaded by a body of statistics. (This explains why they are used so infrequently in the antismoking campaigns of the American Cancer Society and the American Heart Association.)

You should remember, finally, that a number by itself means little or nothing. If in a particular year Montreal leads the major leagues with 179 double plays, what does that mean? That it has a fine second baseman? That it has poor pitchers? That its home park has an Astro-turf infield? Who knows? When 46 of 100 beer drinkers who "regularly drink Budweiser" preferred an unmarked mug of Schlitz (in a 1980 New Orleans test), what does that prove? Probably that most drinkers can't tell one beer from another. What can you conclude about an $18,000 annual salary, a 150-word poem, a $7.95 meal? Not much. An important quality of statistical argument was expressed in a scene in *Annie Hall:* The lovers, played by Diane Keaton and Woody Allen, are asked by their psychiatrists how often they have sex. She responds, "All the time. Three times a week." And he says, "Hardly at all. Three times a week."

EXERCISES

How reliable are these statistical arguments?

1. If you begin having your hair styled, are people going to think you've gone soft? Half the Los Angeles Rams' line has their styled. If you want to laugh at them, go ahead. We don't.
2. Researchers report that the average man makes up his mind in six short seconds whether or not he wants to know a woman better.
3. Listerine Antiseptic stops bad breath four times better than toothpaste.
4. We need more federal aid to local schools. There are still 1,400,000 illiterates in the United States.
5. On "Solidarity Day" (September 19, 1981), thousands of union workers massed in Washington to protest Reagan administration economics. U.S. park police estimated the crowd at about 260,000. AFL–CIO officials called it half a million.
6. Leo Guild's book *What Are the Odds?* reports that a young person with a broken engagement behind him is "75 percent as happy" as one who was never engaged.
7. Wartime statistics: Last week the Viet Cong lost 1231 men. American and Vietnamese losses were moderate.
8. Every year Americans waste 3.8 billion gallons of gasoline by driving inefficient or untuned engines.
9. Using a simple cipher (A= 6, B = 12, C = 18, etc.), the words KISSINGER

and COMPUTER both total 666, the number of the Antichrist. Certainly, this proves something.

10. Jaguar advertisement: "You'll get 14 MPH from Park Avenue to Wall Street and 20 MPH from Beverly Hills to Palm Springs."

11. It is estimated that each year, some 10 million wise Americans spend $500 million on essential life-building food supplements and vitamin capsules. Can 10 million Americans be wrong?

ESSAY ASSIGNMENTS

Write an essay either affirming or opposing one of these statements. The material you encounter in your background reading will include statistical argument; so should your essay.

1. American industry *is* fighting pollution.
2. We need gun-control laws to curtail crime.
3. Sex education leads to promiscuity, pregnancy, and disease.
4. It's proved: Cigarette smoking causes lung cancer.
5. IQ tests do not prove anything.
6. American income-tax laws should be revised.
7. Statistics demonstrate that X is a mistake. (Fill in the X.)

ISAAC ASIMOV

The Case Against Man

The first mistake is to think of mankind as a thing in itself. It isn't. It is part of an intricate web of life. And we can't think even of life as a thing in itself. It isn't. It is part of the intricate structure of a planet bathed by energy from the Sun.

The Earth, in the nearly 5 billion years since it assumed approximately its present form, has undergone a vast evolution. When it first came into being, it very likely lacked what we would today call an ocean and an atmosphere. These were formed by the gradual outward movement of material as the solid interior settled together.

Nor were ocean, atmosphere, and solid crust independent of each other after formation. There is interaction always: evaporation, condensation, solution, weathering. Far within the solid crust there are slow, continuing changes, too, of which hot springs, volcanoes, and earthquakes are the more noticeable manifestations here on the surface.

Between 2 billion and 3 billion years ago, portions of the surface water, bathed by the energetic radiation from the Sun, developed complicated compounds in organization sufficiently versatile to qualify as what we call "life." Life forms have become more complex and more various ever since.

But the life forms are as much part of the structure of the Earth as any inanimate portion is. It is all an inseparable part of a whole. If any animal is isolated totally from other forms of life, then death by starvation will surely follow. If isolated from water, death by dehydration will follow even faster. If isolated from air, whether free or dissolved in water, death by asphyxiation will follow still faster. If isolated from the Sun, animals will survive for a time, but plants would die, and if all plants died, all animals would starve.

It works in reverse, too, for the inanimate portion of Earth is shaped and molded by life. The nature of the atmosphere has been changed by plant activity (which adds to the air the free oxygen it

Source: "The Case Against Man" from the book *Science Past—Science Future* by Isaac Asimov. Copyright © 1970 by Field Enterprises, Inc. Reprinted by permission of Doubleday & Company, Inc.

could not otherwise retain). The soil is turned by earthworms, while enormous ocean reefs are formed by coral.

The entire planet, plus solar energy, is one enormous intricately interrelated system. The entire planet is a life form made up of nonliving portions and a large variety of living portions (as our own body is made up of nonliving crystals in bones and nonliving water in blood, as well as of a large variety of living portions).

In fact, we can pursue the analogy. A man is composed of 50 trillion cells of a variety of types, all interrelated and interdependent. Loss of some of those cells, such as those making up an entire leg, will seriously handicap all the rest of the organism: serious damage to a relatively few cells in an organ, such as the heart or kidneys, may end by killing all 50 trillion.

In the same way, on a planetary scale, the chopping down of an entire forest may not threaten Earth's life in general, but it will produce serious changes in the life forms of the region and even in the nature of the water runoff and, therefore, in the details of geological structure. A serious decline in the bee population will affect the numbers of those plants that depend on bees for fertilization, then the numbers of those animals that depend on those particular bee-fertilized plants, and so on.

Or consider cell growth. Cells in those organs that suffer constant wear and tear—as in the skin or in the intestinal lining—grow and multiply all life long. Other cells, not so exposed, as in nerve and muscle, do not multiply at all in the adult, under any circumstances. Still other organs, ordinarily quiescent, as liver and bone, stand ready to grow if that is necessary to replace damage. When the proper repairs are made, growth stops.

In a much looser and more flexible way, the same is true of the "planet organism" (which we study in the science called ecology). If cougars grow too numerous, the deer they live on are decimated, and some of the cougars die of starvation, so that their "proper number" is restored. If too many cougars die, then the deer multiply with particular rapidity, and cougars multiply quickly in turn, till the additional predators bring down the number of deer again. Barring interference from outside, the eaters and the eaten retain their proper numbers, and both are the better for it. (If the cougars are all killed off, deer would multiply to the point where they destroy the plants they live off, and more would then die of starvation than would have died of cougars.)

The neat economy of growth within an organism such as a human being is sometimes—for what reason, we know not—disrupted, and a group of cells begins growing without limit. This is the dread disease of cancer, and unless that growing group of cells is somehow stopped, the wild growth will throw all the body structure out of true and end by killing the organism itself.

In ecology, the same would happen if, for some reason, one particular type of organism began to multiply without limit, killing its competitors and increasing its own food supply at the expense of that of others. That, too, could end only in the destruction of the larger system—most or all of life and even of certain aspects of the inanimate environment.

And this is exactly what is happening at this moment. For thousands of years, the single species Homo sapiens, to which you and I have the dubious honor of belonging, has been increasing in numbers. In the past couple of centuries, the rate of increase has itself increased explosively.

At the time of Julius Caesar, when Earth's human population is estimated to have been 150 million, that population was increasing at a rate such that it would double in 1,000 years if that rate remained steady. Today, with Earth's population estimated at about 4,000 million (26 times what it was in Caesar's time), it is increasing at a rate which, if steady, will cause it to double in 35 years.

The present rate of increase of Earth's swarming human population qualifies Homo sapiens as an ecological cancer, which will destroy the ecology just as surely as any ordinary cancer would destroy an organism.

The cure? Just what it is for any cancer. The cancerous growth must somehow be stopped.

Of course, it will be. If we do nothing at all, the growth will stop, as a cancerous growth in a man will stop if nothing is done. The man dies and the cancer dies with him. And, analogously, the ecology will die and man will die with it.

How can the human population explosion be stopped? By raising the deathrate, or by lowering the birthrate. There are no other alternatives. The deathrate will rise spontaneously and finally catastrophically, if we do nothing—and that within a few decades. To make the birthrate fall, somehow (almost *any* how, in fact), is surely preferable, and that is therefore the first order of mankind's business today.

Failing this, mankind would stand at the bar of abstract justice (for there may be no posterity to judge) as the mass murderer of life generally, his own included, and mass disrupter of the intricate planetary development that made life in its present glory possible in the first place.

Am I too pessimistic? Can we allow the present rate of population increase to continue indefinitely, or at least for a good long time? Can we count on science to develop methods for cleaning up as we pollute, for replacing wasted resources with substitutes, for finding new food, new materials, more and better life for our waxing numbers?

Impossible! If the numbers continue to wax at the present rate.

Let us begin with a few estimates (admittedly not precise, but in the rough neighborhood of the truth).

The total mass of living objects on Earth is perhaps 20 trillion tons. There is usually a balance between eaters and eaten that is about 1 to 10 in favor of the eaten. There would therefore be about 10 times as much plant life (the eaten) as animal life (the eaters) on Earth. There is, in other words, just a little under 2 trillion tons of animal life on Earth.

But this is all the animal life that can exist, given the present quantity of plant life. If more animal life is somehow produced, it will strip down the plant life, reduce the food supply, and then enough animals will starve to restore the balance. If one species of animal life increases in mass, it can only be because other species correspondingly decrease. For every additional pound of human flesh on Earth, a pound of some other form of flesh must disappear.

The total mass of humanity now on Earth may be estimated at about 200 million tons, or one ten-thousandth the mass of all animal life. If mankind increases in numbers ten thousandfold, then Homo sapiens will be, perforce, the *only* animal species alive on Earth. It will be a world without elephants or lions, without cats or dogs, without fish or lobsters, without worms or bugs. What's more, to support the mass of human life, all the plant world must be put to service. Only plants edible to man must remain, and only those plants most concentratedly edible and with minimum waste.

At the present moment, the average density of population of the Earth's land surface is about 73 people per square mile. Increase that ten thousandfold and the average density will become 730,000 people per square mile, or more than seven times the density of the workday population of Manhattan. Even if we assume that mankind will somehow spread itself into vast cities floating on the ocean surface (or resting on the ocean floor), the average density of human life at the time when the last nonhuman animal must be killed would be 310,000 people per square mile over all the world, land and sea alike, or a little better than three times the density of modern Manhattan at noon.

We have the vision, then, of high-rise apartments, higher and more thickly spaced than in Manhattan at present, spreading all over the world, across all the mountains, across the Sahara Desert, across Antarctica, across all the oceans; all with their load of humanity and with no other form of animal life beside. And on the roof of all those buildings are the algae farms, with little plant cells exposed to the Sun so that they might grow rapidly and, without waste, form protein for all the mighty population of 35 trillion human beings.

Is that tolerable? Even if science produced all the energy and materials mankind could want, kept them all fed with algae, all educated, all amused—is the planetary high-rise tolerable?

And if it were, can we double the population further in 35 more years? And then double it again in another 35 years? Where will the food come from? What will persuade the algae to multiply faster than the light energy they absorb makes possible? What will speed up the Sun to add the energy to make it possible? And if vast supplies of fusion energy are added to supplement the Sun, how will we get rid of the equally vast supplies of heat that will be produced? And after the icecaps are melted and the oceans boiled into steam, what?

Can we bleed off the mass of humanity to other worlds? Right now, the number of human beings on Earth is increasing by 80 million per year, and each year that number goes up by 1 and a fraction percent. Can we really suppose that we can send 80 million people per year to the Moon, Mars, and elsewhere, and engineer those worlds to support those people? And even so, merely remain in the same place ourselves?

No! Not the most optimistic visionary in the world could honestly convince himself that space travel is the solution to our population problem, if the present rate of increase is sustained.

But when will this planetary high-rise culture come about? How long will it take to increase Earth's population to that impossible point at the present doubling rate of once every 35 years? If it will take 1 million years or even 100,000, then, for goodness sake, let's not worry just yet.

Well, we don't have that kind of time. We will reach that dead end in no more than 460 years.

At the rate we are going, without birth control, then even if science serves us in an absolutely ideal way, we will reach the planetary high-rise with no animals but man, with no plants but algae, with no room for even one more person, by A.D. 2430.

And if science serves us in less than an ideal way (as it certainly will), the end will come sooner, much sooner, and mankind will start fading long, long before he is forced to construct that building that will cover all the Earth's surface.

So if birth control *must* come by A.D. 2430 at the very latest, even in an ideal world of advancing science, let it come *now*, in heaven's name, while there are still oak trees in the world and daisies and tigers and butterflies, and while there is still open land and space, and before the cancer called man proves fatal to life and the planet.

DISCUSSION QUESTIONS

1. An extended section of this essay compares the growth of human population on earth to the growth of a cancer in a body. Is this a reasonable analogy? Comment on the range of meaning it expresses.
2. The author compares the population of the earth in Julius Caesar's time and at present. Where could he obtain these numbers? Do you have any reason to doubt their reliability?
3. When he indicates the total mass of living objects on earth to be perhaps 20 trillion tons (200 million tons are human beings), the author admits these are not precise figures but are "in the rough neighborhood of the truth." How might these estimates be obtained? Do you have any reason to doubt their reliability?
4. In what sense is the exactness of such figures irrelevant?
5. How reliable is Isaac Asimov as a scientific authority?
6. When the author envisions a world on which every square mile has "three times the density of modern Manhattan at noon," a world without "oak trees . . . and daisies and tigers and butterflies," he is not talking simply of the inevitable extinction of mankind. What is he warning us of?
7. How does the author suggest the necessary worldwide birth control be achieved?

SUSY SMITH

ESP

Ever since the earliest days of psychical investigation, researchers have been trying to find out why ESP happens, and hoping to understand all of its characteristics. Yet through all experimentation, then and subsequently, *psi* (as the psychic power is often called) has remained so elusive and unfathomable that no exact explanation of it has ever been formulated.

Because of this, research has tended to take the direction of trying primarily to indicate ESP's existence and to prove that it is repeatable. Tests have been made over and over again for almost a century with the object of identifying various forms of extrasensory perception and very little more. One wonders why it seems necessary for researchers to repeat this so endlessly, until it is realized that because of psi's very intangibility, proving its existence on acceptable scientific grounds becomes an enormous challenge.

The importance of tests which would utilize chance probabilities was remarked by Gurney: "Of course the first question for science is not whether the phenomena can be produced to order, but whether in a sufficient number of series the proportion of successes to failure is markedly above the probable result of chance." This basic statement has been repeated incessantly by others.

Although Gurney spoke so wisely of chance, it is Professor Charles Richet of France who gets credit for the initial use of the mathematics of chance in evaluating results of telepathy tests. And in 1885, Sir Oliver Lodge, another great physicist who interested himself in psychical research, proposed that conclusive evidence for telepathy might be produced by card-guessing in quantities. He worked out a mathematical formula for estimating the number of hits above those to be expected by chance. When the probability of naming the right card on the basis of chance was known, it was easier to compute how much evidence of telepathy the results showed. While an experimenter in chemistry might be content to achieve a result in which the odds were 20-to-1 against chance, in a subject as offbeat as psychi-

Source: Reprinted from *Esp for the Millions* (Los Angeles: Sherbourne Press, Inc., 1965), pp. 46–61.

157

cal research it seemed imperative to devise a system in which results could be estimated which were 200-, 2,000- or 20,000-to-1 against chance. With card tests repeated endlessly (known as quantitative testing) such results could be achieved.

Although some of these first tests were surprisingly well done, they are not now considered to have been as carefully executed as are those which have been conducted in recent years. With the new techniques he devised, Dr. J. B. Rhine can take the credit for having made quantitative testing for ESP acceptable and successful. Before he started in this field, Dr. Rhine had previously worked for many years with plant physiology and botany, in which he took three degrees at the University of Chicago. His wife, Louisa, was also a graduate in that field. When they encountered some impressive reports of paranormal events, the Rhines became interested in psychical research. After a year in which they both studied psychology at Harvard under Professor William McDougall, they were more than ever taken with parapsychology, in which McDougall had a keen interest.

When McDougall was called to the chair of psychology at Duke University he soon made a professional opportunity in parapsychology available to the Rhines. From 1930 to 1934 they carried forward pioneer experimental investigations in telepathy and clairvoyance, using students as laboratory subjects.

Dr. Rhine knew that, in order to break down the persistent opposition to paranormal phenomena, it would be necessary to find a method of examination which paralleled the laboratory techniques of other scientific research. He also knew that in order to rule out the argument that ESP was nothing but pure chance or coincidence, he would have to repeat his experiments in even greater numbers, and that he would have to perform each test under such rigid control that there could be no question of sensory cues. Helped by advances in the science of statistics, Rhine was able to devise techniques which made a very large number of experiments possible. First acting as agent (or conductor of the test) himself, Dr. Rhine found the students responding to his stimulating personality with cooperative enthusiasm. He soon had a few star performers who were able to produce outstanding ESP.

The tests were made with what were at first called the Zener cards (now usually referred to as ESP cards). In a pack of twenty-five playing-size cards there are five each of five different symbols: circle, square, cross, star, and wave. When the cards are run face down, by the mathematics of probability the subject would expect to guess one symbol correctly out of five trials. Running the entire twenty-five cards, the subject may be expected to average five chance hits. Repeatedly getting more than five hits is an indication of extrasensory perception, but it is only when hundreds of runs have been made and the score is still higher than chance that the test can be considered significant.

Since the time that these cards were first used at Duke, there have been millions of runs made, under conditions varying to indicate whether the ESP is to be identified as telepathy, clairvoyance, general ESP, or precognition.

In 1934 a book entitled *Extrasensory Perception* by Dr. Rhine appeared. In it were accounts of the tests which had been run at Duke; and with its publication a new era in psychical research began. The Pearce-Pratt experiment, the book's most startling feature, introduced Dr. Rhine's research assistant, J. Gaither Pratt, and Hubert E. Pearce Jr., a ministerial student since deceased. Pearce was such an outstanding subject that he would average from six to eleven hits per run at any experimental session. Once, in an informal but nonetheless impressive set of circumstances, he scored a perfect run of 25 hits.

In this experiment which Rhine and Pratt carried out with Pearce in August and September, 1933, the aim was to set up conditions which would exclude all the factors that could reproduce extrachance scores except ESP. Dr. Pratt handled the pack of cards (known as the target pack) whose symbols were to be guessed by Pearce. He was in the Social Science Building at Duke. Pearce was seated 100 yards away in a reading cubicle in the stacks at the back of the Duke Library.

At the start of each session the two men synchronized their watches. After Pearce left for his cubicle, Pratt shuffled the cards and placed the pack at a left-hand corner of his table. At the agreed-upon starting time Pratt removed the top card and, without looking at it, placed it face down on a book in the middle of the table and left it there for a minute. He then removed the card, still face down, to the right-hand corner of the table and immediately picked up the next card and put it on the book. This routine was continued until all the cards were transferred, one at a time, to the other corner. Thus twenty-five minutes were taken for each run of twenty-five trials. Pratt then looked at the faces of the cards and recorded in duplicate the order in which they had fallen and, as a safeguard, before he met with Pearce, sealed one copy in an envelope for delivery to Dr. Rhine.

In the meantime, Pearce had put down on his record sheet during each minute the symbol which he thought was on the card Pratt had in position at the time. At the end of the run he, too, made a duplicate of his record of the twenty-five calls and sealed one copy in an envelope for Rhine's records before checking his duplicate with Pratt. Thus each one of the men had individual records which they could check independently of the others. In this way, also, any question of the individual good faith of any one of the three was disposed of.

Two runs through the pack were made per day and the total series consisted of 12 runs of 300 trials. The number of hits expected on a theory of pure chance was 20 percent of 300 or 60 hits. Pearce obtained a total of 119 hits or just one short of double the number expected from chance. His average run score was 9.9 hits per 25 or 39.7 percent of the total trials made. A score as large as 119 hits in 300 trials would be expected to occur by chance only once in approximately a quadrillion (1,000,000,000,000,000) of such experiments. The experimenters were sure, therefore, that every reasonable man would, without further argument, join them in dismissing the chance explanation. Their optimism was magnificent!

There are no known sensory processes that could be supposed to operate under these conditions. No type of rational inference could apply to a case of this kind. They, therefore, could hardly help but decide that, whatever clairvoyance or the extrasensory perception of objects *is*, this was a case of it. It was a case in which results were obtained under the strictest control ever until that time observed.

The report of this Pearce-Pratt experiment initiated what Dr. Rhine calls "what was doubtless the most heated controversy American psychology has ever experienced." The results of the experiment were attacked on the grounds of poor observation, mathematical inadequacy, and even fraud.

But some of the criticism, or hypercriticism, while it might not have applied directly to the Pearce-Pratt experiments, could still be helpful in a general way to all ESP testing. So it was taken very seriously by Drs. Rhine and Pratt and their associates. They made efforts to correct anything to which these complaints might intelligently apply.

For instance, it was pointed out that if the Zener cards were too thin, some persons might be able to read through their backs the symbols on their faces. Against the contingency that this might possibly have been the case, Dr. Rhine immediately saw to it that new decks were made of thicker material.

Another criticism: there was always a possibility that the sender, unknown to himself, might give certain unconscious cues which made the receiver's accurate guessing possible. Involuntary whispering might occur or the sender's facial muscles might contract with the potential that anyone familiar with muscle reading could know which was the key symbol. Though certain sounds emitted by the agent might be far too faint for a guesser in the next room to be consciously aware of, yet they might be of sufficient intensity to register at a subconscious level, it was suggested. It was also insisted that checks be made to see if the sender was unconsciously reacting to a particular symbol by coughing, or tapping his feet.

The problem of inadequate shuffling of the cards was a more intelligent point. It was suggested that during repeated shufflings by hand it might be possible for several cards to stick together. So hand shuffling was discontinued altogether and shuffling machines were substituted. Special cuts were also concocted to eliminate any possibility of interference from the mind of the subject, in case such might be occurring. In many tests now performed a table of random numbers is used to prepare the deck so that each symbol is bound to be in a scientifically haphazard position.

There were also accusations that errors in recording must have been made in order to account for the greater-than-chance results. To check this, numerous re-evaluations were made of a great many previously scored tests. In one exhaustive recheck of 500,000 card matchings, only 90 mistakes were found. Seventy-six of those turned out to be hits which had not been recorded! It is now accepted from many rechecks of both successful and unsuccessful data, that no errors in checking were sufficient to affect results significantly.

To counteract the assumption that his mathematics might be wrong, Dr. Rhine called in the American Institute of Mathematical Statistics for an appraisal of his conclusions. Their reply, after a thorough checking of the procedures used at Duke, was: "On the statistical side recent mathematical work has established the fact that, assuming that the experiments have been properly performed, the statistical analysis is essentially valid. If the Rhine investigation is to be fairly attacked, it must be on other than mathematical grounds."

While spending years giving careful consideration to all the criticism of their previous work, Drs. Rhine and Pratt were at the same time conducting numerous experiments to see if results above chance could still be obtained when safeguards were set up against all counter-hypotheses that had been suggested. They could.

One of the most striking of these new tests was the Pratt-Woodruff series carried out in 1939. This experiment was designed to meet all the criticisms that had flourished during the years of controversy. It was carried out with more controls against all possible error than any other experiment which had ever been devised. I won't go into detail about how this was conducted, but the results were that in 2,400 runs through the pack of cards there were 489 hits above the number to be expected by chance. The likelihood that this could occur by chance is around one in a million.

Right after the publication of Rhine's book in 1934, psychical researchers had all been exuberant. But it was then found that others could not duplicate the amazing achievements of Rhine and Pratt. The English parapsychologists, particularly, became very discouraged after running numerous series of tests and always coming out with chance results. Eventually however, G. N. M. Tyrrell, a former radio engineer who had deserted electronics for the challenge of this new field of interest, was able to produce the same kind of well-founded results that distinguished Rhine's work. And his personality and techniques threw light on Rhine's accomplishments as well as his own, for Tyrrell had the same rare combination of qualities needed for dealing with so elusive a trait as ESP, hidden as it is in the subconscious. Tyrrell possessed not only scientific training but also a sympathetic approach which never impeded a subject who might be hesitant and doubtful of his extrasensory powers. In addition he had the ability to make a general conception from apparently unrelated particulars. After the report of Tyrrell's test was published, parapsychologists realized that it was also these qualities in Rhine that were largely responsible for his achievements.

Tyrrell was keenly aware of a fact that most researchers, intent on making their experimental conditions as like as possible to those of the physical sciences, had tended to forget; physical conditions are not the only ones operative in ESP. Psychological conditions, he told his fellow experimenters with some emphasis, were equally important. The reason they were surprised at being unable to duplicate Rhine's successes was their own *a priori* conception of ESP. They assumed it to be a fixed characteristic possessed by A, but not by B, and one which could always be revealed by a simple test with a pack of cards. But they were wrong. That so many percent of Dr. Rhine's subjects scored high did not imply that the same percentage would do so anywhere, in any conditions. The experimenter's task, said Tyrrell, is to remove the subject's inhibitions—to induce the faculty to work—to get the extrasensory material externalized. This needs personal influence.

Tyrrell's first successor to achieve fruitful results was W. Whately Carington, who devised a system of testing for ESP which used statistical methods of assessment with pictures of objects instead of the monotonous ESP cards.

His procedure was simple enough. At 7:00 on ten successive evenings, he would hang up one of a series of ten drawings in his study. Each drawing depicted a single target object which had been chosen at random. They remained there with the door locked until 9:30 the next morning. Between those hours his subjects—he had 251 of them, all living at a distance—were asked to draw what they imagined the target object to be. This series of ten constituted one experiment. After a gap in time the procedure was repeated. When a group of experiments was over, the shuffled drawings from the whole group were sent to an outside judge for matching up with the shuffled originals.

These experiments with drawings were a marked success, for the hits were significantly more than one would expect from chance. But in addition the experiments gave some clues about ESP which had not previously been suspected. Carington found, for instance, that percipients seemed to pick up ideas more often than visual forms, also that it did not seem to matter whether the target was actually drawn, so long as the agent had thought of it. But the most unexpected relevation was of the existence of "displacement."

Hits on a particular target were naturally most frequent on the night it was drawn. If the target on Monday was a pyramid, most percipients who drew pyramids drew them on Monday. But some people also drew pyramids on Sunday or Tuesday, even sometimes two days before or two days after Monday. This really started Carington to thinking. If hits on a target drawing could occur both before and after that drawing was made, what about card-naming experiments? Maybe similar displacement had occurred in them.

At Carington's urging, Dr. S. G. Soal, who had previously done many unsuccessful tests with the Zener cards, now re-evaluated his results with respect to displacement. He discovered that two of his subjects, Basil Shackleton and Gloria Stewart, had been scoring hits on either the card before or the card following the target. This seemed to have occurred with such regularity that Dr. Soal was encouraged to attempt new tests with these subjects. He took even more extreme precautions than before, but he had remarkable success this time.

In a grand total of 37,100 trials for telepathy, Miss Stewart hit the target card 9,410 times. Chance expectancy for this number of trials was 7,420 hits. Her results showed odds against chance in the neighborhood of 10^{70}-to-1.

Basil Shackleton was also successful in telepathy tests, especially when checked for displacement. He struck the plus- 1 card (the one immediately following the target card) 1,101 times in 3,789 trials, which represents odds against chance of 10^{35}-to-1.

Dr. Soal, like Carington, became bored to death with ESP cards. Abandoning the impassive Zener symbols, he substituted cards on which were vividly colored pictures of an elephant, a giraffe, a lion, a pelican, and a zebra. The more photogenic fauna were gratefully received by his subjects. For a long series of tests, the subject's interest declines and ESP declines with it. Then what is known as "psi missing" occurs. At some point along the seemingly interminable runs, the percipient will suddenly start hitting consistently lower than chance expectancy because he is utterly fatigued and bored. This is another indication that ESP exists, and is an unconscious power; for if he consciously tried to miss he couldn't succeed at it any better than he could make successful *hits* by consciously trying to do so.

Other characteristics of ESP have been established by laboratory experiments, such as the fact that time and space have been found to affect psi not at all. In the Pearce-Pratt tests, the two protagonists were 100 yards apart. Further tests were performed in England with subjects as distant as Scotland, Holland, and the United States, and in the United States with subjects in India. The far-away guessers did just as well as those close at hand. Illness was no obstacle to extrasensory perception, and although mental state affected it, physical conditions apparently did not.

Despite all the brilliant, if sporadic, achievements of the laboratory in demonstrating ESP by quantitative experiments, in spite of exhaustive and successful efforts by dedicated workers, the returns have been all too meager. Nevertheless, it can be truthfully said that for all its shortcomings, quantitative testing served its purpose well and thoroughly in establishing investigation of the paranormal as a legitimate scientific pursuit.

However, as has been noted, testing endlessly with cards is a highly boring procedure, because conclusions can be reached only by the assembling of overwhelmingly repetitious numerical data. There are, fortunately, other means which can be used for testing. These are called "Qualitative," and involve the drawing of pictures and other more spontaneous and interesting techniques. As Whately Carington showed in the tests he devised, they can also be controlled and evaluated statistically. And so at the present time the trend in formal experimentation is away from quantitative testing and toward the qualitative.

A simple example of a qualitative test is for me to think very firmly of a picture—say of a hat. You, in another room, trying to capture my thoughts, draw a picture of a hat and so identify it. If we could do anything so successful as this repeatedly, it would seem fairly evident to anyone, wouldn't it, that telepathy on your part is indicated?

A series of tests which gave this kind of interesting evidence was undertaken by the well-known American author, Upton Sinclair, and his wife, Mary Craig Sinclair. After watching a young man's feats of apparent telepathy, Sinclair and his wife had become curious, although they were doubtful of the genuineness of the performance. Mrs. Sinclair decided to resolve her doubts by learning "to do these things myself." In the experiments she attempted, Mrs. Sinclair was the percipient and her husband the agent. On a few occasions her brother-in-law, R. L. Irwin, who lived forty miles away, acted as agent.

The experiments usually followed this uninvolved procedure: The agent would make a set of drawings of fairly simple things—a bird's nest with eggs, a helmet, a tree, a flower—and enclose each one in its own opaque envelope. Then, or later, Mrs. Sinclair would relax on a couch, take the envelopes in hand one at a time, and after she believed that she knew its contents, she would draw them. She spent three years at this kind of testing. Out of 290 drawings, 65 were hits, 155 partial hits, and 70 failures. This is an extremely good rate of success. Upton Sinclair was convinced by it of the existence of telepathy. In his book, *Mental Radio,* he wrote:

> *For the past three years I have been watching this work, day by day and night by night, in our home. So at last I can say that I am no longer guessing. . . . Regardless of what anybody can say, there will never again be a doubt in my mind. I KNOW!*

DISCUSSION QUESTIONS

1. The author describes the educational background and experience of Dr. and Mrs. Rhine, as well as their relationship to Professor McDougall. Is this a preface to her argument or part of it?
2. The author reports that Hubert Pearce once scored a perfect run of 25 hits, then calls that "impressive." Why does she use such a weak adjective to describe a seeming miraculous event?
3. One aim of the Pearce-Pratt experiment was "to set up conditions which would exclude all the factors that could reproduce extrachance scores except ESP." Were all such factors excluded? Can anything other than ESP explain the 1 in 1,000,000,000,000,000 results?
4. What is implicit in the criticism that some of the ESP results could have derived from see-through cards or from muscular cues?
5. The Pratt-Woodruff experiments were designed to answer all early test criticisms, and they produced a 1 in 1,000,000 result. Describe the controls that assured the tests' scientific character.

6. What advantages do these features give to individuals seeking to prove the existence of ESP?

> *psychological conditions*
> *displacement*
> *psi missing*
> *qualitative experiments*

7. The Upton Sinclair experiments produced 65 hits, 155 partial hits, and 70 failures. What is a partial hit?

8. Describe a test that you believe would prove the existence of ESP. Would it frustrate the efforts of a clever magician?

GEORGE DELEON

The Baldness Experiment

The winos who hung around my Brooklyn neighborhood in 1950 were not funny. With their handout hands, reeking breaths, and weird, ugly injuries, they were so self-rejecting that you could bark them away even while you shoved them a nickel. My friends and I didn't think they were funny, but we observed one thing that always busted us up. Almost without exception, they had all their hair.

Seriously: we never saw a bald bum. Have you? When was the last time you remember a street alky stumbler with nothing on top?

Black, white, old, young, short, tall, all of them had a full mop. And hair that wouldn't quit. It leaped up as if it were electrified, or shagged down in complete asocial indifference, or zoomed back absurdly neat, gray-black and glued. Inexplicably, it seemed that boozing burned out the guts but grew hair.

Fifteen years later, I offered this observation to my undergraduate classes in the psychology of personality. Then, one semester, I decided to get past the laugh, integrate my present self with my past self, and actually test the hypothesis that booze grows hair.

I conceived a simple investigation, with the class participating as co-researchers. In the project, we'd get some real data on the density, or rather the incidence, of baldness in a random sample of rummies. The tactic was to beachhead ourselves on the Bowery in New York City, fan out in teams of two, and gradually move up from somewhere around Prince Street to 14th Street, the end of the bum region.

On two successive Saturday mornings, the whole research outfit—me, four men, and two women—met on the corner of Bowery and Houston to carry out the plan. Every other derelict who was not unconscious was approached, talked to, and looked at. Since no one usually walks up to a rummy except cops and other rummies, something seemed to happen when two pretty young students of mine would say, "Sir, I'd like to ask you a few questions." The winos would rock a bit and—no kidding—you could almost see a little ego emerging.

Source: Reprinted from *Psychology Today Magazine.* Copyright © 1977 Ziff-Davis Publishing Company.

In planning the research, I decided that we should gather as much information as we could that might be relevant to the experiment. We decided to mark down answers to questions about age, race, ethnicity, marital status, family baldness, drinking life, etc. We even asked our subjects where they usually slept (in or out of doors), figuring that, too, might influence their hair growth.

While one team member interrogated, the other circled around the subject, studying the head, raised and lowered, to observe the pate. Subjects were evaluated on a four-point baldness scale as hairy, receding, bald pate, or totally bald.

Interesting problems developed from the beginning; what appeared to be simple was really complex. When do you call a guy bald? What does "receding" mean? (We dispensed with the use of rulers or vernier calipers, assuming that, bombed or not, the derelict would shuffle off as soon as we pulled out any kind of hardware. We felt grateful that he tolerated the paper, pencils, and questions.) So there was no quantification, no precision. We simply had to make quick judgments.

Our teams interviewed over 60 Bowery subjects, paying them a quarter a pop, all of which came out of my pocket. Back at the school, the data were tallied and, sure enough, the results confirmed my intuition. Only about 25 percent could be called receding or totally bald, with the remainder being pated or hirsute. I had been right all along, and we reported the results to the class.

But it turns out that the skepticism of annoyed youth may actually be the quintessence of good scientific research. After I enjoyed the laughs and took a few bows, a number of students, not on the teams, were quick to raise some sharp objections.

First, and most obvious, was that we needed to study baldness in a group of nonderelicts in order to make proper conclusions. Second, wasn't it possible that the teams had been influenced by my colorful classroom predictions about hairy bums and had tended to judge the subjects as nonbalding?

The criticism was first rate. I knew that because it threw me into an immediate depression. I hated the students who offered it. I also knew that we'd have to do the whole study again with new teams and new derelicts. This time, nonderelicts would have to be included, too, and I would offer no advance hypothesis that might bias, in my favor, the way kids looked at heads.

I waited a whole academic year, got a new personality class, and this time took no chances. During the lectures, it was necessary to arouse the interest of the class in the broad issue of bums and baldness. So I suggested that derelicts were a special group of people who seemed to lose their hair sooner and more completely than other men. In short, I lied. Morality aside, it was a tough one to tell because I feared that it would shape the kids' perception the other way. They might actually see receding hairlines and shiny heads where there really was only hair. But I had to take the risk of betting against myself to make the win more sure.

Out on the turf again a new and larger research squad of six men and six women worked over five straight Saturdays. They did the Bowery in pairs, interviewing about 80 derelicts.

We also went after a comparison group. Any man walking in or out of Bloomingdale's or cruising along 5th Avenue in the 50s was operationally defined as a nonderelict. These fine fellows we decided to call "sterlings." "Sterling" male shoppers in tweeds were stopped on a random basis in front of Bloomingdale's revolving doors. They were put through the whole routine of questions about drinking, age, etc., and their heads were carefully checked out. One difference was that we were too embarrassed to hand them quarters, so we didn't. Then, about a month later, to extend our control group, I sent five squads into a faculty meeting at Wagner College and got the same information on 49 college professors in one sweep.

Happily, the new set of derelict data turned out the same as the old, and the results of the three comparison groups were more striking than expected. When the information was presented simply as nonbald versus balding (which combined receding plus pated plus total), we found that 71 percent of the college professors were balding, 53 percent of the sterlings, and, of the derelicts (both years), only 36 percent (see Figure 1).

There were no ethnic or racial differences, nor were the other factors in the questionnaire very important. Still, age must matter, and it does.

Under age 25, we found 17 (21 percent) sterlings, but only one derelict and no professors. In fact, the average age of the sterlings was 37.5, while it was 47.5 for the other two groups. This makes sense, since it takes a lot of years to become either a derelict or a college professor.

Figure 2 shows the percentage of balding across several age levels. Naturally, the older men in all groups contain a greater proportion of hair losers. But after age 40, the differences among the groups are fascinating. The sterlings and professors reveal similar rising percentages, with the profs leading. The derelicts, however, in the years 41 to 55, actually show a slight decrease, and of the 50 guys on the Bowery past age 55, only 44 percent showed signs of balding as compared with about 80 percent of the oldies in the other groups. So

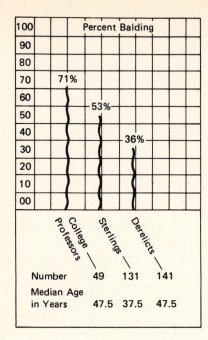
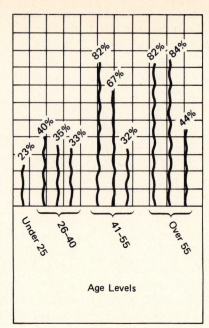

the stereotype of the balding egghead professor is not contradicted by these data. For the Bowery bum, there's no doubt that he simply keeps his hair.

Now comes the hard part: what does it all mean? Though it did not show up in our data, I'm sure that genetics is relevant. Even so, what is the likelihood that only the bums have fewer bald daddies? Not much.

These results also rule out ethnic and racial factors. Hair and air didn't go together, since the derelicts who said they usually slept out were no less bald than those who snoozed in the dorms of the flophouse hotels.

Are the bums breezier and more carefree? Calm or numbed so that they don't feel the stress that most of us do? Is it the food they eat, or don't eat?

No. We concluded that it must be the alcohol and some resulting biochemical activity. It happens, since completing the study, that I've learned that medical literature does point to some interaction between liver damage, alcohol metabolism, the female hormone estrogen, hair growth and retention. Seems reasonable to me.

If so, I'm elated that our finds are valid. But, in a way, it doesn't matter. The whole trip started for me back in Brooklyn, as a joke. Later, my students and I really observed, recorded what we saw, and attempted to draw conclusions. Seeking the truth is always an adventure; the scientist is in all of us.

DISCUSSION QUESTIONS

1. The author reports three separate readings of the derelict-baldness issue: his observations as a youth, the first study he and his class made, and the final study. Since they all came to the same conclusion, why is the final study more significant than the others?
2. Why did the teams ask questions about age, race, ethnicity, marital status, family baldness, drinking habits, sleeping place, and so on? Why didn't they just check hair?
3. Explain the following:

    a. why the first research team interviewed only every other derelict
    b. why they made no precise measurements of the derelict's hair
    c. why the author lied to the second research team about what he expected to prove
    d. why the derelicts were compared to men around Bloomingdale's and to professors
    e. why the author offered an age analysis at the end

4. "Black, white, old, young, short, tall, all of them had a full mop. And hair that wouldn't quit." What is the tone of this essay? Does the tone add to the author's case?
5. Baldness is usually considered a genetic factor. How does the author explain this away? Is he persuasive?
6. What is amusing about defining male Bloomingdale shoppers as "nonderelict"?
7. "Now comes the hard part: what does it all mean?" What does this sentence tell you about statistics?
8. How effective is the author's writing style?

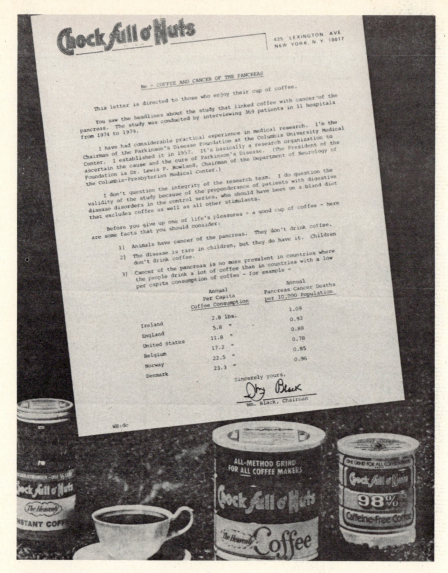

Chock full o'Nuts

425 LEXINGTON AVE.
NEW YORK, N.Y. 10017

Re - COFFEE AND CANCER OF THE PANCREAS

This letter is directed to those who enjoy their cup of coffee.

You saw the headlines about the study that linked coffee with cancer of the pancreas. The study was conducted by interviewing 369 patients in 11 hospitals from 1974 to 1979.

I have had considerable practical experience in medical research. I'm the Chairman of the Parkinson's Disease Foundation at the Columbia University Medical Center. I established it in 1957. It's basically a research organization to ascertain the cause and the cure of Parkinson's Disease. (The President of the Foundation is Dr. Lewis P. Rowland, Chairman of the Department of Neurology of the Columbia-Presbyterian Medical Center.)

I don't question the integrity of the research team. I do question the validity of the study because of the preponderance of patients with digestive disease disorders in the control series, who should have been on a bland diet that excludes coffee as well as all other stimulants.

Before you give up one of life's pleasures - a good cup of coffee - here are some facts that you should consider:

1) Animals have cancer of the pancreas. They don't drink coffee.

2) The disease is rare in children, but they do have it. Children don't drink coffee.

3) Cancer of the pancreas is no more prevalent in countries where the people drink a lot of coffee than in countries with a low per capita consumption of coffee - for example -

	Annual Per Capita Coffee Consumption	Annual Pancreas Cancer Deaths per 10,000 Population
		1.09
Ireland	2.8 lbs.	0.92
England	5.8 "	0.88
United States	11.8 "	0.78
Belgium	17.2 "	0.85
Norway	22.5 "	0.96
Denmark	23.3 "	

Sincerely yours,

Wm. Black, Chairman

WB:dc

ALL-METHOD GRIND FOR ALL COFFEE MAKERS

Chock full o'Nuts

The Heavenly Coffee

INSTANT COFFEE

ONE GRIND FOR ALL COFFEE MAKERS
98%
Caffeine-free Coffee

DISCUSSION QUESTIONS

1. The author lists six countries and gives information about their coffee consumption and incidence of pancreatic cancer. Why these six countries?

2. The author questions the hospital study because the control group contained too many "patients with digestive disease disorders." What does he mean here?

Argument for Analysis
PART II

Do not despise prophesying, but
test everything; hold fast what
is good.

ST. PAUL, 1 THESSALONIANS

ROGER PENSKE

Fifty-Five Is Fast Enough

In 1972, the winning car in the Indianapolis 500 was clocked at an average speed of 162.962 m.p.h., a record that stands today. The car, which I owned, was driven by my friend Mark Donohue. Three years later, Donohue crashed and was fatally injured while practicing for the Grand Prix in Austria. He was not yet 39.

Professional race drivers deliberately accept the risks of high speed and the ever-present possibility of sudden death behind the wheel. But for thousands of ordinary motorists every year, death on the highway is all too often unnecessary.

I am a lifelong racing enthusiast, first as a driver and today as a car builder and team owner. I am also a firm believer that speeding motor vehicles belong *only* on racetracks, not on public highways. Yet one of our most effective safeguards against needless highway slaughter—the national 55-m.p.h. speed limit—is today under severe attack from increasingly vocal skeptics around the country.

Some leaders of the anti-55 movement ought to know better. These are the racing enthusiasts who have been conducting a national publicity campaign to discredit and repeal the 55 limit. Their campaign, aimed at dedicated racing fans, has been very influential. And why not? Auto racing is currently the country's fourth most-popular spectator sport. Already this year, bills to raise the speed limit have been introduced in six states.

Active in the anti-55 campaign are two of the largest-circulation magazines for motor-racing fans, *Car and Driver* and *Road & Track.* Last September, John Tomerlin, *Road & Track's* highway-affairs analyst, told a national meeting of state traffic-safety officials that the federal government's claim that 55 saves lives and fuel cannot be documented. Also figuring in the campaign against the law were delegates to the Republican National Convention, who adopted a platform plank attacking the national speed limit as an invasion of states' rights.

In addition, critics contend that enforcement costs too much

Source: Reprinted with permission from the 1981 *Reader's Digest.*

175

and diverts police from more important work, that it is creating a nation of scofflaws since no one obeys it, and that it amounts to "Big Brotherism." Let's examine these charges:

CHARGE: The 55-m.p.h. limit is just another example of Washington-imposed Big Brotherism.

FACT: Shortly after the Arabs shut off the oil in October 1973, the Emergency Highway Energy Conservation Act became law, requiring all states to impose a highway speed limit of 55, or risk losing federal highway funds. But 28 states had already jumped ahead of Big Brother by imposing 55 (and in some cases, 50) on their own. The National Governors Association and the heads of all state law-enforcement agencies continue to support the 55 limit. And public-opinion polls consistently show that about 75 percent of drivers also support it.

CHARGE: The 55 law doesn't save lives.

FACT: Though the speed limit was imposed to save fuel, not lives, its safety benefits became apparent shortly after it was enacted. In 1974, the first year of 55, auto fatalities dropped by more than 9000. Critics say that the reduction was because Americans drove less in 1974 than in 1973. But the decrease in miles traveled was only 2.5 percent, compared with a 16-percent fatality drop.

Traffic engineers attributed the reduction in highway accidents to something called "traffic pace." When all drivers travel at about the same speed, which tends to happen under the 55 law, there is no need to weave from lane to lane to pass. But when speed limits go up, the faster cars are continually zooming around the slower ones, creating prime conditions for accidents.

And consider this: If you do have a crash at 70 m.p.h. or faster, your chances of survival are 50–50. Cut your speed to between 50 and 60 m.p.h., and the odds climb to about 31-to-1 in your favor.

According to the U.S. Department of Transportation, strong enforcement of 55 could forestall as many as 415,000 injury-producing accidents over the next ten years, and save up to 32,000 lives.

CHARGE: Drivers ignore the 55 limit.

FACT: A certain percentage of drivers *always* exceed the speed limit. Yet the latest speed-monitoring reports from states around the country indicate that the average speed on roads posted for 55 is less than half-a-mile-an-hour over the limit.

CHARGE: Police are taken off more important work to enforce 55, and the law costs too much to enforce.

FACT: The U.S. National Highway Traffic Safety Administration reports that "no significant redistribution of resources results from the 55-m.p.h. speed limit." Police are *not* being pulled off more important duties to enforce 55. And critics who argue that enforcement of the speed limit wastes tax dollars aren't aware that states spend only a small percentage of their law-enforcement budgets for 55. In any case, states will always have to enforce *some* kind of speed limit, whether it is 40, 55 or 70. The cost doesn't vary significantly for different speeds.

CHARGE: The 55 limit saves an insignificant amount of fuel.

FACT: The exact amount of savings varies with the vehicle, but cuts in fuel use when speed is reduced from 70 to 55 m.p.h. commonly range from 15 percent to 30 percent.

In 1978, the Department of Transportation estimated that Americans were saving 1.5 billion gallons of motor fuel a year as a result of 55. Recent analyses, which take into account today's more fuel-efficient engines, show that savings of motor fuel attributable to 55 now amount to 3.4 billion gallons a year—about 3 percent of our total consumption.

Critics claim time and money would be saved if trucks and buses were exempt from 55. Again, wrong. According to fleet companies, slower speeds improve fuel mileage for trucks and buses, and cut maintenance costs. For example, Consolidated Freightways, the nation's second-largest regulated motor carrier, changed gear ratios to limit top speed on its rigs to 57 m.p.h., and thus realized 8-percent better fuel economy. United Parcel Service conducted fuel-consumption tests with identical tractor-trailers, one driven at 55 m.p.h. and the other at 65 m.p.h. The 55-m.p.h. truck got 32-percent better fuel economy. And so it goes around the country: truck fleets *are* saving because of the 55 law.

Americans have had seven years to evaluate the 55-m.p.h. speed limit. *All* the evidence is favorable. The law saves gas. *And* lives.

The Nutty ACLU

It has come to the point where the activities of the American Civil Liberties Union are ridiculous.

A UPI dispatch from Providence, Rhode Island, indicates that the Rhode Island branch of the ACLU says that a state health department rule requiring college women to be inoculated against German measles is discriminatory.

The ACLU director, Steve Brown, says that the rule requiring all college women between 15 and 35 entering the state colleges for the first time to be vaccinated should apply also to male students and asked the health department to change it: Unless a change is made, he says he will file a sex discrimination complaint with the U.S. Department of Education.

Apparently the ACLU does not understand that inoculation for German measles is very important for women because, without it, if they get German measles during pregnancy, this could have very unfortunate results on the child they are carrying.

To the best of this writer's knowledge, the ACLU has not yet proved that men can have babies.

Source: Editorial from the *Manchester (N.H.) Union Leader*. Reprinted from the *Independent American* (February 26, 1981), p. 2.

Some want to keep our land unspoiled. Some want to explore it. We want to explore without spoiling.

There's a strange either-or proposition building up in this country.

It's one that says either we completely preserve our public lands by turning them into permanent wilderness, or we tear them up and exploit them to the fullest for their natural resources.

We've got to believe there's an acceptable middle ground between these two extremes.

At least that's what all of us at Atlantic Richfield believe. And so do the many Americans who have invested with us.

Look at the facts. Our public lands currently supply an estimated 10% of our energy. Yet they actually contain about one half of all our known domestic energy resources — vast amounts of coal, oil shale, tar sands, crude oil and natural gas.

Over 40% of the 760 million acres the federal government owns has been withdrawn from mineral mining or leasing.

Another 25% has been placed under regulation that effectively precludes oil, gas and mining operations.

All without ever finding out first, through preliminary exploration, what the resource potential of that land really is.

The desire for land that stands pure and pristine is certainly understandable. But, surely, in these times of scarcity, our need for energy and mineral resources is just as pressing. We know for a fact that exploration can easily be conducted in an environmentally sound manner.

Doesn't it then make sense that we invest in exploring and evaluating our public lands before classifying them as wilderness or otherwise, and locking them up forever?

At least then we could make sure we're doing the right thing.

Or so it seems to us at Atlantic Richfield.

There are no easy answers.

ARCO

Atlantic Richfield Company

ERICA ABEEL
The Love and Rage of Jean Harris

The contrast resonates with a cruel irony. On March 10, 1980, Dr. Herman Tarnower plans to have dinner with current girlfriend, Lynne Tryforos. Around 1 P.M., he returns home from the Scarsdale Medical Group to see to the wine. On March 10, 1980, Jean Harris, his companion of fourteen years, entertains ideas of a different order. She writes a will, scrawls several "suicide notes," then drives five hours through rotten weather—to end a life.

Whose is not clear. Prosecutor George Bolen contended Harris shot Tarnower four times in a jealous rage over his affair with her younger rival. Defense lawyer Joel Aurnou contended Tarnower was killed in a "tragic accident" when he tried to prevent Harris, suicidally depressed over pressures at work, from shooting herself. In his camp, Bolen had plausibility and the famed "Scarsdale Letter," which torpedoed Harris's claim that she viewed her rival with equanimity. In his camp, Aurnou had a host of forensic experts, who went on interminably about perforations of the flesh, and who offered rebuttals to all the points scored by Bolen. But Aurnou had a more redoubtable weapon: impassioned female identification with the accused.

Without impugning the American legal system, let me say that this whole business is a bit of a circus, and I have no great faith that any definitive picture of the truth will emerge. I wonder whether both sides aren't right: Jealous rage and suicidal feelings are not incompatible; Harris could have set out for Purchase, New York, with one motive, then segued into another. She may have intended only that the doctor dissuade her from her own bullets. No stranger to self-deception, Harris herself may no longer know what she intended—if she ever knew in the first place.

But then I am less interested, finally, in the central question of Jean Harris's intentions than in all the side issues. I am interested in what drove her to this act, which, in effect, was a figurative suicide. I am interested in why women identify so powerfully with

Source: From *Savvy* magazine, pp. 208–211, 219 "Without Consolations" (under the title "The Love and Rage of Jean Harris") in *I'll Call You Tomorrow, and Other Lies Between Men and Women* by Erica Abeel. Copyright © 1981 by Erica Abeel. By permission of William Morrow & Company.

181

Harris—thereby conferring on a sordid *crime passionnel* the status of media event. In Jean Harris women see themselves and the woman they fear becoming, fight not to become, just missed becoming. They feel, there but for the grace of God go I. They read her story as a cautionary tale: For fourteen years a man and a woman keep company outside traditional structures, and he ends up with money, power and love. And she? Play it like Jean and you end up crazy, in the slammer, or dead.

No one would have noticed, of course, if the man and the woman had been undistinguished. Herman Tarnower was not only the noted cardiologist and author of *The Complete Scarsdale Medical Diet,* he had symbolic credentials as well. In a culture that worships slimness, he was the Guru of Lean—and, for many women, perhaps the ultimate authority figure. Before her fall as headmistress of the tony Madeira School, Harris was the ultimate in respectability. While the general public voyeuristically enjoys the contradiction between the outer and the secret Harris—behind the starchy façade lay twisted passions—women perceive a more threatening dimension: Harris's considerable professional achievements could not save her, as they so often do men, from emotional mayhem.

Women also view with disquietude her age. While the sexual vitality of 69-year-old Tarnower would be found admirable, enviable, almost mythic—an avid middle-aged woman is an embarrassment, slightly grotesque. In popular fantasy, Harris at 56 should have been more concerned with losing her teeth than with losing her lover. As a spurned middle-aged woman, she reminds women of their own age-related vulnerability. Her example suggests that continuing desire will be greeted with the "jeers" she alludes to in the notorious "Scarsdale Letter"—as if the sexually vital woman of middle years were on a par with some village freak. (With her porcelain features, blue eyes, celestial smile and intense manner, Jean Harris, for the record, is mesmerizingly lovely—despite her travails, and the fact that some days she resembles Ophelia among the water lilies, dressed by Chanel.)

But the case goes beyond personalities; it raises larger controversial issues, reducing dinner parties in Scarsdale, I hear, to shouting matches between the sexes. In a sense, along with Jean Harris, Tarnower's life style is on trial. By all accounts an excellent doctor, Tarnower was devoted, with the tunnel vision peculiar to lifelong bachelors, to his own pleasures: food, wine, travel, expensive forms of hunting—and "thoroughbred women," in *Time* Magazine's phrase. His was a life of serial loves—with overlap—Jean Harris being the next-to-last. In the public fantasy, Tarnower personifies a hedonistic dues-free existence exempt from long-term commitment, responsibility, and that aging face across the breakfast table. Exempt from pain: Since he didn't really need or care about anyone, as Harris maintains, he was invulnerable. Exempt from reality: unmarried, he told Harris, he would never have to know about her mother's nursing home. To many men, Tarnower is a folk hero of the narcissistic age, the guy who could—well, almost—get away with it. Even the rabbi who presided at Tarnower's funeral praised his "desire for personal independence," comparing it, with dubious taste, to Einstein's.

Women do not share this admiration, as the defense lawyer well knows. Women feel the alleged murderer is equally a victim—not of bullets but of antihuman, degrading treatment; of the venerable male practice of enjoying a woman during her "prime," then trading her in for a new model. The housewives who commute four hours to watch this real-life soap see a woman who put in fourteen years of devotion, rewarded in every arena but love with at least a pension and a gold watch, who is then "discarded like garbage."

Of course one had come to expect almost anything in an age of *Tout Est Permis,* when men and women have fewer rational claims on each other's loyalty than ever before. But along comes an educated woman of substance who snaps. Who goes crazy. And it is a curious thing, but she is not alone in the craziness. One can dismiss as fringe loonies the fans writing Harris, "The bastard got what he deserved." But what is one to make of all the tranquil, sane women who applaud her?

Surely, with Harris's .32 many women vicariously gunned down their own little traitor. But there's something more: While no one would seriously maintain that a man who displeases ought to be shot through the head, neither would one be happy seeing him walk away scot-free from despicable behavior. The uneasy gratification women feel at Harris's act is really nostalgia for a sense of moral obligation—which may well reflect some permanent human need. In sympathizing with Harris, one is not condoning murder but rather affirming the idea that people are responsible to one another; they can't blithely plunder another human being; that a major reform in sexual manners is in order. . . .

Recklessly insisting on the primacy of love at any price, Harris lived out every woman's worst potential. She is, I suppose, an anti-role model. But Jean Harris will not easily leave us alone because of the larger lesson. Her adventure mocks the liberated pieties of people who believe that social attitudes have kept pace with women's aspirations. For fourteen years, Harris and her lover lived outside tradition as independent "equals"—so adult, so evolved—yet in the twilight of that affair they hardly came out equal. Tarnower ended up with money, prestige, social opportunities and a devoted young mistress to grace his twilight years. And Harris ended up with little money, unemployment, dwindling social opportunities, and the conviction that at 56 her life as a woman was over. Lacking a calling for spinsterhood and for single-minded devotion to career, she believed her *life* over. Put melodramatically, you could say she ended up with nothing. Hers is a cautionary tale without consolations. I pity the men and women of the jury who judge her.

SHAPING UP AMERICA'S ECONOMY IS GOING TO TAKE GUTS AND HARD WORK. AND NOBODY EVER SAID IT WOULD HAPPEN OVERNIGHT.

Remember how frightening it was when the prevailing economic wisdom in Washington seemed to be, "Let's wait awhile and hope things get better on their own?"

Obviously, things didn't get better. And people got tired of waiting. So they voted Republican for a change in 1980; because President Reagan and the Republicans in Congress had the ideas to cure the economy and the guts to turn them into workable programs.

In less than one year, the Republican leadership has already:
• Taken an ax to the sickest, most extravagant budget in our nation's history.
• Cut federal income tax rates for all Americans.

• Begun to curb the bureaucrats who have saddled us with unworkable and unnecessary federal rules and regulations.

There is a fresh wind of change blowing through Washington, cleaning out the dust and debris left by an ineffective leadership that did not know how to listen to the people. The Republicans are listening; they're working hard to solve our problems.

It took a long time to get us into this economic mess. Nobody ever said that getting us out would be easy. Nobody said it would happen overnight.

But think how much easier the job will be if we all work at it together.

REPUBLICANS.
Leadership that works. For a Change.

Paid for by National Republican Congressional Committee, Cong. Guy Vander Jagt, Chmn.;
Republican National Committee, Richard Richards, Chmn.;
National Republican Senatorial Committee, Sen. Bob Packwood, Chmn.

Source: Reprinted with permission from the National Republican Congressional Committee, the Republican National Committee, and the National Republican Senatorial Committee.

WILL DWYER II

The Infant Formula Issue

Before taking on the topic of how I believe the United Nations is making mischief for the world of journalism and the world of business, I would like to recognize and thank two men of Rome who have made my visit possible. They are, of course, Bob and Robbie Cunningham of the *International Daily News.* Without their willingness to suggest with whom and where I should speak and without you honoring their invitation by your attendance, my visit would have little meaning.

I also would like to express my public appreciation to Prince Suderi, president of the International Fund for Agricultural Development (IFAD), for his generosity in asking me to meet over lunch with his top officials tomorrow in order that we might discuss matters of common concern.

All of us in journalism seem constantly to be searching for the inviting lead, those few well-chosen words that bring the reader, viewer, or listener immediately into involvement with our story. Here is one that worked that way with me: "The United Nations is impotent, yet not harmless."

It's the lead from an article that appeared in the *Chicago Sun-Times* on December 30, 1980. The headline under which it appeared read "UN Hatches Plan to Muzzle World News Flow" and the article's author, Shirley Hazzard, deserves credit for the inviting lead.

But more important than the style of the story was its substance. The author, a ten-year employee of the U.N. Secretariat, related the UNESCO plan to establish an international code of ethics for the communications media. She detailed its dangers and challenged the press to "spread the alarm."

I feel fate led me to the Hazzard story; my coming across it resulted from a curious confluence. It happens that her warning about what UNESCO had in mind for journalists was reprinted from the Chicago newspaper in the January 9 issue of the *Congressional Record,* the very issue in which a U.S. Congressman had reprinted

Source: A speech delivered at the Stampa Estera, Rome, April 15, 1981.

the text of a commentary I had written warning about another U.N. agency, the World Health Organization (WHO).

How unusual, I thought. Normally, the press and business have little in common. Both sectors of our society have problems, to be sure. But, usually, they are so apart that the press and business seem to have antagonistic interests.

The more I have investigated these two issues and the two U.N. agencies, UNESCO and the WHO, responsible for their creation, the more I am struck by their inimical identity. UNESCO wants to license journalists and require us to conform to a code of ethics it would write and enforce. The WHO wants to ban totally the product advertising of infant formula in all countries of the world and forbid product sampling even to doctors and nurses.

My interest in the infant formula issue grew out of detecting a potential for inconsistency by the U.S. government. Where on the one hand, the Reagan mandate of last November clearly was for less government control over enterprise, I found on the other that a corps of American government bureaucrats—those whose ranks are unaffected by political fortunes or presidential elections—were continuing to commit U.S. support behind the WHO's marketing code proposal.

Not only was this the situation in my own country, I discovered it in the United Kingdom as well. Mrs. Thatcher and Ronald Reagan may be two peas in the same pod when it comes to free market economics, but they are both served—perhaps, ill-served—by government professionals who, in too many cases, find controls quite congenial.

At the WHO Secretariat in Geneva, the coordinating center for the movement to harness the baby food business, I asked U.N. officials how and why this all had come about.

And, it is what I have been able to assess about the evolution of this code proposal—and it applies in like manner to the UNESCO journalism code—that really is what I want to relate to you. It is frankly a process that best can be described as an intellectual disgrace. It represents the consequences of misinformation, of free market advocates' failure to challenge baseless attacks, and of the erosion of national sovereignty.

In describing this to you, let me also underscore the timeliness of the matter. Push has come to shove. In less than three weeks, the World Health Assembly, the plenary body for the WHO, will convene for the month of May in Geneva. The hottest item on its agenda is a recommendation from this January's meeting of its executive board calling on the Assembly to enact a sharply-restrictive marketing code for infant formula.

Clearly, because some of the proposed provisions actually would violate the laws of several developed countries, quick and unanimous action by the WHA is unlikely. The U.S., for example, would have to oppose any ban on advertising since the Supreme Court has granted commercial expression virtually the same "free speech" protection that the First Amendment secures for political statements. Similarly, where the WHO formula code would require cooperative action by several baby food manufacturers to restrain certain trade practices, this would be the basis for anti-trust charges in America.

If we look then at how reported contentions move from conversation to regulation, it seems necessary to first examine the validity or accuracy of the platform that supports such political processes. As a reporter, that's where I began.

There are four charges made by social activists, both in and outside of the WHO, about the infant feeding issue:

1. *The industry opposes breast feeding and promotes its products to the detriment of nature.*
2. *Infant formula availability is responsible for the decline of breast feeding in developing countries.*
3. *Baby formula, typically a powdered milk, causes malnutrition, even death.*
4. *The marketing methods of the formula industry are inappropriate or overly aggressive.*

In the same order, let me tell you what I found from looking into these allegations and checking them against the knowledge of those who actually have been in those areas of Third World nations where the problems are said to be acute.

1. Promotion of formula is influential. However, its influence is not on whether or not a new mother chooses to breast feed but upon those mothers who can't, don't, or won't elect nature. In other words, the advertising affects the choice of which supplement, not whether to supplement. Thus, formula really is in competition with buffalo and goat's milk or other questionable foods.

2. It is the whole pattern of urbanization and improvement of economic status that has produced dramatic social shifts. More women are working than ever before. Consequently, fewer women are breast-feeding.

3. A professor in my community of Los Angeles said infant formula caused the death of 10 million babies. Every independent investigation of his contention comes up with no basis for that number.

I interviewed several public health workers from lesser developed
countries, and they assured me that even taking into account that formula may be mixed with water from polluted supplies, survival
chances still are better for the baby fed with formula than with any
other supplement or substitute for breast milk.

4. There was a basis for contending that formula sales practices were not always appropriate. However, whatever the competitive
passions were that led to such bold behavior, they now have been
checked by the industry's own action. The principal practices currently used to market these products are essentially the same as those
used by pharmaceutical companies with their nonprescription drugs.
In short, it is geared primarily to health professionals.

Now, ask yourself, why haven't those with the most to lose in
this battle, namely, the companies that make formula addressed these
points in a similar manner? Certainly, they know this story. They
have the facts.

I happen to think most business people are terrified by controversy. They bite their lips and suck their thumbs, just so long as they
don't have to confront their critics. And then they wonder why so
much regulation is befalling them.

In the case of the WHO and the marketing code, or UNESCO
and the journalism code, the coersive proposals have never been
forced into the arena of rugged intellectual combat where free-market
spokesmen might challenge the bases for regulation. In fact, it's the
aggressive adversary who tends to dominate most of what the public
hears. And, why not? It's not so easy to report what isn't being said.

There is another phenomenon in this process. It's the neutrality ploy or the "we're not involved in that matter" response.

As I prowled the WHO corridors in Geneva on several occasions, I learned that once an infant formula code was voted in, the
agency's Secretariat would seek a similar set of restrictions on the
pharmaceutical and chemical industries. So I called more than a
dozen executives in these industries both in the U.S. and in Europe
asking for a reaction on marketing codes. Every one of them told me
that as long as they weren't in the immediate sights of the formula
code, they were keeping strictly neutral.

It kept reminding me of Dante's admonition about the hottest
spot in hell being reserved for those who in the midst of crisis declare
neutrality.

If the infant formula debate is to be positioned correctly,
it will require that the leaders—public and private—of the developed countries move to the front. They will have to make plain to
the WHO delegates and those who instruct them that an international

health organization has no business in determining market specifics.

There is room for a WHO role, a quite legitimate one. It is for the May Assembly to write and adopt a set of principles giving guidance to member states of the U.N., to health professionals throughout the world, and to industrial marketers, on how all can cooperate in the promotion of breast feeding. Taking that much more positive tack would see light replacing heat in this overall debate.

Regrettably, I don't expect this to happen. I expect the forces of regulation will prevail as they often do when free men are not sufficiently watchful.

I am grateful for your interest and your kindness in letting me offer for your consideration my point of view. Now, I look forward to your questions.

Source: National Catholic Reporter/Bill Toohey. Reprinted from the *National Catholic Reporter* (August 14, 1981), p. 11.

CLARENCE B. CARSON

How Sound Is Social Security?

The Reagan Administration has come forth with its plan for solving the problems of Social Security. Unless something is done to alter current trends, the projection is that the retirement fund will run out of money sometime in 1982. The Congressional Budget Office estimates that by 1986 the fund will lack $63.5 billion needed to meet its obligations, and that by 1990 it will be short twice that much.

Let's face it, the Social Security program is a time bomb. It will remain so, unless and until the most drastic changes are effected to make it actuarially sound. Tinkering with its benefits, delaying for a few months the paying of some cost-of-living increase, removing the penalties for working past 65, feeding some concocted figures about future prosperity into a computer and reading them through rose-colored glasses won't cure Social Security. One might as well claim to cure patients of terminal cancer by applying a Band-Aid and regaling them with the statistics for cures in cases of early detection.

Since the basic fallacy in the Social Security program is the same as that in *chain-letter schemes,* I shall use that illusion to point it up and show what the government has done. I am not denying, of course, that those who get in on the ground floor of an extensive chain-letter campaign might not get handsome returns from their initial investment. For all I know, it may be possible for them to increase their wealth a hundredfold; or, for that matter, a thousand. It is those later on the chain who are the victims.

The United States Postal Service holds that chain-letter schemes are fraudulent, and participants in such undertakings are subject to prosecution for fraud if they use the mails. That in itself might not be persuasive, but the points they advance are convincing. There are two basic reasons why chain-letter schemes cannot work as claimed. The first is that no more money can come out than went in. On its face, that has to be true. Therefore, if some get more out than they put in, this must be balanced by an equal amount which others put in that they do not get out.

The chain-letter enthusiast thinks he has a way around this

Source: Reprinted from *The Review of the News* (June 3, 1981), pp. 31–32.

difficulty; a way implicit in the promise of wealth to all participants. It is that there is an infinite or unlimited number of people who can be successively drawn into the chain. That is not the case, of course. Despite the world population explosion of the last two centuries, there are still only enough people on this planet to sustain the chain-letter undertaking for a short while. Postal Service sleuths have worked all this out mathematically, I am told, but I had trouble with the old math, and my mind is proof against both the new math and computations which run to more than six figures. With an unaccustomed burst of faith, however, I am willing in this case to take their word for it.

Thus far, everything said about chain-letter schemes, except their being illegal, is applicable to Social Security as well. That is, those who got in on the ground floor could get much more out of it than they put in. (I had a great step-uncle who made one small payment, a few dollars at most, retired, lived into his nineties, and drew many thousands in benefits.) But it is also true of Social Security that no more can be taken out (plus interest, in the case of Social Security) than has been put in. It follows, too, that if some do get more than was put in, this must be balanced with an equal amount from others who get less. So far as having an unlimited number of people to which it can be extended, Social Security is worse off than chain-letter schemes. In theory, chain letters could be sent anywhere in the world; whereas, Social Security extends only to the population of the United States.

There are some differences, however, between chain-letter schemes and the Social Security program. They are not essential, but they do help to explain why Social Security has not long since met the fate of chain-letter schemes. The first difference is that participation in Social Security is compulsory. Participation in chain-letter schemes is voluntary, and they soon peter out because of it. People break the chains for a variety of reasons, plus no reason at all: skepticism, good sense, carelessness, just never got around to sending it off, and the like. On the other hand, Social Security secures participation with the aid of the ubiquitous hand of the I.R.S.

Second, Social Security is built upon a delayed system of payment of benefits. It is possible to pay into it for the better part of a lifetime before any benefits become due. This is why I referred to it as a time bomb.

Third, Social Security has been able to expand its income gradually in three ways. (1) It has expanded the portion of the population covered, being extended to more and more kinds and categories of income producers. (2) It has increased gradually the amount of the tax on incomes and has, at the same time, extended the amount of income subject to the tax. (3) Incomes have risen with inflation; and, in conjunction with the above, more and more money has been poured into the coffers of the fund.

Even so, time is running out. The bomb is ticking louder. There is no longer any Social Security fund to speak of. It may be possible to defer the day of reckoning by reducing benefits here and there, but the program will never be economically sound until benefits are realistically geared to contributions. If that should happen, however, the program might no longer be politically attractive. In which case the Postal Service might finally get around to making an adverse ruling against the use of the mails by Social Security.

Talisman Changes Lives for Millions

An extraordinary phenomenon is sweeping the North American continent, it was learned from reliable sources here recently. A well-known but little understood woman who calls herself Madame Zarina is possessed by a power that allows her to dispense most of life's good things to whomever owns her specially designed Talisman.

Money, wealth, happiness, love and prosperity unfold the moment the famous Zarina's Talisman is worn or carried. What is this Talisman? It is a specially minted coin that mysteriously converts upon the wearer or carrier an almost certain propensity for happiness and success in every venture of life. There is only one stipulation, however. Instructions must be followed meticulously because for some peculiar reason the effectiveness of the Talisman is dependent upon them. A set of these instructions is enclosed with each Talisman.

People who have worn or carried this mystical Talisman have reported an almost immediate reversal of their luck. Most report that sooner or later their lives are radically changed. Others report a gradual, though definite, change.

Madame Zarina is not available for comment though reporters have been dogging her footsteps for many months now. Maybe that's the key to her success: Complete secrecy. And inaccessibility.

Now for those of you out there who are straining at the bit to change your luck, here's how to do it. Simply send $2.00 for each Aluminum Talisman, $4.00 for each Bronze Talisman, or $8.95 for each Electro-Plated Gold Talisman to Madame Zarina, E28-C P.O. Box 12, Rouses Point, N.Y. 12979.

Source: Advertisement reprinted from the *National Examiner* (July 14, 1981), p. 7.

"What do you expect? They don't let us pray anymore."

Source: Reprinted from *The Churchman* (November 1980), p. 7.

WILLIAM E. GARDNER
The Closet Society—A Fable

A group of people enter a large room. None of them had ever been in that room before. They sit around the room conversing with one another, observing the architecture of the room, the decorations, etc. Finally one of them gets up from his chair and walks slowly around the room, making a rather close scrutiny of things. He comes to a closed door on one side of the room, puts his hand on the door knob, and tries to open it. But it is fastened. He looks at it, tries once again to open it, and finally gives up this attempt; and then he remarks to the rest of the group, "I wonder what's in this closet?" Whereupon, others, who had not been paying attention to his actions, become interested. Some of them arise from their places and try to open the door. More interest is now generated, and they begin to speculate on the contents of the closet.

One says, "The room is clean, so probably there are brushes, mops, and other cleaning supplies in the closet."

Another says, "I think that is where the wood for the fireplace is kept." And so they have a friendly discussion over the possible contents. And this goes on for some time, each one having his own ideas of what's in the closet.

Then a newcomer walks into the room and, after greetings and introductions, someone tells him about their discussion and asks his opinion as to what's in the closet. He looks at the door, goes over and tries unsuccessfully to open it, looks at it some more, looks at the room and its construction, and finally asks, "How do you know it's a closet?" The group is suddenly very silent, until one of them speaks up, "We've already decided it's a closet. What we are doing is speculating on its contents."

"But," says the newcomer, "how do you know it's a closet?"

"It has to be a closet. Every room like this has to have a closet."

Others take up the argument. "Did you ever see a large room like this without a closet?"

And as they argue with the newcomer, they become more and

Source: Reprinted from *The Churchman* (April–May 1981), p. 12.

more convinced of their position, and eventually the newcomer real-
izes that he has touched off a sensitive argument and that he is not
very popular with his questioning the validity of their position, and
he takes his leave.

When he is gone, one member who is speaking frequently
enough to take on the role of leader says, "That was an uncomfortable
time. Why did he have to come in and spoil things when we are all
getting along so well?" The others agree.

"Do any of you doubt that this is a closet?" No one doubts.

"Then let's get organized and prevent anything like that from
happening again."

And soon they have organized the Closet Society.

"Let us elect a secretary, and he can write into the minutes
that we all agree that this is a closet, but that each one may have his
own ideas as to what's in the closet."

"I move we put a sign on that door, saying, 'CLOSET'" And
this is done.

Eventually, other newcomers enter the group and enjoy the
standing debate as to the contents of the closet. But, occasionally, a
newcomer asks the forbidden question: "How do you know it's a
closet?"

By this time the organization is strong enough to have a police force, which takes out such radicals and has them shot or burned
at the stake.

And, as time goes on, the minutes of that first meeting become
a Constitution which cannot be amended, and the writings of members of the group concerning the contents of the closet are compiled
in a sacred book; and there is not just one little original sign on the
closet door, but a larger one over it, and another saying, "This IS a
CLOSET," and others at the entrance of the room—"This way to the
CLOSET."

Members of the Closet Society take part in the annual Fourth
of July parade and have become the solid citizens of the community.

But once in a while, the peace of mind ordinarily enjoyed by
the Closet Society members is disrupted by some radical who asks the
searching question, "How do you know it's a closet?" And now, instead
of shooting such people or burning them at the stake, they are turned
over to the Anti-Closet Activities Committee, which has a way of effectively ruining the reputations of such inquisitive and radical people.

Sign This Congressional Petition and

STOP ABORTION!

Thousands of innocent babies are killed <u>every</u> <u>day</u> here in America!

Here are the facts:

1. Last year, approximately 1.5 million unborn babies were killed by abortion!

Hitler murdered 6 million Jews during his reign of terror. We kill that many unborn babies in just 4 years. And we consider it legal!

2. Abortion has become a legalized method of birth control! 30% of all women who become pregnant choose to end their pregnancy by abortion.

3. According to the U.S. Supreme Court, it is legal to kill a baby IF:

(a) The baby lives inside the mother and is less than 3 months old. (Some states allow abortion up to 6 months!)

(b) The mother wants the baby killed.

(c) The doctor is willing to do the killing.

We must not stand by and allow the slaughter of millions of infants to continue.

A Human Life Amendment to the Constitution could restore full protection of the law to all living humans, born and unborn, in all states.

Your signature urgently needed!

You can help save the lives of unborn babies by urging your Congressmen to support a Human Life Amendment.

We need one million Americans to sign this petition immediately, and we will deliver the results of this

This ad paid for by Moral Majority, Inc., Jerry Falwell, President.

petitioning to the Congress of the United States.

It's time for all moral Americans to speak up against abortion!

▌Sign This Petition Today!▐

Petition to the Congress of the United States

I oppose the killing of innocent babies through legalized abortion.

I urge you to support passage of a Human Life Amendment or any effective pro-life legislative effort.

Signed _____
Name (Print) _____
Address _____
City _____ State _____ Zip _____

SAM1H

Mail this petition to: Jerry Falwell
Moral Majority, Inc.
National Capitol Office
P.O. Box 190
Forest, Virginia 24551

Any contributions to help pay for this campaign are urgently needed and appreciated.

VIRGINIA SOUTHARD

The Ethics of Nuclear Power

In the Sept. 6, 1980 issue of *America,* Frederick S. Carney purports to discuss "An Ethical Analysis of Nuclear Power." So distorted, inaccurate and incomplete a presentation requires, in fairness, a response from a qualified professional.

I write as a lay Catholic who has devoted 10 years to the study of the problems of nuclear power. I write as the chairperson of the citizens' organization that first opposed and has litigated the licensing of the ill-fated Three Mile Island plant since 1972 and as a former Harrisburg, Pa., resident who directly experienced the T.M.I. accident in 1979, and I am also a person who has had cancer. With these qualifications, I wish to assert that the ethical analysis of nuclear power must be considered in the context of the realities of the nuclear fuel cycle as it operates today, not in "theoretical" or "calculated" analyses of safety that disregard the biological and medical evidence of the cancer and genetic damage that result from exposure of human beings to ionizing radiation. Indeed, I feel that the lack of consideration of the health effects of ionizing radiation and of the nuclear waste problems raises a question as to the validity of the entire article.

As a Catholic, I also strongly object to Mr. Carney's assumption that human life, which is held to be a sacred gift from God by all Christians, can be considered subordinate to "our industrial base" to the extent that any impairment of it from whatever cause could be catastrophic to our society and devastating to a wide range of intrinsic values to which we are committed. Such an assumption is not an acceptable value judgment for the commercial use of nuclear generated electricity with its risk from unwanted radiation damage and catastrophic accident.

The entire Carney article was written without reference to the well-established and accepted fact that any exposure to radiation, including natural background, may damage the genetic material of the person exposed, resulting in defects, premature disease or death in that person's progeny. The author fails to acknowledge the equally

199

well-established fact that all exposures to radiation increase the risk of injury and disease to the one exposed, which, due to the latency period between exposure and appearance of the damage, may not be diagnosed for many years.

There is no discussion of the bases for the existing Federal radiation standards. These standards assume that benefits are resulting to society that equal the injuries, which the standard setters admit are occurring, from the allowable radiation levels now being received by the public from the nuclear industry.

So misleading and tortuous are the logic and argumentation of his value analysis and so incorrect are the data on energy needs and effects that the reader is hard-put to address every point. For example, the illogic of Carney reasoning may be seen in his treatment of safety and human life as "relative values." He concludes that "persons should have freedom when its exercise does not harm others." Yet the increases in man-induced radiation in the environment from nuclear energy exemplify the imposition of a burden without choice upon the individual citizen. An individual does not have the right to decide for himself if he wishes to incur the increased risk of radiation-related disease or genetic injury to his descendents that may be caused by exposure to emissions from nuclear power will ascertain how many people will actually die or have been injured as a result of the release of radiation at T.M.I. The author may be unaware that radiation monitors in the plant were off scale in the early days of that accident and that there were no ground-level thermoluminiscent dosimeters in place between 2.6 and 9 miles of the plant for the first three days of the accident—information contained in the H.E.W. report cited by Mr. Carney. In view of the uncertainty of doses received and of further releases that may occur during the clean-up period and of the dose-response relationship of low-dose radiation, the residents of central Pennsylvania face an agonizing future during the next decade or more for the well-being of themselves and their children.

The author provides an energy growth scenario that assumes the rates of increase that characterize an earlier period of American history; yet he dismisses conservation lightly and expresses his personal but unsubstantiated doubt that solar, wind, biomass, geothermal, hydro and other low-polluting renewable energy sources will be brought on line by the year 2000. Others among us, who treasure human life for its intrinsic value as God's gift, may be more willing to conserve to bring about that transition to "soft energy" sources.

Nuclear power is, in fact, an almost trivial energy source (less than 3 percent of total energy supply in the United States today). Although the 74 reactors licensed to operate in our country are capable of producing 13 percent of our electricity supply, Mr. Carney may not be aware that in most of the months since the T.M.I. accident began, fewer than 55 of the 74 licensed reactors have been in operation in any month. The outages result from unresolved safety problems, from serious accidents, from backfitting requirements, from seismic uncertainties, and maintenance or refueling. As Amroy B. Lovins has shown, nationwide we get more energy from wood, and the Department of Energy is now demonstrating the use of wood to generate electricity on a commercial scale far more safely than nuclear power.

While Mr. Carney suggests that the United States engages in "humanitarian assistance to—persons in the third world—to overcome their poverty," we Americans, who comprise only 6 percent of the world's people, are consuming between 30 percent and 50 percent of the world's available resources. Is the complex, very expensive, high technology of nuclear power really of importance to the urban poor or rural villagers who cannot afford food to nourish their children, much less electricity?

Nowhere does this author discuss radioactive wastes; the lack of criteria for radioactive waste management, the lack of exposure standards, the lack of demonstration of waste storage, transportation accidents, diversion for use in atomic bombs, or the true costs of ultimate disposal. There is no discussion of the ethical implications of routinely releasing low-level radioactive wastes into our environment. Nor does the writer justify exposures which take place unbeknown to the recipient of a radiation dose.

Since the appearance of Mr. Carney's article in September, the Nuclear Regulatory Commission has proposed to deregulate certain radioactive wastes so that by dispersion and dilution they will be dumped into our community sanitary landfills and sewage systems. Also, under recently proposed regulations, the N.R.C. would allow the recycling of contaminated metals, such as copper, nickel and iron, for use in a wide variety of consumer products, including cooking pots, toys, cars and coins. It is a cheaper solution to low-level waste disposal than the use of regulated, supervised and monitored burial sites. Can it be ethical for our society to indulge itself in the use of an energy source which produces long-lived, highly toxic wastes before providing that these wastes can and will be safely disposed of? For many of your readers who live by the word of God, the answer can only be "No!"

Finally, I cannot accept Mr. Carney's position on values and disvalues: "We must ask whether deep within the moral roots of our civilization we have held and do hold today, that either the instrumental value of safety or the intrinsic value of human life is an absolute value. Is either a value that takes precedence over every other value, a value for the sake of which we would sacrifice any other value that comes into conflict with it? The answer I think is no."

The Gospels record for us the absolute value which Jesus places on love of God and love of neighbor, that two-fold love which is at the heart of Christian existence. This is my position.

Smoking's other hazard.

You see it in every cigarette advertisement.

Artfully tucked away in the least conspicuous corner of the ad is an obligatory warning: "The Surgeon General has determined that cigarette smoking is dangerous to your health."

But the Surgeon General, if he were an accountant, could have determined still another kind of danger.

Cigarette smoking is also a clear, present, and continuing hazard to your pocketbook—even if you don't smoke.

Every year, while smokers all around you are losing their health, you are losing at least $250 in ways you may not even suspect.

Not surprisingly, the tobacco industry sees it differently.

America's oldest industry, as it is fond of calling itself, has summoned econometric models to prove its "dramatic" contribution to the nation's Gross National Product.

But this is roughly akin to the convicted felon who claims he's helping the economy, because his imprisonment creates jobs for judges, jailers, and manufacturers of steel bars.

Like the view from a prison cell, a tobacco apologist's perspective is likely to be somewhat limited.

It ignores the heavy burden of smoking-connected costs which fall on everyone—but with special unfairness on non-smokers:

There are higher fire insurance costs than there should be, because a major cause of all fires is smoking.

Higher prices for virtually any product you buy, because smoking increases absenteeism—and consequently manufacturing costs, by billions of dollars annually.

Higher health insurance premiums, because smoking costs the nation more than $20 billion a year in hospital care and physician services.

And, of course, higher taxes. To support the loan program which the Government operates for tobacco farmers.

How much does all this come to?

Estimates vary, but a fair guess seems to be approximately $50 billion.

To offset this, Federal, state, and local authorities collect about $6.5 billion a year in tobacco taxes.

This leaves every man and woman in the U.S. with the tab we mentioned earlier: approximately $250 a year each in support of a product for which almost nobody has a good word to say—not even smokers themselves.

Indeed, nine out of ten smokers today would like to quit. But the help they are receiving from their Government is pitifully inadequate—two million dollars on antismoking activities, compared to a *billion* dollars which the cigarette companies are currently investing in their advertising campaigns.

We spend more money to combat alcoholism and teenage pregnancy than to help people fight their smoking addiction. Yet cigarettes take more lives than liquor. And unwanted babies, tragic as they are, cost the nation far less than the economic pressures created by tobacco.

It's time we recognized smoking for the dual threat that it is—not just to every smoker's heart and lungs but to the body politic as well.

For its economic health, America must kick the smoking habit.

RODALE PRESS, INC.
Emmaus, PA 18049

Rodale publishes: *Prevention, Rodale's New Shelter, Organic Gardening, Bicycling, Executive Fitness Newsletter, The New Farm,* and *Theatre Crafts,* as well as hardcover and paperback books under the Rodale imprint. The company also produces films and television programs.

Source: Reprinted with permission from the Rodale Press.

LEOPOLD TYRMAND

The Sharks

Nixon had to go, whatever his deserts or failings, because the liberal establishment in the media hated him, for various reasons. It's natural that a Supreme Court featuring four Nixon appointees, including the Chief Justice, would elicit similar feelings from the liberal muckrakers. They have long seemed like sharks cruising toward blood in the water. Since the Warren Burger court has recently taken a stand against some of the more indecent transgressions of the so-called free press, thereby earning its hateful wrath, some kind of vendetta was inevitable. This book is nothing but rabid, unabashed revenge, adorned with the bogus righteousness of service to the republic. A massive effort to drive its message into the nation's consciousness is being made by the most powerful centers of opinion making, which smacks of ideological collusion.

Muckraking is called "New Journalism" these days, which makes it no less smelly; its intentions are simply veiled with a thicker layer of mendacity and false civic virtue. Its most potent device is a sort of "reconstituted-lemon-juice" style: the muckrakers simulate and counterfeit situations and conversations which they have never seen, attended or listened to, which they learned mostly from biased, often dishonest, informants, and which they peddle as reality. They are about as real as reconstituted lemon juice. Mr. Woodward is one of the most prominent exponents of the genre: to an unprejudiced eye, his "work" is no less than despicable.

Source: Book review reprinted from *Chronicles of Culture* (January–February 1980), p. 32.
Bob Woodward and Scott Armstrong: *The Brethren: Inside the Supreme Court;* Simon & Schuster; New York.

RAFE KLINGER

Face-to-Face with a Space Beast!

Arlin Gilpin was a curious young man when he grabbed his pistol and went to investigate the mysterious orange light near his home.

Minutes later the 19-year-old youth was babbling insanely—and his hands had turned green.

Arlin and three other witnesses told The NEWS of one of the most chilling UFO encounters ever—the night they met a huge space alien with red-orange eyes like burning coals.

"There was a form there, but I can't describe it," said Arlin's mother, Cathy, of Casey County, Ky., who also saw the unworldly creature.

"It didn't seem to want to hurt anyone—but I would never try to follow one again."

Arlin's nerve-shattering encounter left him with green hands and a purple-colored burn mark under his right eye. Incredibly, the marks vanished by the next morning.

"I haven't any idea what I saw," Arlin told The NEWS. "It wasn't anything of human form."

The nightmare encounter occurred the night of March 11, outside the homes of the Gilpin and Wethington families in a sparsely-populated area.

Arlin and his mother were watching TV when they heard a strange sound like an electrical pump or drill outside their house.

Looking out the window, they saw a glowing orange ball of light setting over the woods near their acreage. Thinking it was a car that had run off the road, Mrs. Gilpin got in her car and drove out after it.

As she approached, she could see a large glowing ball of light which kept dancing away from her as she approached.

Mrs. Gilpin was frightened and wanted to turn around.

"But I got this weird feeling that it was pulling me to it," she said.

Terrified, she forced herself to turn the car around and drove away.

Source: Reprinted from *Weekly World News* (June 30, 1981), p. 15.

Meanwhile, Arlin had telephoned his nearby aunt and uncle, Candy and Carroll Wethington. Then he grabbed his pistol and went out to investigate.

As Arlin walked toward the woods, two orange dots "like eyes" suddenly appeared just a few feet in front of him.

"It was like there wasn't anything there, but there was. The eyes were above me and it wasn't a human figure. It seemed like a great big giant ape, but I couldn't tell.

"I'm 6-foot-1, and it was much bigger, more than seven feet."

Shocked by the sudden appearance, Arlin called out and then fired.

"I shot at it and it just disappeared," he said. "I'd say it was something from outer space. I don't know of anything on earth that I could shoot at from that close and it could just disappear."

Arlin started walking back toward the Wethingtons' house. When he turned, the orange eyes appeared behind him again. He turned and went up to them and raised his pistol.

"I kept trying and trying to pull the trigger—but I couldn't pull the trigger. It seemed like it wouldn't let me."

Arlin was terrified. He rushed into his aunt's house totally panic-stricken.

His aunt, uncle and two other relatives there were consoling his mother who had driven to their home.

When they saw him, they were stunned. His hands had turned green!

"It looked like a powder was covering them," said Candy Wethington. "But it wasn't a powder. It wouldn't rub or wash off."

Arlin was terrified and babbling wildly. His relatives calmed him and took away his gun. Then, they all gathered around a table to sip coffee and discuss the strange things they had seen.

Suddenly without a word, Arlin stood up and walked out the door. Candy and the others looked out the window and saw him standing at the end of the walkway talking to something with glowing orange eyes.

"I got this feeling while I was in the house that I had to go outside," Arlin recalls. "It was waiting for me.

"It seemed like it was trying to talk to me, but I couldn't understand it. It was making electronic sounds.

"I still couldn't make out its shape in the dark. Then, it just touched me—on the cheek.

"It was like a shock—like when you bump into an electrified fence—only it went from my cheek down through my whole body.

"I wasn't afraid. It seemed like when it touched me, it was letting me know that it could do whatever it wanted to—and I couldn't stop it."

Arlin walked back into the house. On his cheek was the burn mark. Candy said the glowing dots stayed for a moment and then just vanished.

Arlin says that he hasn't suffered any ill effects from his encounter with the being.

"I don't know what it was," he said. "I just think it must be from another planet.

"I have this feeling that it's going to come back. It may not come back here, but it'll come somewhere."

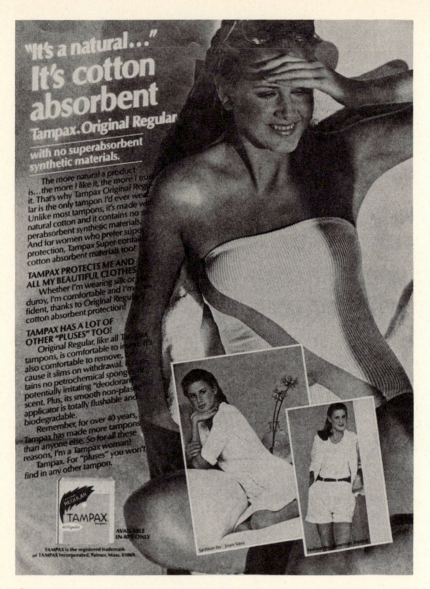

Source: Courtesy of TAMPAX Incorporated, Palmer, Mass.

ROBERT J. CARLEY

The Libertine Equation

The programs and actions growing out of libertine thought and its ideologies, have put society in bondage to the indifferent with disturbing consequences. It strikes me in this manner.

Ultra liberal thought in its libertarian way, racing on its erratic course deep within the sanctuary of man and woman, soon bursts forth upon society. Confused, discontented, immoral, demanding, abusive, with no restraints and in their frenzy call it freedom.

This is not freedom, this is an abuse of freedom in which society becomes a slave to turbulent thought, shiftlessness and wanton desires.

It is a delusion, the leading of individuals the wrong way down a one-way street. It is an intellectually organized view and principle presented in such a way, even though it is misleading, to meet the permissive demands of the time. This sort of libertine equation has just about bankrupted society morally and financially.

Society and religion must find a way to unwind from this dangerous thought that knows no evil, sees no evil, hears no evil; that has no moral or financial balance; that plays upon the weaknesses of human nature to gain its popularity. This kind of speculative philosophy has been the scourge of nations down through the ages.

Every so often history repeats itself and moral society has had to deal with this type of thinking and behavior. If in this present day and time it is allowed to continue, everyone will be engulfed in this delusion. For when the bell tolls, it tolls for all.

May I say in all fairness, while we cannot condone disoriented, undisciplined runaway thoughts and actions, we also cannot allow narrowness and cynicism to govern our lives. Both can be ruinous and so cloud the mind to reality and sane thought.

Source: Letter reprinted from *Mobile Press-Register* (October 3, 1981).

GORDON'S DIDN'T GET TO BE
THE WORLD'S LARGEST SELLING GIN
WITHOUT MAKING AN EXCEPTIONAL
MARTINI.

Largest selling gin
in England, America, the world.

The Execution of Steven Judy

The Execution of Steven Judy in Indiana last week was the fourth since the U.S. Supreme Court's 1977 decision to allow capital punishment. Judy's government-sanctioned killing drew some protests and press coverage, but not nearly as much as the earlier executions. It seems we are adjusting to the new standard. We should not.

The crimes of the 24-year-old Judy, the rape and murder of a young woman and brutal killings of her three children, were hideous acts. Judy's apparent failure to show remorse was incomprehensible, the product of a twisted and sad life. There was not much appealing in his personality.

Nevertheless, his was a human life, just like those he ended. The issue here is the right of any of us, represented collectively in our government, to decide to take steps to end human life. After periods of finding reasons to void the stark commandment, "Thou shalt not kill," church teaching more recently has clearly opposed capital punishment.

Life is a gift of God and it is sacred. We are "temples of the Holy Spirit," even the murderers among us. The Steven Judys must be locked up; society must be protected. But capital punishment is wrong, just as wrong as abortion, euthanasia and all forms of destruction of human life.

Source: Reprinted by permission of the National Catholic Reporter, P.O. Box 281, Kansas City, Mo. 64141.

IMPORT BUYERS ARE LOSERS

When they buy imported clothing, cars, appliances, trucks, and other overseas products, they lose jobs for American workers — jobs which can eventually mean losing their OWN jobs.

They lose because the unemployed can't buy the products and services of the import-buyers.

They lose in paying for welfare, food stamps, social programs and needs of the unemployed American workers.

They lose when skills and factories essential to our national defense deteriorate from neglect and leave the nation vulnerable.

They lose money at home and overseas. They lose by weakening our economy which endangers our freedom.

Don't be a loser...
BE A WINNER!
BUY AMERICAN!

Security and prosperity begin at home.

UAre Winners with UAW

Better Buy American –
and Get a Better Buy!

International Union UAW
Region 8 T. Michael Director

Alabama State,
UAW Community Action Program Council
Ray Madison, President

THOMAS E. BLACKBURN

If You Can't Rely on Jeane Dixon...

Now I ask you, if you can't rely on Jeane Dixon to tell you what is going to be going on, whom can you rely on?

I ask because competition among seers is one of the last functioning free markets in this era of big oil, big steel and big food. Hardly a trip to the supermarket goes by without an offer from this publication or that to tell you, "Exclusive: psychic talks to Elvis and learns Jackie's future."

People read this stuff, and I've always wondered what they were reading and whether they were finding out what was going to happen before Dan Rather told them. Haven't you ever thought it would be fun to save a set of psychic mumbo-jumbo and see how the predictions turned out?

I did. That is why I have in front of me Jeane Dixon's semian-nual predictions for the first six months of 1981—95 pages issued by her *Los Angeles Times* **Syndicate.**

Among the shocks Dixon didn't prepare us for last December were the assassination attempt on President Reagan, Ted Kennedy's divorce announcement, all the Cabinet names, the successful space shuttle flight, the baseball strike and the Israeli attack on the Iraqi nuclear reactor. Dixon talked about Carol Burnett for a whole page without mentioning the libel judgment.

Dixon didn't mention Alexander Haig, but she did wrongly predict Henry Kissinger would be back in an official capacity by spring. She said the star of the cabinet would be the (unnamed) secretary of energy who, of course, turned out to be good old whassisname, the root canal man.

It turned out that it was impossible to keep a box score on her hits and misses. I can't separate her predicting from her pontificating. She expected the hostages to be released after Jimmy Carter left office and Reagan settled in. Elsewhere, she indicated that Vice Presi-

Source: Reprinted by permission of the National Catholic Reporter, P.O. Box 281, Kansas City, MO. 64141.

dent George Bush might spend part of March negotiating the release or welcoming them home.

She can claim to be right about Carter being gone before the hostages—by 25 minutes—but in the total context, her guess was no better than everyone else's.

And the more specific she gets, the more often she is wrong.

A big, favorable response didn't follow Ronald Reagan's actions on Jan. 11 and 12 because he was out of the news, getting a haircut or something, when Dixon said he'd wow us. She was also wrong about Prince Charles shunning marriage and Queen Elizabeth butting into British politics, about Hollywood's "real life shooting" like J. R. Ewing's; about Ringo Starr staying out of sight (he married an actress); about Reagan and Menachem Begin hitting it up in a chummy relationship; about Dan Rather getting in trouble in February for rash behavior and about the shoot-outs in city streets that would be part of the fad for things western.

She keeps her batting average up with obvious predictions, like showers in April. Al Jolson hit that one 50 years ago. Such hits, however, call attention to other misses, like failure to tell us about drought in 46 states.

Dixon said Senator Paula Hawkins would charm us but didn't warn us about two more publicized fellow freshmen senators, John P. East and Jeremiah Denton. She wrote about Barbara Mandrell's television show as if it would be another "I Love Lucy." Well, it wasn't cancelled.

Almost anyone can do the sort of thing Dixon does. A Wrigley Field regular can predict, when the Cubs have the tying run on second with no one out in the bottom of the ninth, that the run won't score. I've done that one many times myself.

This is not to pooh-pooh extra-sensory perception. Events take their direction from their own rhythm and dynamics which may be picked up subconsciously by an observer who doesn't quite know how he or she does it. But the rhythm and dynamics come from the people involved, not Capricorn or Tarot cards. Most of us get hunches like Dixon's, but few make a living at it, and of those who do, few are as respectable as Dixon. Which is what makes the normalness of her success rate so surprising.

Her psychic powers don't make her political predictions any more accurate than David Broder's or her suggestions to the stars any sounder than Rona Barrett's. So what's so psychic?

Psychic fans may be expected to trumpet her prediction about the assassination attempt on Pope John Paul. Here is what she said: "Authorities will uncover an outlandish plot against the Pope by one of the foolish splinter groups in Italian radical politics."

"Uncovering a plot" when the shooting starts is hardly an action by "authorities," and what the shooting had to do with radical politics remains to be revealed.

The impressive thing in 95 pages is not Dixon's so-so psychic power but her politics, which track neatly with the Reagan wing of the Republican party. Her adulation of Reagan stops little short of idolatry. "His ascendancy to the presidency," she says, "will be merely (sic) another step in fulfilling his destiny. . . ." What's next? Pope? The Nobel Prize for physics? An Academy Award?

She is so attuned to and approving of the current political order that her success rate should go up in the Reagan years. She predicts what it will try to accomplish. Wonderful things are in store for the cities, she says, when they get something she only describes vaguely. What she is describing is the "enterprise zone" proposal. She makes it sound like it comes from psychic vibrations. Actually, it comes from Heritage Foundation publications. The Puerto Riconization of American cities is what she is talking about. She assures us we'll love it.

The heavy element of wish fulfillment accounts, no doubt, for why she failed to warn us about the socialist victory in France with (shock! gasp!) Communists entering the government.

She doesn't approve of Reds. One thing she did promise was that high officials would flee China and reveal the awful things going on behind the Bamboo Curtain during the past six months. Instead, Haig flew to China and declared it almost a free world ally. Dixon got double-crossed on that one.

But if you can't rely on Dixon to tell you when a Red leopard is going to change its spots, you can't rely on psychics for anything at all, can you?

"If you concentrate on my accomplishments and abilities as a professional, in time you'll be able to overlook the fact that I'm a woman."

Source: © 1978 by National Review, 150 East 35th Street, New York, N.Y., 10016. Reprinted from *National Review* (July 7, 1978), p. 821.

MARTIN RIDGEWAY
Marriage and Catholic Doctrine

Editors:

Neither your article "Synod 'Secret' Poll" (NCR, Nov. 28) nor the family synod itself speaks to my problem.

I am a divorced Catholic who has remarried. Joan and I are active members of Holy Family parish. I have petitioned the diocesan marriage tribunal for an annulment. Laura, my former wife, is cooperating with me in seeking this. She too is remarried to a Catholic.

During the long annulment proceedings, I have met the various biblical and ecclesiastical statements relating to my case. And I am confused.

1. *Under the Old Testament law, I could put Laura away for any cause I thought sufficient. (Hillel, the Jewish scholar, listed as an adequate cause "burning the bread.")*
2. *Of course, under the law, I wouldn't have to put Laura away in order to wed Joan. I could keep any number of legal wives.*
3. *Jesus (in Matthew) suggested I could put Laura away if she were guilty of fornication.*
4. *Jesus (in Mark) said I could not put Laura away for any cause.*
5. *He said specifically that divorced persons living in subsequent marriages are guilty of fornication.*
6. *The new family synod has ruled that Joan and I can be full sacramental members of the church if there is no sex in our new marriage.*
7. *The Vatican has approved only one form of birth control: celibacy (either total or periodic). St. Augustine held out for total celibacy.*
8. *And finally, there is Pope John Paul's recent statement that it is sinful for any man to look after his wife with lust in his heart.*

Source: Letter printed in the *National Catholic Reporter* (January 9, 1981), p. 10.

I don't know how I'm supposed to respond to this maze of doctrine, but it does make me yearn for those Old Testament days.

Still, it seems to me if I stick with the Gospels, I'm all right.

Following Jesus (in Matthew), I can put Laura away if she is guilty of fornication. Following Jesus (in Mark), she *is* guilty of fornication because she's living in a new marriage. Consequently, I should be able to put her away and wed my present spouse. (Laura can do the same with me.)

The problem is the Church, which keeps putting those prohibitions on sex in marriage. I can't look after my wife in lust. I must use celibacy to achieve birth control. I can keep my new marriage only if it is totally sexless.

Well, if I can't have sex in my new marriage (and Laura can't in hers), how can we commit the fornication necessary for us to put each other away and validate our new marriages and become once again full members of the Church? This is Catch-22 morality.

I will appreciate any clarification one of your writers might give me on this situation. He might begin by advising me if it is lawful to lust after my ex-wife. I have to meet Laura every other Wednesday at the marriage tribunal, and she's looking good.

Reviewing Scientific Data

For scientists the basic assumption with assumptions is to assume nothing. Last March 2, when 40 young scientists, all winners in the Westinghouse Science Search, gathered in Washington, D.C., to exhibit their projects at the National Academy of Science, several popularly held assumptions fell at approximately 32 feet per second per second, with atmospheric variables, of course.

ASSUMPTION: By high school age, girls naturally gravitate to the arts, but have little head or taste for math and science, which demand the skills more characteristic of boys. The first prize winner, however, was Amy Sue Reichel, who admittedly is a serious painter and pianist. Westinghouse gave her the $12,000 prize for an experiment in genetic factors in immunization.

ASSUMPTION: Non-English-speaking students have difficulty adjusting, invariably fall behind in their studies and drain the resources of their schools. Possibly, but Tan Dinh Ngo, 16, was such a student when he arrived in New York last year from his native Vietnam not knowing any English. His work in numbers theory, it is true, failed to place in the top 10, but as finalist he made the trip to Washington.

ASSUMPTION: New York City schools are ineffective because of racial tension, violent crime, narcotics and political bureaucracies. This collapse of a school system is being repeated in other cities across the country. Some collapse. Six of the ten prize winners came from city schools and a seventh from a near suburb. An objective analysis of the data supports the thesis that some effective education is going on in the private and public schools in New York.

Source:: Reprinted with permission of America Press, Inc., 106 West 56th Street, New York, N.Y. 10019. © 1981. All rights reserved.

219

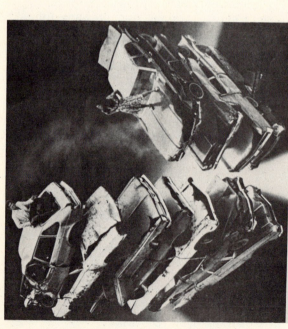

JOHN MERROW

The Tuition Tax Dodge

(A DUBIOUS IDEA WHOSE TIME HAS COME)

The man from New Hampshire had never heard of a "tuition tax credit" but he thought it sounded like a good idea. He and his wife were both working, he said, and because their state doesn't provide kindergarten, they had to send their daughter to a private school. He wouldn't mind, he said, "getting some of that tuition money back at tax time."

This may be his year. A tuition tax credit bill came close in the last Congress (passed the House, lost narrowly in the Senate). This Congress is more conservative, and President Reagan, unlike his predecessor, supports the idea, as does the secretary of education. The idea is simple: if you send your child to a private school or college, you may subtract from your tax bill a specified amount (but not more than half) of the tuition. How much credit parents get depends on the bill, but the most publicized, the Moynihan-Packwood-Roth bill, provides $250 in the first year, $500 thereafter. Anyone who owed the IRS less than the credit would get the money in cash.

Tuition tax credits may have friends in high places in Washington, but most liberal and public education groups oppose them. The *New York Times* and the *Washington Post* are condemning the idea with even more vigor than they did last time around. Other opponents are calling tuition tax credits a "pernicious danger" to the public schools, a "blatant raid on the Treasury," and—at least by implication—a threat to the stability of the Republic. Thirty organizations, including the PTA and associations of school principals, superintendents, school boards, and teachers have formed the National Coalition for Public Education to fight against tuition tax credits.

The opponents have a lot of ammunition available to fire at tuition tax credits, though some shells are more explosive than others.

Source: Reprinted by permission of *The New Republic,* © 1981 The New Republic, Inc.

First is the constitutional or "church-state" argument: because about 85 percent of nonpublic school students are in parochial schools, giving tax credits amounts to state establishment of religion, which is expressly forbidden by the Constitution. Earlier attempts to aid nonpublic schools have been overturned on this ground, notably in the Supreme Court's rejection of New York State's plan, in the 1973 *Nyquist* decision. Supporters of tax credits argue that their legislation is different because the credits will go to families, not to religious schools or to churches. Senator Moynihan argues that if all religions are eligible (as they are under his bill), then no one religion is "established." If tax credit legislation passes, there is sure to be a church-state court test.

Another argument is that tax credits will go, indirectly, to white-only, segregationist academies (true), and directly to parents who are purposely buying segregated education (also true). Moreover, credits will encourage segregation-minded parents with children still in public school to flee (probably true). On the other side of the case, it's good to remember that private schools are, on the whole, more integrated than public schools. It isn't strictly true—as often claimed—that tuition credits benefit the rich the most. The prime beneficiaries, in fact, would be middle-class families. Most parents paying $4,000 to $5,000 to send a child to Andover or Groton don't need, and probably don't care about, a $500 tax credit. Parochial school tuition, though, is normally in the $400 to $1,200 range. Poor people would not benefit unless they could find a way to come up with half their children's tuition money, and then benefits would be delayed each year until after tax time.

There is a big question whether the U.S. can afford the cost in lost tax revenues, which opponents such as Senator Ernest Hollings of South Carolina estimate will be four billion dollars a year. Because most members of Congress seem to have taken vows at the altar of the balanced budget, passage of tuition tax credit legislation would seem to mean even deeper domestic budget cuts, presumably from programs such as Title I, school breakfast and lunch, CETA, and other programs that help the poor.

It seems clear that tuition credits would be yet another advantage for private over public schools. Already public schools are required to serve everyone, but the private schools are selective, and don't have to enroll—or keep—the handicapped, the unmotivated, the unintelligent, the anti-social, and other hard-to-educate children. It's not fair for government to encourage more "skimming off the cream." Advocates of tuition credits claim that parents of private school students have to pay taxes to support public schools and tuition and that this is not fair. By that faulty logic, though, people who belong to country clubs or drive to work in their own cars should get tax credits for those outlays because, after all, their taxes are already paying for public parks and mass transit and they shouldn't have to "pay twice."

Tuition credits seem to invite the federal intrusion into education that conservatives claim to abhor. Who, for example, will distinguish between real and phony private schools? The logical investigator is the IRS rather than state education authorities. In reality, the IRS might do the job better. Private schools in most states are virtually unregulated, having only to meet fire and health code standards and teach U.S. history. Fear of federal "meddling" does seem to have diminished, perhaps extinguished, the enthusiasm that fundamentalist Christian schools once had for tuition tax credits. Other private schools, like those in the National Association of Independent Schools, are talking bravely about finding "workable solutions."

Despite their dislike for each other, both U.S. teacher unions, the National Education Association and the American Federation of Teachers, vigorously oppose tuition tax credits. Part of their reasoning is that with public school enrollment already declining, teachers cannot support anything that might shrink the student population further. Teaching jobs are at stake, in their view. The fact is, though, that nobody knows how many students would leave for private schools if tuition tax credits pass. Some opponents predict a whopping five percent—more than two million students. Other observers predict almost no movement, on the grounds that the tax credit is too small to induce parents to change. If the pessimists are right, though, tuition credits are likely to undermine public education and to spawn creation of thousands of new private schools, some of which will specialize in mischief as much as education.

All this represents a strong case against tuition tax credits, but there is one good argument on the other side: the need to shake up the public schools and the monopolistic-minded people who run them. Public educators as a group have forgotten that they work for the public. They have built up bureaucratic walls to protect themselves and have coated their policies in layers of jargon. It will take a drastic threat to make them responsive. Congressional and presidential moves toward tuition tax credits might do the trick. Clearly there are exceptions to the pattern of inadequacy in the public schools, but too few. Tuition tax credits are probably bad education policy and bad tax policy, but the threat they pose just might force the public schools to improve the quality of the education they offer and scare them into opening their doors to parents. Something has to do this, and soon.

Source: Reprinted with permission from Philip Morris.

JAMES J. KILPATRICK

Sin, Sex, TV

The dictionary defines "crusade" as a remedial enterprise undertaken with zeal. People who act with zeal perforce are zealots, and zealots are first cousins of fanatics, and all this is why the Rev. Donald Wildmon and his followers give me the blue willies.

The Rev. Mr. Wildmon, as you may have read, is engaged in a crusade against sex and sin on television. He rounded up 4,000 like-minded volunteers across the country, and for three months these observers solemnly annotated every shot, every kiss, every damn or hell and every jiggle on the tube. When they were done, the reverend ran the results through a computer. Then he put some heavy pressure on the sponsors of the programs deemed most objectionable.

The Procter & Gamble people, who spend almost $500 million a year on TV advertising, quickly got the point. Said board chairman Owen Butler to the networks: "I can assure you that we are listening very carefully to what they say." Mr. Butler thought the reverend's National Federation for Decency was expressing "some very important and broadly held views about gratuitous sex, violence and profanity."

For a while there was talk of a boycott against the products of the offending sponsors, but that talk has subsided. The writers and producers of such bummers as "The Dukes of Hazzard" have stopped muttering about censorship and artistic freedom. For the time being the controversy has blown over, but my blue willies remain. Two of the best rules for happy human relations are "Live and let live," and "Mind your own durned business." Why don't we observe them?

These issues ought to be decided in the marketplace. That is one of the things a free society is all about. Implicit in the intolerance of the Wildmon crusaders is the prospect that if they don't like a particular program, nobody else should be able to see it either. That is zealotry in action, and it is an ugly business.

The Mississippi reverend says his crusade is supported by five million families in all 50 states. Maybe yes, maybe no. That leaves roughly 54 million other families unaccounted for. Ninety-eight percent of all these families have television sets, and there is this interesting characteristic about those TV sets. Every one of them has a little switch that is lettered in this fashion: "On" and "Off."

Nothing in this world—no law, no regulation, no economic pressure, nothing at all—compels the reverend and his friends to watch "Dallas" or the "Dukes" or "Flamingo Road." His 4,000 observers and the members of his five million families are freeborn American citizens. It is a reasonable presumption that every one of them is capable of manipulating the little switch. All they have to do in order to avoid offense is to turn the switch to "Off."

Commercial television, let us remember, is just that—a commercial enterprise. The folks at Procter & Gamble are not sponsoring particular programs out of altruistic motives. They are not concerned with promoting art, but with selling soap. Once a program fails to attract sufficient viewers to sell sufficient soap, the program will be dropped. This is how the marketplace works.

But the manipulation of the little switch, it seems to me, ought to be by individual decision and not by mass persuasion. Live and let live! It is not essential to a contented and productive existence that we watch television by day and by night. There are books to be read, and letters to be written, and pickles to be pickled, and a thousand other enterprises and amusements to pass the time. What do Mr. Wildmon's five million families do when they are being offended by "Three's Company"? Maybe they could just sit around the kitchen table and talk. It's a wholesome thought.

One of these days, these essentially trivial exercises in censorship will be trampled underfoot by technology. Before this century ends, all of us will have access to TV entertainment across the whole spectrum from good works to go-go girls. Come the millennium, these crusaders will be out of work—and not a day too soon.

Did Soviet Secret Police Plot Shooting of Pope?

There always seems to be a suspicion of a conspiracy whenever a head-of-state or any other important figure is felled by an assassin's gunfire. Whether the victim dies or not, the suspicion generally remains until the case is solved or dimmed by time.

What brings this to mind is a recent British television program that reported both the Vatican and Italian security services suspect the Soviet KGB of involvement in the attempted murder of Pope John Paul II.

The motive, according to this TV broadcast, was the pope's defense of the independent Solidarity labor union's stand against the communist government in his native Poland.

The same current affairs program suggested that Mehmet Ali Agca, the 23-year-old Turk convicted of shooting the pope, was accompanied by another gunman at the time of the shooting. That Ali Agca was not a lone fanatic but part of an international conspiracy with roots in East bloc countries.

That is easy to believe. Whether the Soviet KGB was involved in the shooting or not, there is still room for suspicion of a communist conspiracy. Meantime, this is one case that deserves continued attention from every civilized government.

Source: Editorial reprinted from *Mobile Press* (September 8, 1981), p. 6A.

HERE'S WHAT'S <u>NOW</u> BEING SAID ABOUT OTHER PEOPLE'S CIGARETTE SMOKE.

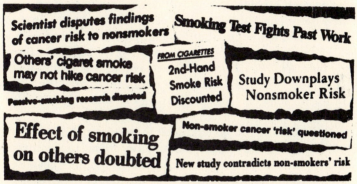

Several months ago, headlines around the world trumpeted alarming news. A Japanese study was claiming that non-smoking wives of smokers had a higher risk of lung cancer because of their husbands' tobacco smoke. That scared a lot of people and understandably so, if this claim was the last word.

But now new headlines have appeared. First, because several apparent errors are reported to have been found in the Japanese study—raising serious questions about it.

Second, because Lawrence Garfinkel, the statistical director of the American Cancer Society who is opposed to smoking, published a report covering 17 years and nearly 200,000 people in which he indicated that "second-hand" smoke has insignificant effect on lung cancer rates in nonsmokers.

For more information on this important public issue, write Scientific Division, The Tobacco Institute, 1875 I St., N.W., Washington, D.C. 20006.

BEFORE YOU BELIEVE HALF THE STORY, GET THE WHOLE STORY.

WILLIAM F. BUCKLEY

The Hysteria About Words

Have you noticed that the use of an unusual word sometimes irritates the reader to such a point that he will accuse the user of affectation, than which there is no more heinous crime in the American republic? The distinguished political and social philosopher and columnist Russell Kirk used the word "energumen" to describe, in his Introduction to my book *Rumbles Left and Right,* whom it is I agitate against, and one reviewer fairly exploded with annoyance. Now the word in question means "someone possessed by an evil spirit" and fanatically addicted to a particular idea—can you think of a better word to describe certain kinds of people who seek to reorder public affairs according to their hypnotic visions? Should one refuse to use a venerable word for which there is no obvious synonym simply because it is a word that does not regularly appear in the diet of the average reader?

I raise the problem because I am often accused of an inordinate reliance on unusual words and desire—as would you in my shoes, I think—to defend myself against the insinuation that I write as I do simply to prove that I have returned recently from the bowels of a dictionary with a fish in my mouth, establishing my etymological dauntlessness. Surely one must distinguish between those who plunder old tomes to find words which, in someone's phrase, should never be let out, belonging strictly to the zoo sections of the dictionary, and such others as Russell Kirk, who use words because (a) the words signify just exactly what the user means and because (b) the user deems it right and proper to preserve in currency words which in the course of history were coined as the result of a felt need.

There is a sort of phony democratic bias against the use of unusual words. Recently I heard a young movie actress being interviewed on a radio station. She was asked by her interrogator what it meant to be an actress and replied that an actor's life was "multifaceted." "What are you trying to pull on me?" demanded the radio announcer. Sweetie pie ran, panicked, from the argument—what else, in

Source Reprinted from editorial column, *The National Observer* June 15, 1963.

the democratic age, when it is deemed an effrontery on the democratic ideal to use a word that is not used twice a week by Little Orphan Annie? "I'm sorry I used such a fancy word . . . I guess I don't really know what it means . . . I should have said, there are lots of aspects to being an actress." Democracy won the day, and the show droned on.

Awhile ago I was on Jack Paar's program, and he asked me a number of questions having to do with this and that, which I tried, vainly, to answer as best I knew how. I wrote about that experience in *Rumbles* and described the ensuing tantrum of Mr. Paar and his associates, who steamed on and on about my ideological vices, expressing special outrage at my unintelligibility.

It is a curious thing, this universal assumption by a number of prominently situated opinion, or rather mood, makers that the American people are either unaware of the unusual word or undisposed to hear it and find out what it means, thus broadening not merely their vocabulary—that isn't the important thing—but their conceptual and descriptive powers. Those who say that the average American is incapable of appreciating the meaning of the word "energumen" are, in my humble judgment, nuts. The average American is, in Franklin P. Adams' phrase, above average, and his intelligence is not tied umbilically to Jack Paar's antiintellectualist muse. It is curious that a man who is offended by the use of the word "multifaceted" or "energumen" is perfectly capable of expressing a sentence of death-defying mechanical complexity. I am, unfortunately, innocent in the world of science, and I wish I knew what in the world the TV hawker is talking about when he reels off something having to do with a "double action injector system in the valve mechanism," but it does not occur to me to suggest that he is putting on airs; it occurs to me to rue my patently inadequate knowledge of my mechanical *abc's*.

The point about unusual words is that they are as necessary to philosophy, economics, esthetics, and political science as they are necessary in the world of higher mechanics, in which so many people, displaying the natural American genius, are so much at home. It is possible, I suppose, to describe the refinements of an Astrojet fan-injection blah blah blah engine in words understandable to me, but the exercise is not often resorted to, because the manufacturers assume a certain level of mechanical literacy, as they assume that those who do not have it ought not to set the standards for those who do have it. So it is in other fields, which is why, in my judgment, when Mr. Russell Kirk uses the word "energumen," he should be allowed to use it, and the thing for book reviewers to do when they come upon it, if they are unfamiliar with it, is not to pout, but to open a dictionary and see if the word is one whose meaning they wish to learn. They must guard against going about like antiliterate energuments.

NO RELIGIOUS GROUP SHOULD FORCE YOU TO PRACTICE WHAT THEY PREACH.

Right now the United States Senate is holding hearings on a Constitutional Amendment to outlaw abortion.

This effort, backed by a handful of Senators, seriously threatens the religious freedom of every American.

If they succeed, you will be forced to accept, as law, one narrow religious and moral belief. Even if it is not your own. Your church's. Or your synagogue's.

The Religious Coalition for Abortion Rights of New York State represents most of the country's major religions. We are organizations like the American Baptist Churches, N.Y.S.; the N.Y. Federation of Reform Synagogues; The Episcopal Church; The United Presbyterian Church, Synod of the Northeast; the United Church of Christ and The United Methodist Church, whose positions on abortion you might not be aware of.

We believe abortion is an individual decision. And therefore your God-given right. While we support a woman's choice to become a mother, we also support her choice not to. But most importantly, we feel no religious group has the right to use the power of politics to impose their beliefs on you.

Yet this is precisely what the Constitutional Amendment would do. By outlawing abortion, it will rob you of the right to make your most personal decisions according to your own conscience.

By your support of the Religious Coalition For Abortion Rights, we can work together to stop this small group from forcing you to practice what they preach.

Our country's most cherished inalienable right is being threatened: Freedom.

RELIGIOUS COALITION FOR ABORTION RIGHTS

American Baptist Churches, New York State
American Jewish Congress, Women's Division
B'nai B'rith Women, District #1
Catholics for Free Choice
The Episcopal Church, Dioceses of New York, Central New York and Rochester
Lutheran Church in America, Upper New York Synod
National Council of Jewish Women, State Public Affairs Committee
National Federation of Temple Sisterhoods, District #3
New York Federation of Reform Synagogues
New York Society for Ethical Culture
New York State Council of Churches
Religious Society of Friends, Long Island, New York and Purchase Quarterly Meetings
Unitarian Universalist Association, Metropolitan New York and St. Lawrence Districts
United Church of Christ, New York Conference and Metropolitan Association
United Methodist Church
United Presbyterian Church, U.S.A., Synod of the Northeast

PERSONAL FREEDOM IS AS SACRED AS RELIGIOUS FREEDOM.

Source: Reprinted with permission from the Religious Coalition for Abortion Rights of the State of New York.

Do You Read Small Ads Like This?

As part of an advertising program we will give a pair of genuine diamond stud earrings to every reader of this publication who reads and responds to this printed notice before Midnight, Aug. 17, for the sum of $5 plus $1 shipping and handling. There is no further monetary obligation. [Each diamond of the pair is a genuine .25 pt 10-facet round diamond and will be accompanied by our Certificate of Authenticity to that effect.] This advertising notice is being placed simultaneously in other publications. If you see it in more than one publication, please let us know, as this information is helpful to us. Should you wish to return your earrings you may do so at any time to the address below and receive a full refund. There is a limit of one (1) pair of diamond earrings per address, but if your request is made before Aug. 9, you may request a second pair by enclosing an additional $5 plus $1 shipping and handling. No request will be accepted past the dates noted above; your uncashed check will be returned if postmarked later than those dates. Please enclose this *original* notice with your request; photocopies will not be accepted. Send appropriate sum together with your name and address to: **ABERNATHY & CLOSTHER, LTD., Diamond Earring Advertising Program, Dept. 668-29, Box 1310, Westbury, New York 11590.**

Source: Reprinted from *National Examiner* (July 14, 1981), p. 26.

CHARLEY REESE

Israel Has Legitimate Claim to Gaza Strip

Until by happenstance I became interested in the history and culture of the Middle East, I never realized the extent of anti-Semitism in the world and the outright double-dealing that greed for Arab oil will produce.

I can demonstrate the double-standards which Israel is subjected to by telling you about the West Bank. This area is called Judea and Samaria by the Israelis and it is called Israeli-occupied Arab territory by the Arabs. The U.S. State Department, which has opposed the State of Israel since before it was even created, calls the Israeli settlements in the occupied territory "illegal."

What are the facts? Title to Judea and Samaria rested with the Ottoman Empire for about 400 years. When the Empire was dissolved at the end of World War I and France and Great Britain were carving up the Middle East between themselves, Great Britain obtained from the League of Nations a mandate to govern the territory we call Palestine.

What excuse did Great Britain use to justify assuming trusteeship over Palestine? The Balfour Declaration. Great Britain was explicitly granted the Palestine Mandate for the expressed purpose of establishing a national home for the Jewish people. There has never existed an independent nation called Palestine. Britain and France established the boundaries.

It didn't take long, once oil was discovered in the Middle East, for the British to decide that the destiny of the British Empire more profitably lay with the Arabs instead of the Jews. Four-fifths of Palestine were lopped off to create Trans-Jordan for the sole purpose of installing Abdullah, the grandfather of King Hussein, on a throne.

In 1948, when the British were finally driven out of what remained of the Palestine Mandate, and the United Nations voted to partition it, giving part to the Jews and part to the Arabs, the Arabs refused. The area was invaded by the Arab nations in an attempt to

Source: Reprinted from the *Pensacola Journal* (November 7, 1981), p. 8A.

drive the Jews into the sea. Jordan occupied what we now call the West Bank and East Jerusalem. Egypt occupied Gaza. Jordan illegally annexed the West Bank and East Jerusalem, areas it had taken by force in an act of war. Only two nations recognized the annexation. Egypt ruled Gaza like an occupied territory. From 1948 to 1967, there was no talk in Egypt or in Jordan of an independent Palestinian state. There was no talk of granting autonomy to Palestinians.

In the 1967 War, which Egypt and Jordan initiated, Israel captured the West Bank and Gaza. The war ended with a cease fire. When a war ends with a cease fire, both parties remain where they were when the cease fire began until a peace treaty is negotiated. This is both customary and legal under international law. The sovereignty of the occupied territory is decided at the time the two parties make a formal peace treaty and establish permanent boundaries. (At the present, Israel and Jordan remain legally at war.)

This is exactly what Israel and Egypt have done. In negotiating a peace treaty, Israel agreed to return the entire Sinai to Egypt (the Egyptians have never claimed sovereignty or title to Gaza). Jordan, however, has refused to sit down with the Israelis and negotiate a peace treaty. Therefore, Israel has continued to occupy the West Bank. After 13 years of waiting, the Israelis annexed East Jerusalem. Jerusalem, by the way, has had a Jewish majority since well into the 1800s. Jordan never had a legitimate claim to it.

Please note that at no time in the last 480 years has any Arab nation had a legitimate title to the land now called the West Bank. The area went from the Ottoman Empire to Great Britain to occupation by Jordan to occupation by Israel.

The Israeli occupation of the West Bank and Gaza is perfectly legal under international law. The claim that it is Arab territory is spurious. The issue of whose land it is remains to be decided. Until it is decided, the Israelis have a legal right to establish as many settlements in it as they choose. The demand that Israel return the West Bank as a pre-condition to any talks is laughable. There is no basis in international law whatsoever for such a ridiculous demand. What do you think we would have done if Japan had said it would not talk peace in 1945 until we returned Okinawa and withdrew all of our forces from the Japanese mainland? We'd still be there.

Eight Rules for Good Writing

PART III

What matters is that we get done what we
have to do and get said what we have to say.

DONALD J. LLOYD, *"Our National Mania for Correctness"*

Eight Rules for Good Writing

The succeeding pages will show you how to write clear, straightforward prose. This is the language you would use in explaining a situation or arguing an issue. It expresses itself in a direct, informal style.

There are other styles of writing. For an inaugural address or a theological essay, you will want a more formal, balanced presentation. For an emotional appeal or an angry condemnation, you may want a more colloquial or slangy style. But such occasions are rare. The informal style recommended here will serve you in almost all writing situations. You can use it to propose marriage, explain entropy, or plead not guilty.

The eight rules that follow should make you a better writer. They include material you need to know, and they omit areas you do not need to worry about. The intent is practical—not to tell you about "good writing," but to show you how to achieve it.

These rules will be sufficient for most people on most writing occasions. The weak student who cannot recognize a sentence and does not know that a period goes at the end of it will need additional help, as will the refined writer who seeks a singular style. Nevertheless, the rules can help most people become fluent, correct, and effective writers.

RULE 1: CHOOSE A SUBJECT YOU CAN WORK WITH

Choosing a subject is one of the hardest parts of writing, and perhaps the most important. In most writing situations, of course, you do not have to choose a topic. You want to write the power company protesting the latest rate hike. You have to write a thank-you letter to your aunt. Your boss asks you to prepare a marketing report. In these cases the subject is there, and you have to tell a particular audience about it.

Still there are occasions when you select a topic for an essay or speech. And there are times when you might be given a general subject ("The American Dream" or "Tomorrow's Promise"), but you can approach it in a number of ways. You need to recognize the problems in making a choice.

To produce a good essay, you should choose a topic that will interest your audience, that lends itself to detail, and that can be covered in a prescribed number of words. (The point here will be clearer if you recall the last dull sermon you heard.)

If you were assigned to write a 500-word theme for a general audience (think of the people you see around you in class or at a movie), how good would these topics be?

1. "Death Awaits All Men"

Unless you are going to write of something unusual—an exploding sun, the bloody prophecies of Revelation, or the mathematics of entropy—this will be a boring subject. When you write of "all men," you tend to say what everyone knows.

2. "My Brother, the Practical Joker"

This topic concerns an individual person rather than all men. The experience, however, is pretty close to that of all men. Most people have met practical jokers. Unless your brother's jokes are particularly brilliant or outrageous, you would do better with another subject.

3. "I Am Sure I Have Pierced Ears"

This subject does not lend itself to detail. What can you write after the first sentence? Who would be interested?

4. *The Sun Also Rises*—Hemingway's Masterpiece"

This topic is interesting and rich with detail, but it is more suitable to a 300-page book than a 500-word theme. If you wish to write on a novel, you must restrict yourself to one feature of it. Here you could limit yourself to one character ("Robert Cohn—the Outsider") or to one fairly defined theme ("Fishing in Spain—A Symbolic Quest").

Remember that, almost invariably, your tendency will be to choose a subject that's too broad rather than one that's too narrow.

5. "Hank Aaron Was a Better Hitter Than Babe Ruth"

This could be a good choice. The subject would interest many readers. It provides a lot of detail—comparison of number of times at bat, number of hits, quality of opposing pitchers, the kinds of baseballs used, sizes of stadiums, and so on. The theme—if you keep the focus on batting and avoid discussions of fielding, baserunning, and personality—can be finished in 500 words.

Another element that makes this a good subject is that it presents a minority view, something that always adds interest. "Cleanliness Is Important" is a vague truism, but "Cleanliness Is Dangerous" could make a fascinating theme.

6. "How to Clean a Bassoon"

This subject lends itself to detail; it can be covered in 500 words; and it is beyond the experience of "all men." But, for whatever reason, it would have little appeal for most readers.

> <

Of course, a knowledgeable and creative writer can make any subject interesting. And one can imagine singular readers who would respond to any topic. These exceptions, however, do not change the situation for you. You must try to choose a subject that will keep the interest of a fairly general audience.

EXERCISES

Which of these subjects would be more likely to produce an acceptable 500-word theme? Why?

1. The Virtue of Thrift
2. Space Travel Will Have a Drastic Effect on Contemporary Art
3. A Sure Way to Pick Winners at the Dog Track
4. The Importance of a College Education
5. Richard Nixon and the Watergate Tragedy
6. My Brother Collects Green Stamps
7. Dogs Are Better Than Cats
8. Drag-racing Cars Perform Mathematically Impossible Feats
9. Ethnic Humor
10. Aspirin, Bufferin, Anacin—Somebody's Lying
11. The World Is Ending: Prophecy, Weaponry, and Ecology

RULE 2: GET YOUR FACTS

An interesting theme has to be specific. No one can write a compelling essay on entropy or Hank Aaron or space-age architecture or much else without seeking out a body of factual information. Writing involves research.

Unless you are writing from personal experience, you will probably want to build your theme around people you can quote and facts you can bring forward. You obtain such material from a number of sources.

Visit the Library

Large stores of information can be unearthed by using the card catalog and the *Reader's Guide.* The card catalog lists author, title, and subject for every book in the library. The *Reader's Guide,* under subject headings, lists magazine articles printed over the years. (You can find the magazines in the periodicals section or on microfilm.)

This list illustrates some of the titles available to you and the kinds of information they contain.

> *Acronyms and Initialisms Dictionary*
> (What is the NAFGDA?)
> *American Movies Reference Book*
> (Who won the Academy Award as Best Supporting Actor in 1966?)
> *Bartlett's Familiar Quotations*
> (Who said, "A reformer is a guy who rides through the sewer in a glass-bottomed boat"?)

Baseball Encyclopedia
> (Who was the only major league pitcher to pitch two consecutive no-hit games?)

Benet's *Reader's Encyclopedia*
> (Who is the hero of Henry James's *The American?*)

Black's Law Dictionary
> (What is the Miranda Rule?)

Book Review Digest
> (When David Garnett's *Shot in the Dark* was published in 1959, how did critics react to it?)

College Handbook
> (What is the ratio of male-to-female students at Loras College?)

Crime in the United States (The FBI Report)
> (How many aggravated assaults were reported in Madison, Wisconsin, in 1975?)

Current Biography
> (Name the two daughters of jazzman Chuck Mangione.)

Cyclopedia of Literary Characters
> (Name the Three Musketeers.)

Dictionary of American History
> (Who founded the NAACP? When?)

Dictionary of American Slang
> (What is a "hodad"?)

Dictionary of Classical Mythology
> (Who is Aemonides?)

Encyclopedia of the Opera
> (Why couldn't Hoffmann wed his beloved Olympia?)

Facts on File
> (Why was New York Police Chief John Egan sent to prison in 1974?)

Famous First Facts
> (Who received the first kidney transplant?)

Funk's *Word Origins and Their Romantic Stories*
> (What is the source of the word "tantalize"?)

Gallup Poll
> (In 1977, what percentage of Americans believed that homosexuality is a condition some people are born with?)

Gray's Anatomy
> (If you strain the muscles of your thenar eminence, where do you hurt?)

Guinness Book of World Records
> (How long was the world's longest hot dog?)

International Who's Who
> (Who is Gaetano Cortesi?)

Interpreter's Bible
> (What did Jesus mean when he said it is easier for a camel to go through the eye of a needle than for a rich man to enter the kingdom of God?)

McGraw-Hill Encyclopedia of Science and Technology
> (What are the characteristics of synthetic graphite?)

Menke's *Encyclopedia of Sport*
> (What golfer and what score won the U.S. Open in 1963?)

Mirkin's *When Did It Happen?*
> (Name two famous composers born on May 7.)

The Murderers' Who's Who
> (How did an ear-lobe figure in the "death" of murderer Charles Henry Schwartz?)

Oxford Companion to Music
> (What is the Impressionist School of music?)

Oxford English Dictionary
> (When was the word "fair" first used to mean average?)

Prager Encyclopedia of Art
> (What is the real name of the painting usually called *Whistler's Mother?*)

Rock Encyclopedia
> (Who was the lead singer in the original Jeff Beck Group?)

Statistical Abstract of the United States
> (How many American women used poison to commit suicide in 1976?)

Telephone Directory (any large city)
> (If you want tickets to a Chicago White Sox game, where should you write? What 800-number can you call?)

The Way Things Work
> (Why doesn't the ink leak out of your ball-point pen?)

Webster's Biographical Dictionary
> (What is Mary McCauley's better-known name? Why is she famous?)

Webster's Dictionary of Proper Names
> (When and what was the Chicken War?)

Webster's Geographical Dictionary
> (In what county and state is Black River Falls?)

Who's Who in American Women
> (What is Linda Ronstadt's birthday?)

World Almanac
>   (Name the junior senator from Oregon. What is the
>   capacity of the Notre Dame stadium?)

World Encyclopedia of the Comics
>   (What was Blondie's maiden name?)

Also, make particular use of the *New York Times Index.* This gives you references to names mentioned in that information-packed newspaper. Many libraries have collections of the *Times* dating back to the 1890s, on microfilm. Learn to thread the microfilm projector, and you can have a fine time reading how Red Grange scored four touchdowns in 10 minutes or how Neal Armstrong landed on the moon.

You will need all these sources to provide facts for your essays.

Don't be afraid to ask for help in the library. Most librarians are nice people.

Use Your Telephone

Libraries employ reference people who spend a good part of every day answering questions over the phone. If you need to know Babe Ruth's batting average in 1928, you can either find the answer in a baseball almanac or phone your local reference librarian, who will look up the information and call you back.

You can phone others too. If you need to know whether there is an apostrophe in "Diners Club," call an elegant restaurant and ask the cashier. If you have a brief legal question ("What would it cost to change my name?"), phone a lawyer. If you need to know the current price for waste paper, call a junk yard. For specific information, don't be afraid to call your priest or banker or news reporter or sheriff or insurance agent. Most of these people are willing to help you, and many will be happy to.

Write for Facts You Need

Many sources are available to you. United States government agencies will send you documents on a range of subjects. Organizations with a message will send you stacks of literature. (Both the American Cancer Society and the Tobacco Institute have pamphlets on smoking and health.) You can base your writing on materials from Liberty Lobby, Common Cause, the National Rifle Association, the Confraternity of Christian Doctrine, the Non-Sectarian Committee for Life, the Moral Majority, the National Organization for Women, and similar groups.

Two sources deserve special mention. If you want the script of a particular news program (say, "Sixty Minutes"), write and the network will send you a copy. For anything related to new laws, politics, or government programs, write your congressman. From a congressman, you will *always* get an answer.

> <

If you make the effort, you will find plenty of information to give meaning and interest to your writing.

Warning: Get your facts right. Errors of fact in your writing are just like misspellings and agreement errors. They make you look careless or ignorant. In persuasive writing, they are fatal.

EXERCISES

Use your library and other resources to locate this information.

1. What was the front-page headline and the sports-page headline in the *New York Times* on the day you were born?
2. What is the source of these lines? (a) ''The reports of my death are greatly exaggerated.'' (b) ''When in doubt, punt.'' (c) ''My pen is breathing revenge.''
3. Distinguish between Gresham's Law, Parkinson's Law (No. 1), Vernon Law, the Landouzy-Grasset Law, and the law of filial regression.
4. Who was president of the Anti-Saloon League in 1919?
5. In football, both the Pittsburgh Panthers (college) and the Chicago Cardinals (professional) were said to have ''dream backfields.'' What player was a member of both?
6. What did Wallace Stevens mean when he wrote ''The only emperor is the emperor of ice cream''?
7. Identify as many of these as you can:

Marcus Arelius Arnheiter	*Major Major Major Major*
Sir Toby Belch	*Three-card Monte*
Jay Berwanger	*Major Ogalvie*
Amelia Bloomer	*John Peel*
Peaches Browning	*Benjamin Franklin Pinkerton*
Dr. Kenneth Edelin	*Lydia Pinkham*
Gallant Fox	*Ofissa Pop*
Dr. Rosalind Franklin	*Peter Quint*
Hoot Gibson	*Bobby Shaftoe*
Edward Mortimer Gilbert	*Jill St. John*
Thomas Gradgrind	*General Guy Sternwood*
Pete and Frank Gusenberg	*Art Tatum*
Huncamunca	*Helen Twelvetrees*

RULE 3: LIMIT YOUR TOPIC TO MANAGEABLE SIZE

Most writing is subject to space and time limitations. You are preparing a magazine advertisement or a campaign document (one page). You are writing an editorial or a letter to the editor (under 1000 words). You are preparing a sermon or an after dinner speech (20 minutes or less). Rarely will you have an opportunity that will permit, or an audience that will tolerate, a discussion of all aspects of an issue.

Therefore you must limit your topic. Do not, for example, write about "Dieting." Even "Crash Dieting" is too broad a subject. But you can argue that "Crash Dieting Is Dangerous." Similarly, do not speculate about "America's Unjust Drug Laws"; write "Alabama's Marijuana Laws Violate the Fifth Amendment."

This kind of topic narrowing is particularly important when you write argument. A vague and rambling essay is rarely persuasive.

Don't write an "about" theme—that is, a general theme about fishing, about communism, about heart disease, or about love and death. These aren't helped by vague titles like "The Joys of Fishing" or "The Truth About Communism." Such unfocused subjects lend themselves to vague generalizations. They produce themes that lack unity, coherence, and interest.

Your essay is probably unfocused if it discusses unnamed or hypothetical people: "students," "Cora Crazy," "Tom J.," or "a doctor in Florida." When you find yourself writing "some people" or "in life," you can be sure you're in trouble.

A carefully focused theme demands specific detail. You will need these facts if you want to keep your reader awake.

EXERCISES

Limit each of these topics; that is, isolate parts that you can discuss in a 500-word theme.

1. Improving American Education
2. LSD—A Blessing or a Curse?
3. The Assassination of John Lennon
4. Women in Politics
5. God in Everyday Life
6. ABSCAM Evidence
7. Raising Houseplants
8. Travel Is Educational
9. Current Slang
10. Extrasensory Perception
11. Situation Ethics
12. Animals Can Talk
13. Cocaine

RULE 4: ORGANIZE YOUR MATERIAL

Most essays—and indeed most reports and business letters—are made up of an *introduction,* a *body,* and a *conclusion.* The introduction says, "I am going to write about X." The body discusses X in some organized way. And the conclusion says, "That's what I have to say about X." Good writers will keep this pattern from being too obvious, but this is the pattern they will use.

The Introduction

The purpose of the introduction is to catch the reader's attention, announce your subject, and (sometimes) outline the direction of your essay.

The best way to get the reader's interest is to announce your subject and get on with it. You can, of course, try a witty opening ("If my girl had two more IQ points, she would be a tree") or a dramatic one ("I know who killed Jimmy Hoffa"); these might work for you. If you are not confident about such lines, however, it is best to rely on a straightforward opening.

Just say it. Write "America can't afford nuclear power" or "*Dallas* has all the characteristics of a morality play." Then get on proving your point.

Although you may not seek a dramatic opening line, you should try to avoid sentences that turn off your reader. If you begin your essay by saying, "Time is the auction block of the world" or "My brother collects Green Stamps," it probably doesn't make much difference what you write afterward. Nobody will be reading it.

The line in your opening paragraph that announces the main idea or purpose of your theme is called the *thesis statement.* You may include another sentence with it, giving a general outline the essay will follow.

Most topics can be divided into parts. Your essay praising Johnny Bench might discuss his fielding, base running, and hitting. Your argument against abortion might describe the growth of the fetus month by month. Your analysis of a physical or social problem (lung cancer, skyjacking, etc.) might first describe the effect, then indicate some probable causes.

See how these introductions announce the outline of the essay:

There can be no doubt that extrasensory perception exists. How else can one explain the results of the Spranches–Malone experiment conducted at UCLA in 1975?

(The theme will discuss the experiment.)

Legal abortion is necessary. Otherwise we will be back with vast numbers of women getting amateur surgery in bloody abortion mills.

(The theme will discuss earlier years: (1) vast numbers of women and (2) bloody surgery.)

The only way to stop inflation is to raise taxes and impose wage and price controls, but I don't think the President has the courage to support these measures.

(The theme will cover (1) anti-inflation measures—a tax raise and wage-and-price controls, and (2) presidential courage.)

Keep your introductions short.

The Body

The introduction and conclusion are little more than a frame surrounding what you have to say. The paragraphs of the body *are* your essay.

Each paragraph presents a unit of your message. This does not mean that each division of your topic, as announced in the introduction, must be covered in one paragraph. In the anti-inflation theme just introduced, your discussion of wage-price controls might take two, three, or six paragraphs.

Just as the introduction has a thesis statement announcing what the whole theme is about, so each paragraph has a *topic sentence* telling what it will cover. Usually this is the first sentence. Because they show exactly what the rest of the paragraph will be about, these are effective topic sentences:

These gun laws haven't reduced the crime in Cleveland.

Why did the price of electricity go up in July?

Consider what the human fetus can do in its third month.

Secretary Haig was equally unsuccessful with the Italians.

Your paragraph should not bring in material beyond the scope of the topic sentence. In the paragraph about gun laws in Cleveland, for example, you should not discuss other crime-fighting measures in Cleveland; you should not mention crime in Detroit.

Topic sentences are effective in linking paragraphs. In the examples given, the references to *"These* gun laws" and to Secretary Haig's being *"equally* unsuccessful" show a relation to material in previous paragraphs. Words like "therefore," "however," "such," "second," and "similarly" have the same effect.

Within each paragraph, try to give the sentences the same grammatical subject. (In the paragraph on Secretary Haig, the subject of most of the sentences should be "he" or "Haig" or "the Secretary.") If you vary the kinds of sentences, as in the following example, the practice should not seem monotonous.

You frequently hear statements that simply lack evidence. *Advertisements* announce that "Ban is preferred by seven out of ten American women," that "four out of five movie stars use Lustre-Creme Shampoo." *Rumor* whispers that Viceroy filters are made of harmful fiber glass and that drinking fluoridated water can cause brain damage. Such *claims* can safely be ignored until evidence is offered to support them.

A variation popular with *sensational writers* is to make an extravagant claim and point to concrete evidence—which happens to be unavailable. *They* charge that Warren Harding was murdered by his wife and that Franklin Roosevelt was poisoned by the Russians at Teheran—then regret that evidence is lost in the past. *They* affirm the existence of abominable snowmen, the true "Shakespeare," Atlantis, and the Loch Ness monster—then lament that proof remains out of reach. *They* know that UFOs are extraterrestrial spaceships and that a massive conspiracy led to the attempted assassination of President Reagan and Pope John Paul—then insist that law-enforcement agencies are withholding evidence. These too are inductions with an absent sample.

Remember that the grammatical subject is not necessarily the first word of a sentence. It may follow an introductory phrase ("After the dance, *he* . . .") or clause ("When Kathy remembered the accident, *she* . . .").

In some paragraphs, keeping the same subject will prevent you from saying what you want. Or it will make your writing seem stilted and artificial. In such cases, don't do it.

Here's an important point. *Avoid long paragraphs.* Part of writing well is making someone else want to read your work, and people are turned off facing long, block, single-spaced paragraphs. (Think how you feel beginning a chapter in your sociology textbook.) Make use of short paragraphs, headings, blank space between sections, indented material, and similar devices to make your ideas easy to read.

When in doubt whether to begin a new paragraph, *always* begin the paragraph.

The Conclusion

The last paragraph of your essay echoes the introduction. It summarizes and generalizes about the subject discussed.

Unless your paper is long or particularly complicated, you do not need to restate the structural outline ("In this theme, I have discussed first the language of Mark's gospel, then its historical qualities, and finally its theology.") Instead, just give a sentence or two expressing the main point. Here are some acceptable concluding paragraphs:

Mark's gospel is more like a sermon than like a biography. It is a work of profound faith and impressive artistry.

> *No one favors abortion. But we have to admit that, in many cases, it is the only humane alternative.*
>
> *The Spranches–Malone experiment proves conclusively that ESP exists. Now we have to figure out what we can do with it.*

Keep your conclusions short.

EXERCISE

Discuss the strengths and weaknesses of this essay. Consider the thesis statement, the topic sentences, transitions between paragraphs, keeping the same subject within a paragraph, unity of a paragraph, and so on.

POETRY

All my life I have hated poetry. I hated it in high school, in grade school, and in the sophomore poetry course I've just completed here at South Alabama. Why we serious students have to study jingled nonsense, I will never know.

I live in Reedsburg, a community of farmers, tradesmen, and practical people. Nevertheless, the Reedsburg Grade School subjected me to all sorts of frivolous and impractical poetry. From the first grade on, my class endured semester after semester of cute rhyme. We read teddy-bear poems from *Winnie the Pooh.* We read Mother Goose rhymes about Simple Simon and Robert Louis Stevenson poems about a "friendly cow all red and white." We read jingles telling us to drink our milk. I always wonder why the poets didn't just *say* things instead of chanting and jingling them. It was silly.

I had some poetry in Reedsburg High School too. However, I escaped much of it by signing up for speech classes. In speech I studied more sensible subjects. I learned to speak in front of a group. I learned to think on my feet. I learned to make a talk interesting by referring to the audience and adding humor. Most important, I learned to say things directly, without all the cute ornament of poetry.

The sophomore poetry class I've just finished at South Alabama has only made me dislike poems more. Mr. Remington, my instructor, was incompetent. The way he read them, all poems sounded just alike. When he wasn't mumbling about Shelley, we were taking impossible tests on Keats and nightingales. Either it was assumed we knew everything about epics or he was talking down to the class as though we had never heard of metaphor. The day before the final exam, he didn't even show up for class. The whole quarter was a waste of time.

In fact, all the poetry discussions I've had from grade school up to now, have been a waste of time. I just don't like poetry.

RULE 5: MAKE YOUR WRITING INTERESTING

Remember that no one *has* to read your essay. And if people have to hear your speech, they don't have to pay attention. The burden is on you to make your subject interesting.

This is not a huge task. If you have a topic you think is important, and if you present it with clarity and specific detail, your reader or listener will probably be interested.

Generally, you maintain interest by avoiding certain practices that deaden language.

Truisms

Do not say what everyone knows.

Don't be like actress Brooke Shields who told a congressional sub-committee: "Smoking can kill you. And if you've been killed, you've lost a very important part of your life."

Your readers will not be thrilled to hear that third-degree burns are painful or that the president of the United States bears great responsibilities. Don't write "Every great man has moments of profound sorrow, but Thomas Eaton's life was genuinely tragic." Write "Thomas Eaton's life was tragic."

Clichés

Some phrases have lost meaning through overuse. Your writing will lose emphasis and interest if you use tired language like this:

acid test
and . . . was no exception
at your earliest convenience
bottom line
cloud nine
constructive criticism
couldn't care less
few and far between
first and foremost
in a very real sense
is invaluable
last but not least
let's face it
needs no introduction
nitty-gritty
on the other hand
shot in the arm
slowly but surely
sneaking suspicion

snow job
status quo
to make a long story short
to touch base with
viable alternative

Many words and phrases from current slang ("bad," "get down," "make the scene," "heavy," etc.) are objectionable because they have been overused, and not because they are informal.

A good rule: If you suspect a particular phrase is a cliché, it is. Write something else.

Remember that avoiding a cliché can produce a rich substitution. A CBS sports announcer once described Green Bay quarterback Bart Starr as (not "cool as a cucumber" but) "cool as the other side of the pillow."

Generalized Language

The point cannot be overemphasized: *To be interesting, you must be specific.* Write of real things. Use specific names, numbers, places, dates, and quotations. You can, for example, refer to the same man in a number of ways:

an athlete
a ball player
a baseball player
an infielder
a first baseman
a Philadelphia first baseman
Pete Rose

Always choose the most specific word that serves the purposes of your essay. An effective message uses proper names.

Generally, your writing will be more interesting if you avoid the words "good," "bad," and "said."

Substituted words are almost always more meaningful. Instead of "good," write "even-tempered," "inexpensive," "compassionate," or "crisp." Instead of "bad," write "moldy," "pretentious," "degenerate," or "unfair." The word "said" is always acceptable, but you can add richness to your prose by substituting "whispered," "suggested," "boasted," "conceded," or "gasped." In argument the word "claimed" is often useful. (Try never to write "stated.")

Similarly, try to avoid forms of the verb "to be," that is, the words "is," "are," "was," "were," "am," and "been." Much of the time, you will have to use these words, of course, but substitutions are invariably more detailed and effective. For example, "Sue Walker *was* injured" becomes "Sue Walker smashed two bones in her right foot." And "The weather *was* horrible" becomes "Eight inches of snow fell on Buffalo yesterday." (Some scholars have designated the English language without "to be" forms as "E-prime.")

The best way to win interest is to force a lot of real names and numbers into your prose. Don't write:

> *His cousin drove me to a nearby woods, and we sat drinking beer and listening to music until very late.*

Write:

> *Ginger drove me over to Johnson's Woods, and we sat in her new Toronado till four in the morning. We drank three six-packs of Coors and listened to all her Frank Zappa tapes.*

At best, this kind of writing doesn't just tell you of an event. It shows it to you.

Inflated Language

Except in rare cases, you will want your writing to be clear. To do this, keep your language as simple and direct as possible. When addressing a general audience, try to avoid these kinds of expressions:

> Foreign words—*bête noir, ne plus ultra, coup d'état*
> Learned words—*penultimate, symbiotic, alumna*
> Poetic words—*repine, oft, betimes*
> Technical words—*input, persona, societal*
> Odd singular and plural forms—*datum, stadia, syllabi*
> Literary allusions—*Lot's wife, protean, the sword of Damocles*
> Current in-words—*parameter, viable, ambiance*

Such words are more acceptable if you are writing for an educated or specialized audience. But a really fine writer probably wouldn't use them there either.

Write words you would say. Don't use "in view of the above" or "for the above reasons"; write "consequently" or "for these reasons." Try not to use "the addressee," the "executrix," "the former," or "the latter"; write "Robin Carpenter" (or "she" or "her"). Never refer to yourself as "the writer" (or "we"); say "I."

> <

The next time you hear a dull lecture or sermon, don't tune it out. Ask yourself why it is dull. Probably it is a collection of truisms, clichés, and vague or inflated phrases. You can learn from such examples.

EXERCISES

Rewrite these sentences. Make them more likely to sustain the interest of a general audience.

1. This insult was the last straw. I decided to leave Marcie, and I spent the next few hours preparing for the trip.
2. The Book of Jonah illustrates the ludicrous intractability of a particular mind-set.
3. Scott Daniel was a fine basketball player. I believe he was the best to play in the league in the last twenty years. He was really fine.
4. Vis-à-vis our tête-à-tête, I must say the rendezvous filled me with ennui.
5. We will never know everything about the atom, but some of the recent discoveries have been fascinating.
6. Driving the L.A. freeway is like crossing the river Styx.
7. In the following weeks at school, I worked frantically. Every day I became busier and busier.
8. As we entered the restaurant, David stated that the chicken there was good but the service was bad.
9. Anyone can suffer with a rotten tooth or a sprained thumb, but the man with kidney stones endures a superexcruciating kind of pain.
10. In the final analysis, there are few rugged individualists in this day and age who are really down to earth in expressing nothing but the truth about the seamy side of life. Perhaps in the near future . . .
11. Salesmen should cultivate a charismatic emphasis to facilitate contractual negotiations on an interpersonal basis.
12. Graduate school can be a procrustean bed.

RULE 6: MAKE YOUR WRITING EMPHATIC

Sometimes unnecessary words or particular word forms detract from the point you want to make. These recommendations should help you emphasize the important ideas in your writing.

Avoid Wordiness

Unnecessary words may confuse, bore, or antagonize your reader. Say what you have to say as briefly as possible. Too often a series of words exists where one will do.

> *am of the opinion that = believe*
> *due to the fact that = because*
> *the man with the dark complexion = the dark man*
> *people who are concerned only with themselves = selfish people*
> *I disagree with the conclusion offered by Professor Lally = I disagree with Professor Lally*

And commonly one or more words appear where none is necessary.

> Becky ~~really~~ is a ~~very~~ beautiful girl.
> ~~Personally,~~ I agree with him.
> I asked whether ~~or not~~ the twins looked alike.
> I dislike his personality ~~and his temperament.~~
> ~~There were~~ several people at the party ~~who~~ saw the fight.
> And ~~I think it necessary to add that~~ Tom wasn't there.

Don't worry about wordiness when you are putting together the first draft of your essay; just get down what you have to say. Simple, direct prose usually comes with rewriting.

Write in the Active Voice

In active-voice sentences, the grammatical subject is the acting agent. ("The *Brezinsky Commission* has attacked public apathy.") In passive-voice constructions, the subject receives the action of the verb. ("*Public apathy* has been attacked by the Brezinsky Commission.")

You can use the passive voice in sentences where the acting agent is obvious or irrelevant ("the President was reelected") or where you want to deliver bad news and avoid personal involvement ("the decision is to buy our supplies from a different source"—"your contract will not be renewed next year").

Passive voice, however, is generally a bad thing. It doesn't sound natural and seems wordy and evasive. Where you may want particular emphasis, it can produce a mushy effect: "Home runs were hit by both pitchers during the game."

Often, using the active voice means beginning your sentence (or beginning the main clause of your sentence) with acting agents: *we, she, Jim Phillips the Brezinsky Commission,* and so on. This gives force and directness to your prose. Try to avoid forms that keep you from doing this. Here are examples:

> My intention is . . .
> It was soon evident that . . .
> There were . . .
> . . . was seen
> . . . could be heard
> The assumption was that . . .

If you are writing a personal essay, begin most sentences (or main clauses) with *I.*

Think of passive voice as you do a visit to the dentist. It's necessary sometimes, but you want to avoid it whenever you can.

Express Your Main Idea in the Subject-Verb of Your Sentence

Make the subject-verb unit of your sentence express your main thought. Put less important information in modifying phrases and clauses.

Try not to express your main thought as a modifying phrase ("Harold Lord slipped in the outfield, *thus breaking his arm*") or as a *that* clause ("I learned *that Aunt Lynda had been arrested for arson*"). Give your point subject-verb emphasis:

> *Harold Lord slipped in the outfield and broke his arm.*
> *Helen told me the sad news: Aunt Lynda had been arrested for arson.*

Do Not Waste the Ends of Your Sentences

Because the end of a sentence is the last thing a reader sees, it is a position of emphasis. Don't use it to express minor thoughts or casual information. Don't write "Both candidates will appear here in July, if we can believe the reports." (This is correct only if you want to stress the doubtfulness of the reports.) Don't write "Pray for the repose of the soul of Paul Denking, who died last week in Cleveland." (Your reader will begin speculating about the significance of Cleveland.) Notice how emphasis trails away in a sentence like this:

> *The B-1 bomber, a brainchild of the U.S. Air Force and*
> *Rockewell International, is trying a comeback as one of*
> *America's leading defense weapons after President Carter, in*
> *June 1977, put a stop to the plans to complete the project.*

For particular emphasis, write your thought in subject-verb form (see previous section) and give the unit an end-of-the-sentence position. Don't write "The Union reluctantly approved the contract"; say, "The Union approved the contract, but they didn't want to do it."

Because the beginning of a sentence also conveys a degree of emphasis, you should not waste that position either. Try to put words like "however," "therefore," and "nevertheless" in the middle of sentences. ("The postman, however, arrived at five o'clock.") Don't do this if it makes your sentence sound awkward.

Keep Your Sentences Relatively Short

To avoid a monotonous style, you should build your essay with sentences of different kinds and lengths. But using short (or relatively short) sentences will help you avoid difficulties.

When sentences go beyond fifteen or twenty words, punctuation—

which can be a problem—becomes complicated; meaning gets diffuse; their pronouns are separated from the words they refer to; and the reader or listener finds it difficult to see the continuity and may lose interest. Short sentences are better.

When you finish a reasonable-length sentence, fight the temptation to add a line beginning *which* or *when* or *because* or *according to* or some other *ing* form. Put that additional material in a new sentence.

EXERCISES

What changes would make the meaning of these sentences more emphatic?

1. I was born in the city of Chicago, Illinois.
2. Trapped in a drab life with a dull husband, Hedda Gabler shoots herself, partly too because she is threatened by Judge Brack.
3. The eagle suddenly loosed its grip, allowing me to escape.
4. Though I had more than several reasons to dislike and distrust Libby MacDuffee before the accident, I found still more when she tried to take me to court to pay for hospital costs and when she claimed I had had three martinis at the Red Oak Bar an hour (or at the most two hours) before the wreck.
5. Reviewing the past history, we found that the team was weak on basic fundamentals and that the average age of the players was 17 years old.
6. Nevertheless, I must refuse your kind offer.
7. His hope was that he could conquer Paris by June.
8. Although Jeannine feared flying, she took the 9:02 flight from Milwaukee, being already two days late for the convention.
9. This book concerns itself with language intended to deceive.
10. It was greatly feared by the crowd that an honest decision would not come from the referee.

RULE 7: AVOID LANGUAGE THAT DRAWS ATTENTION TO ITSELF

You want your audience to follow your ideas, to see the argument you're developing. Don't break their attention by using odd words or phrases that catch their eye. Try to avoid these distracting forms.

Repetition

Repeating a word for emphasis can be effective ("government of the people, by the people, and for the people"), but often it distracts attention. Avoid repetition of sentence forms ("I went to see the accident. Fifteen people were there. Each told a different story."); of particular words ("Going to school is not going to be easy. If the going gets tough . . ."); and even of sounds ("The black boxer was bloody, beaten, and battered.").

Dangling and Misplaced Modifiers

Make it clear what words your adjectives and adverbs are modifying. You do this by putting modifiers close to the words they refer to. Avoid examples like these:

When nine years old, my grandmother took me to the circus.
He was reported drowned by the Coast Guard.
I *only* shot two deer.
By knowing what you want to say, your essay will progress
    more easily.

Notice that these sentences are clear enough; in context, your reader would know what they mean. But such awkward and even humorous lines draw attention to themselves and away from your meaning.

Elaborate Figures of Speech

A mixed metaphor often produces irrelevant laughter. ("You're the salt of the earth and the light of the world, but you've thrown in the towel.") But even a meaningful figure of speech can be distracting. You could write "Carter steered the ship of state over treacherous seas; he was a star-crossed president." Such a sentence, however, stops the reader. Instead of following the rest of your ideas, he pauses to interpret the metaphor.

You will, of course, want to use figures of speech in your prose. But don't let them obscure your meaning by being too dramatic:

*Auto sales got a big shot in the arm in March from the price
    slashes.*

Or pointless:

Lee Bailey wore a suit the color of a thousand dollar bill.

Or redundant:

At the wedding, the champagne flowed like wine.

Or complicated:

Jesus touched me with the Psalms of his hands.

Keep your metaphors relatively simple.

Faulty Parallelism

You should express coordinate ideas in similar form. You do this mainly to avoid awkward and distracting sentences. Clearly, "I was *alone, uncertain,* and *possessed of a considerable degree of fear"* is less emphatic than "I was *alone, uncertain,* and *afraid.*" Notice how the awkwardness of these sentences weakens their impact:

> The teachers were burdened with *large classes, poor textbooks,* and *the necessity to cope with an incompetent principal.*
> I love *seeing* my daughter and *to hear* her voice.
> For a settlement, I will accept *a new stove* or *having my old stove repaired.*

Some sentences cannot be made parallel. You cannot change "Ted was tall, charming, and wore a blue hat" to "Ted was tall, charming, and blue-hatted." In such cases, write the first units so your reader doesn't expect the final one to be parallel. Write "Ted was tall and charming; he always wore a blue hat."

Awkward Constructions

Try to give your sentences the sound of natural speech. Don't break the continuity with intrusive passages.

> *I promised to, if the expected raise came through, take her to the Grand Hotel.*
> *Her brother, if we can believe local historians (and who can), was a senator.*

Any time your subject is ten words away from your verb, you're probably in trouble.

Avoid noun clusters. Business and technical writers sometimes seek a kind of forceful compression and talk of a "once-in-a-lifetime, million-dollar, career-decision dilemma." And they produce sentences a person has to read twice to understand. It is better to write in a natural speaking voice.

Don't seek a poetic style by inverting word order. Don't write "Quiet was the night" or "The reason for her suicide, we shall never know."

Keep it natural. Where it sounds all right, don't be afraid to begin a sentence with a conjunction or to end it with a proposition. ("And suddenly I realized where the money had come from.") And don't let some dated English textbook persuade you to say, "This is we." You *know* how that sounds.

Abrupt Changes in Tone

Your tone is your personal voice, your way of saying things. This will vary with your audience and your subject. You talk one way to an intimate friend and a different way to a visiting archbishop. You would use formal diction when writing of the United Nations Charter, and you might use colloquial—or even coarse—language in describing your fraternity house.

It is important to keep your tone appropriate and consistent. Don't jar your reader by describing a U.N. Charter provision as a "crap-headed experiment." And don't call your fraternity dining room "a haven of calculated insouciance."

If your tone is light enough to permit contractions (can't, wouldn't), use them right from the beginning of your essay. Don't begin to use them in the middle of a relatively formal paper.

> <

Remember that any time your reader is more impressed by your writing than by your meaning, you have failed. No one can improve on the advice lexicographer Samuel Johnson gave in the eighteenth century. He said, "Read over your composition, and where ever you meet with a passage which you think is particularly fine, strike it out."

EXERCISES

Correct weaknesses in these sentences.

1. Seaver was pitching beautifully until the seventh inning, and then the fireworks fell in.
2. When reading late at night, the book should be held under a strong light.
3. Juan Peron's rise to power was a slow one. There were many pit-stops.
4. We traveled for six days and the car broke down. We hitchhiked to Loredo, and I took a job gardening, I had the car towed into town, but no one there could fix it.
5. I'm sorry about the story, Laurie. It's as bad as your messy essay. I warned you frequently to rewrite your work.
6. Mrs. L. Williamson earned her Ph.D. studying DNA at M.I.T.
7. Cancer hit my family with full force this year, sending two of my aunts to the Mayo Clinic.
8. Professor Dendinger is giving a lecture tonight on student unrest in the faculty lounge.
9. Pamela was pretty, energetic, and carried a file of history notes.
10. The movie producers saw *Heaven's Gate* and immediately removed it from circulation. They could smell the handwriting on the wall.

RULE 8: AVOID MECHANICAL ERRORS

To write effectively, you need to know a number of elementary rules of usage. But there are some you do not have to know. An important truth is expressed in this story:

> *A man went to his doctor and described his ailment. Clinching his right fist tightly, he complained, "It hurts me when I go like that." The doctor prescribed the remedy: "Don't go like that."*

The story tells you many things about writing: how to punctuate long and involved sentences, how to use apostrophes in unusual constructions, how to use quotation marks within quotation marks, and how to spell "infrastructure." The advice: "Don't go like that."

The following rules on punctuation, abbreviation, number, and spelling should take you through most writing situations.

Punctuation

1. Use Commas to Make Your Sentences Easier to Read. Textbooks routinely tell you to put a comma before the conjunction in a compound sentence ("Pam is a good student, but she cannot learn economics"); after introductory clauses ("When I went home, I saw my brother's car"); and before the *and* in elements in a series ("I bought a suit, three ties, and a sweater").

The problem is that many professional writers do not punctuate like this. Hence you may be confused.

A good rule to follow is this: Always use commas in these constructions *when the sentences are long.*

> Arthur had traveled 57 miles through the desert to meet the
>   Prince, and he knew that nothing in the world could make
>   him turn back now.
> When I saw that the young soldier was holding a gun on
>   Martha and me, I became most obedient.
> Suddenly Henry saw that the parable applied to him, that he
>   must change his life, and that the time to start was now.

Similarly, you should always insert commas in these constructions *when there is a danger of misreading.*

> The fox ate three chickens and the rooster ran away.
> When they finished eating cigarettes were distributed to the
>   soldiers.
> They stopped looking for Irene became tired.

If you use normal word order (a "speaking" voice) and keep your sentences relatively short, you should have little difficulty with commas.

2. Use a Semicolon to Show That Two Independent Clauses Are Closely Related. Sometimes you want to indicate the particularly close relationship between two statements. Here you merge the statements into one sentence and connect them with a semicolon.

Her brother has been sick for years; now he is going to die.
To know her is to love her; to love her is a mistake.

This construction often occurs when the second statement contains "however," "therefore," or "nevertheless."

The 747 was two hours late getting into O'Hare; consequently,
he missed his connection to Reno.
Billy wanted to propose during final-exam week; he saw,
however, that this would cause problems.

You can also use semicolons to separate the halves of a compound sentence or the units in a series when the separated passages have commas within them.

My boss, Patrick Henderson, was there; but before I could talk
to him, he fell and broke his arm.
Among those present were Dr. Williams, an English professor;
Mr. Rainey, head of the Presbyterian meeting; and Mrs.
Milliken, president of the P.T.A.

If you have problems punctuating such long sentences, don't write them.

3. Use a Colon to Introduce a Unit. You use a colon to introduce something: an announcement, a clarification, or a formal series.

In May, the professor made his decision: he would leave the
University.
The difference between fathers and sons used to be a simple
one: Fathers earned the money and sons spent it.
Molly excelled in active sports: tennis, swimming, badminton,
and gymnastics.

When a complicated sentence follows a colon, the first word may be capitalized—especially if the sentence is long. ("In May, the professor made his decision: He would leave the university, move to Cleveland, and take a position with the Pater Academy.")

In general, you will never use a colon except after a complete statement. Don't write, "Her favorites were: Andy Williams, Tim Conway, and Brack Weaver." Write,

These were her favorites: Andy Williams, Tim Conway, and
Brack Weaver.

or (better)

Her favorites were Andy Williams, Tim Conway, and Brack
Weaver.

It is permissible to use a colon after "the following." ("He did it for the following reasons: . . .") But when you can avoid it, don't write "the following" at all. It's not something you would *say*. (Write, "He did it for several reasons: . . .")

4. Use an Exclamation Mark to Show Emphasis. Because adding an exclamation mark is an easy way to show emphasis, you may be tempted to overuse it. Try to reserve it for "Wow!" or "Fire!" or some comparable outcry.

Never use two or more exclamation marks to seek additional emphasis. Never!

5. Use a Question Mark After a Direct Question. You will, of course, put a question mark after a question. But be sure it is a direct question.

> *What can they do in 12 minutes?*
> *He asked, "Did you see Sylvia there?"*

Don't use a question mark after an indirect question or after a question form that is really a polite command.

> *She asked if I knew the way to school.*
> *Will you please hand in your bluebooks now.*

Try not to use question marks to express uncertainty or irony.

> *John Wilcox was born in 1657(?) and died in 1760.*
> *Those amateurs (?) made a very good living playing tennis.*

These are weak constructions. Say instead that Wilcox was born "about 1657"; criticize "those so-called amateurs."

6. Use Hyphens to Form Compound Adjectives and to Divide Words at the End of a Line. Use a hyphen to join a compound adjective when it *precedes* a noun. You can say that "the theory was out of date," or you can call it "an out-of-date theory." In such examples, the hyphens make your meaning clearer:

> *a Monday-morning quarterback*
> *a dog-in-the-manger attitude*
> *a long-term investment*
> *germ-free research*

Hyphens are particularly necessary to make sense of the noun-clusters that occur in technical writing. A scientific writer may refer to "polyethylene coated milk carton stock smoothness test results." What does that mean? It becomes clearer with hyphens: "polyethylene-coated milk-carton-stock smoothness-test results." But it is always best to keep the hyphens and rewrite the phrase: "the results of smoothness-tests conducted on polyethylene-coated milk-carton-stock."

Use a hyphen to divide a word at the end of a line. But remember that you must divide the word between syllables ("when-ever," "in-tern," "pho-bia"). You should not divide a word so that only one letter appears on a line ("a-bout," "phobi-a"); and you should never separate a one-syllable word ("doubt," "called," "proved").

If you don't know where to divide a word, consult your dictionary. If you don't have a dictionary at hand, don't divide the word. Write it all on the next line.

7. Use Parentheses to Tuck in Extra Material. Parentheses are useful. They let you include additional information without breaking the continuity of your message. As these examples show, you can tuck in dates, examples, clarifications, and whatever you want.

> *Nicholas wrote* Corners of Adequacy *(1981) to answer charges made against his father.*
> *Dylan Thomas (1914–1953) was a Welchman, a poet, and an alcoholic.*
> *Some foreign words (*gemutlichkeit, *for example) can't be easily translated into English.*
> *His wife (he married about a year ago) was barely 5 feet tall.*

Don't misuse parentheses. Don't use them to set off material that is necessary in the sentence.

> *"Nice" (in the old sense of "discriminating") is seldom used any more.*

And don't use them so often that they call attention to themselves. If you use too many parentheses in your sentence (i.e., more than two or three), you can lose (or antagonize) your reader (especially if he or she is concerned about writing style).

8. Use a Dash Where You Need It. Like commas and parentheses, dashes can be used to set off an element. If you want to set off an idea that is closely related to your sentence, use commas. ("My father, who always loved fruit, died eating an orange.") To set off a unit that is less closely related, use dashes (or parentheses). ("My father—he would have been 39 next month—died eating an orange.")

Indeed, a dash—used in moderation—is acceptable punctuation in many circumstances.

Don't bet on Red Devil—he's a loser.
He thought about the situation for weeks—never able to get it
  all together.
It became clear that only one man could be the murderer—Dr.
  Dorrill.

The dash is a handy mark of punctuation. Just don't overuse it.

EXERCISES

Punctuate these sentences. Insert commas, semicolons, colons,
exclamation marks, hyphens, and dashes where needed.

1. When the outfielder caught the second hand baseball he saw that the hide was torn.
2. Charles Lackey the famous actor died on stage last week
3. He never complained he knew it would do no good
4. The nun asked me if I knew the way to Elm Street
5. During the summer I spent at least eleven thousand dollars on eighteenth century furniture
6. The price and I can't tell you how pleased I am to say this is only $4800.00
7. After six weeks of trying my brother finally learned to play hearts
8. The boy who won first prize a silver cup was our neighbor's son
9. I think *The Iceman Cometh* is the best American play written in this century and I absolutely refuse to teach it to this know nothing class
10. Would you kindly pay this bill by the first of the month
11. The wife got the stereo the television and the Thunderbird but the husband got to keep the dog
12. They insisted on waiting for Rex had never been there before
13. Then he wrote *Getting There from Here* 1955 a play about Nazi oppression

Apostrophes, Quotation Marks, Italics, and Capital Letters

9. Use Apostrophes to Show Possession, to Indicate an Omission, and to Form Unusual Plurals. As a general rule, you show possession by adding *'s* to any singular or plural noun that does not end in *s*.

the dog's collar   *Jim's football*
the woman's hand   *the men's boots*

For nouns ending in *s*, you add either an *'s* or simply a final apostrophe. Punctuate it the way you say it; add the *'s* where you pronounce the extra syllable.

the girls' room   *James's reign*
the Clardys' house   *the Harris's car*

(In describing the Hiss-Chambers case, most commentators write of *Chambers' accusations and Hiss's* response.)

In more complicated usage, it is often better to avoid the issue. Don't speculate on how to punctuate "Charles and Bobs television," "Jesus parables" or "the last three months pay." Write "the television Charles and Bob bought last June," "the parables of Jesus," and "pay for the last three months."

You also use apostrophes to replace omitted letters or numbers in contractions ("I've," "couldn't," "the class of '45") and to form unusual plurals.

> *A good essay is not full of and's.*
> *Today Ph.D.'s can't get a job.*
> *I got one A and four C's.*

Usage is changing here. Many respectable authors no longer use apostrophes in these constructions. They write of "Ph.D.s" and "Cs" and "4s."

If you wonder whether you need an apostrophe with proper names (like "Veterans Administration") or brand names (like "French's mustard"), there is no rule to help you. The correct form is whatever the organizations use. In a difficult case, you may have to consult magazines, advertisements, or letterheads; to phone for information; or even to drive to your shopping center.

You need to include brand names in your writing because such details give color and interest to your prose. But the names do bring apostrophe problems, especially if you're trying to champion "Miller" beer over "Stroh's" and "Coors." This list gives some of the more common trade names and shows how complicated the apostrophe problem can be.

Benson & Hedges cigarettes
Betty Crocker cake mix
Bride's magazine
Brooks Brothers clothes
Campbell's soup
Consumers' Research magazine
Diners Club
Dole pineapple
Elmer's glue
Hertz rent-a-car
Hunt's ketchup
Jergen's lotion
Johnson wax
Kellogg's cereal

Ladies' Home Journal
L'eggs pantyhose
Levi's jeans
McDonald's hamburgers
Myers's rum
Oscar Mayer meats
O'Shaughnessys' whiskey
Parents magazine
Parsons' ammonia
Phillips 66 gasoline
Phillips' milk of magnesia
Planters peanuts
Popeyes chicken
Reader's Digest

Sears	Wilson sporting goods
Stroh Light beer	Woolworth's
Wards	Wrigley's gum

Nobody knows all these varying forms. The difference between a good and a bad writer is that a good writer takes the trouble to check out such things.

10. Use Quotations Marks to Enclose the Exact Words of a Source, Titles of Short Works, a Word Used as a Word, and (Sometimes) Words Used in an Odd or Ironic Sense. Use quotation marks to enclose material taken directly from a book or person.

> *In 1955, Aaron Mitchell wrote that the failure of democracy would derive from the "continuing derision of the mob."*
> *Reynolds said, "There is no reason to suspect murder."*

But don't use quotation marks for a paraphrased statement.

> *Reynolds said that there was no reason to suspect murder.*

Put quotation marks around titles of shorter works: magazine articles, short stories, poems, art works, and songs.

> *"A Rose for Emily"*
> *Frost's "Mending Wall"*
> *Picasso's "Three Musicians"*
> *"White Christmas"*

Titles of longer works are put in italics.

Use quotation marks to indicate you are using a word as a word rather than as a meaning.

> *I can never spell "surgeon."*
> *"Cellar door" has a pleasant sound.*

The usage here varies. Many writers use italics in such instances.

Finally, use quotation marks to show the odd or ironic use of a word.

> *The Prime Minister lifted the first volume of the Encyclopaedia Britannica from his desk and "clobbered" his secretary.*
> *These "teachers" are a disgrace.*

Try not to use quotation marks this way. When you can, just write the words.

Where do you put end punctuation when you are quoting? The rules are uncomplicated. Put periods and commas *inside* quotation marks—

always. Put semicolons and colons *outside.* And put question marks and exclamation marks inside if they are part of the quotation; otherwise, put them outside. These examples show the pattern:

> *"When you come," Nick said, "bring your boat."*
> *Molly had said, "I'll never forget you"; however, she forgot me*
> *in two weeks.*
> *Becky asked, "How long has this been going on?"*
> *Who wrote "the uncertain glory of an April day"?*
> *All I can say is "Wow!"*
> *I did too say "Monday"!*

To show a quotation within a quotation, use single quotes.

> *Jack complained, "I can never remember who wrote 'to be or*
> *not to be.' "*

A better suggestion: Reconstruct your sentence so you don't have to put quotes within quotes.

> *Jack said he could never remember who wrote "to be or not to*
> *be."*

11. Use Italics for Titles of Longer Works, for Foreign Words, and (if you have to) for Emphasis. You indicate *italic type* by underlining.

Use italics to mark titles of longer works: books, magazines, newspapers, movies, plays, operas, and long poems, as well as the names of ships and airplanes.

> Walker Percy's *Love in the Ruins*
> *Psychology Today*
> the *Washington Post*
> *Star Wars*
> *General Hospital*
> *Carmen*
> *Paradise Lost*
> the *Titanic*
> the space-shuttle *Columbia*

Do not use italics (or quotation marks) for the Bible—or books of the Bible—or for famous documents like the Declaration of Independence or the Magna Charta.

A useful rule: Whenever you are in doubt whether to use quotation marks or italics to indicate a title, use italics.

Use italics for foreign words. But remember that many foreign words have now become part of the English language and do not need italics.

He was permitted to graduate *in absentia.*
Do not use clichés.
Kathy has a certain *élan,* but she acts like a prima donna.

What should you do about foreign words that have almost become English ("a priori," "coup d'état," "non sequitur")? When in doubt, don't italicize them.

Finally, you can use italics to give some word a special emphasis.

That's *precisely* the reason I am here.
Virgilia did not merely act like a princess; she *was* a princess.

It is best not to use italics for emphasis, but there are occasions where you will want to.

12. Use Capital Letters with the Names of Specific Persons, Places, and Things. Knowing when to use a capital letter is not always easy, but the main rules are clear enough.

Capitalize the names of *people,* as well as their titles and words derived from their names; *places,* including countries (and national groups), states, counties, cities, and defined areas; *time units* like days of the week, months, and holidays; *religious entities; organizations,* their abbreviations and brand names; *historical* events and documents; *titles* of books, magazines, plays, poems, stories, movies, television shows, musical compositions and art objects; and *structures* like buildings, monuments, airplanes, and ships. These examples show the common usage:

Willy Nelson	*Genesis*
Captain Kirk	*General Motors*
Addison's Disease	*G.M.*
Shakespearean sonnet	*Ovaltine*
Holland	*the Battle of Hastings*
the Dutch	*the Gettysburg Address*
Europeans	*the Magna Charta*
the Riviera	Fear of Flying
California	*Chapter One*
Monroe County	*Epilogue*
Black River Falls	Newsweek
Tuesday	The Importance of Being Earnest
February	*"The Killers"*
Memorial Day	*"Mending Wall"*
God	All My Children
Methodist	*"Margaritaville"*
the Pope	*Beethoven's Seventh*
the Archbishop of Canterbury	*the Empire State Building*

the Washington Monument   *the* Titanic
the Spirit of St. Louis

You should have little problem with such examples.

Some words are capitalized in one context and not in another. They are capitalized when they name or relate to a specific entity. These instances show the distinction:

> *I knew Major Jones.*
> *He rose to the rank of major.*

> *I saw Mother there.*
> *I will see my mother there.*

> *I support the Democratic candidate.*
> *I believe in the democratic system.*

> *I attend Spring Hill Baptist Church.*
> *We drove by a church.*

> *I love the South.*
> *We flew south.*

> *This is the Sewanee River.*
> *We swam in the river.*

> *Turn to Chapter One.*
> *Read the next chapter.*

Any word is capitalized, of course, when it begins a sentence or when it begins a line of poetry.

Do not capitalize words like ''spring'' or ''freshman.''

Finally, there are the words that present problems. The usage of these varies with educated writers, and you may have to make your own decision. Here are some guidelines.

A.M. or *a.m.*   Either form is correct. Just be consistent.

Coke or *coke.*   When a product is vastly popular, its trade name may become the name of the product itself and thus lose its capital letter. This has happened to ''ping pong,'' ''thermos bottle,'' ''kleenex,'' and ''band-aid,'' and is now happening to ''Xerox'' and ''Musak.''

Right now, it is probably best to write ''Coke'' when you specifically mean Coca-Cola, and ''coke'' when you mean any other soft drink.

The Pill or *the pill.*   In general usage, the birth-control pill is distinguished from other kinds of pills. Either capitalize the word or put it in quotation marks.

Roman numerals or *roman numerals.*   Sometimes a national reference becomes part of a common word and no longer conveys a sense of nationality; it may then lose its capital letter. You would not capitalize "dutch treat," "french fries," or "turkish towel."

Some words are still changing. At present, you can write either "Roman numeral" or "roman numeral." But be consistent.

Psychology or *psychology*.   You should always use capital letters with specific courses ("Psychology 201") and lowercase letters with the area in general ("I used psychology to convince my mother"). Capital letters, however, are sometimes used to discuss academic courses in a general way. You could write, "The University has strong programs in Psychology and Sociology, but it is weak in Languages."

Black or *black*.   This can be a sensitive area, and there is no firm, consistent convention to guide you here. A decade ago, the word was routinely capitalized. Thereafter, many people capitalized it when referring specifically to race ("the Black heritage") but not when merely describing something ("the black boxer"). Currently, following the usage of noted black leaders, many writers no longer capitalize "black." But *Ebony* magazine still does.

Judge the likely response of your reader before you choose to capitalize (or not capitalize) "black." No usage is correct if it offends someone you don't want to offend.

Truth or *truth*.   From time to time you will be tempted to capitalize a word to show special emphasis ("Tom and Laura used to be Close Friends" or to show irony ("Carl sees himself as a Very Important Person"). You may want to praise a poet or philosopher by stressing his "continuing pursuit of Truth." Try to avoid using capital letters in this way.

Despite the complexity of some of these examples, most uses of capital letters follow a simple rule. You capitalize proper names—the names of specific persons, places, things, and events.

EXERCISES

In these sentences, add apostrophes, quotation marks, italics, and capital letters where they are needed. Remove them where they are unnecessary.

1. My lawyer asked if I read georges mail. I said never in a million years.
2. My Mother loved to read the *Bible,* especially the story of Moses's flight from Egypt.
3. It became an idée fix: he was sure he could find a word to rhyme with jeffersonian.
4. Kate said my favorite song is Bette Davis Eyes.
5. They worked hard on it, but the boys buick was still a wreck.
6. I prefer Yeats poem that celebrates Ulysses courage.
7. His first poem winter dreams was published in the Atlantic Monthly.

8. The Professor asked In what year did Coleridge write Christobel?
9. No wonder he gets straight Cs in mathematics. His 7s all look like 1s.
10. The details of the coup d'état were published in last sundays New York Times.
11. The best song in hello dolly is hello dolly.

Abbreviations

Because your writing should be an extension of the way you talk, you would do well not to write abbreviations at all. You say words, not abbreviations. Clearly, you would sound unusual talking like this:

> *We'll be there the second week in Feb.*
> *In Madison, Wis., I worked for the Rogers Express Co.*
> *This is the St., but I don't know the No.*

However, many abbreviations *are* words. You would sound odd saying this:

> *I have to hurry to my Reserve Officers Training Corps class.*

> *At two post meridian, she drove her car into the Young*
>   *Women's Christian Association parking lot.*

The rule is to follow your own voice. Write the word where you say the word and the abbreviation where you say the abbreviation. Thus you can write either "television" or "TV," either "CIA" or "Central Intelligence Agency." Probably you would never write "Blvd.," "MSS.," "e.g.," "anno domine," or "University of California at Los Angeles."

There are a few exceptions to this rule. Standard usage dictates that "Mr.," "Dr.," "Mrs.," "Rev.," and comparable abbreviations can be used before proper names. Similarly, it permits you to write "etc." instead of "et cetera." In general, however, you should not use abbreviations that are not also words. (And use "etc." sparingly.)

You use periods after most abbreviations ("B.C.," "p.m.," "M.D."). Some abbreviations, however, are so much a part of the language that they have become words themselves. You don't need to punctuate these acronyms:

UNESCO	*FBI*
YMCA	*NBC-TV*
UCLA	*IBM*

If you have a doubt in such cases, you probably don't need to use the periods.

In writing addresses, use the Post Office abbreviations for the states. Over half of them are simply the first two letters of a one-word state name

("CA" for California) or the first letter of each word in a two-word name ("NY" for New York). Routinely, these are written without periods.

These are the only states for which the Post Office abbreviation is not the first two letters:

AK—Alaska	*MN—Minnesota*
AZ—Arizona	*MS—Mississippi*
CT—Connecticut	*MO—Missouri*
GA—Georgia	*MT—Montana*
HI—Hawaii	*NB—Nebraska*
IA—Iowa	*NV—Nevada*
KS—Kansas	*PA—Pennsylvania*
KY—Kentucky	*TN—Tennessee*
LA—Louisiana	*TX—Texas*
ME—Maine	*VT—Vermont*
MD—Maryland	*VA—Virginia*

You would do well to memorize this list. If you routinely use these abbreviations (instead of "Wisc." or "Ala.," for example), your writing will look more professional.

Numbers

The question is whether to write out a number in words ("three hundred and sixty") or to use numerals ("360"). The usage varies here.

A good general rule is to write out numbers when they are small (say, under 100) and when there are only a few of them in your essay.

> *There were seventy-two people in the plane, but only two of*
> *them were injured.*

On all other occasions, use numerals.

You should always use numerals in dates, addresses, percentages, units of measurement, page numbers, and hours followed by "a.m." or "p.m." Use these forms:

December 15, 1976	*4.2 minutes*
15 December 1976	*page 37*
639 Azalea Road	*8:20 a.m.*
16 percent	*14,987 students*

When writing large numbers, remember that numerals look bigger than words. If you want to defend America's national debt, say it is "ninety billion dollars." If you want to protest it, say it is "$90,000,000,000.00." (A neat, objective practice is to round off figures and write "$90 billion.")

If you have more than several numbers to express, use numerals throughout your essay. But don't begin a sentence with a number.

Spelling

The one best way to improve your spelling is to read extensively.

The best short-term way is to keep a dictionary at hand and to look up words you are in doubt about. You should have doubts when you face plainly difficult words, commonly misspelled words, and words you have had trouble with before.

You should never misspell "rhododendron," "bourgeoisie," "alumnae," and "hieroglyphic." You know these are difficult words; you should consult your dictionary and spell them right. (If you don't have a dictionary, consider using another word.)

Here is a list of the most commonly misspelled words in English. Survey the list. If any one of the words looks unusual to you, circle it. Then try to memorize the correct spelling.

absence	*category*	*forehead*
accept	*cemetery*	*foreign*
accommodate	*changeable*	*fourth*
achievement	*choose*	*government*
acquainted	*colonel*	*grammar*
addressed	*committee*	*handkerchief*
advice	*comparative*	*humorous*
advise	*compliment*	*influence*
AFFECT—EFFECT	*conceive*	*initiate*
aggravate	*conscience*	*intellectual*
all right	*contemptible*	*irrelevant*
allusion	*cooperate*	**ITS—IT'S**
A LOT	*courteous*	*let's*
amateur	*deceive*	*library*
analyze	*desert*	**LOOSE—LOSE**
angle	*dessert*	*mathematics*
apology	*dictionary*	*misspelled*
apparent	*difference*	*ninth*
appreciate	*dormitories*	*occasion*
Arctic	*eighth*	*occurrence*
athletic	*embarrass*	*omitted*
attendance	*environment*	*pamphlet*
believe	*especially*	*parallel*
benefited	*exaggerate*	*perform*
Britain	*excellence*	*permanence*
bureau	*existence*	*personnel*
calendar	*existential*	*persuade*
capital	*fascinate*	*playwright*
capitol	*February*	*politician*

preferred	*restaurant*	*tendency*
prejudice	*rhythm*	*than—then*
PRINCIPAL—PRINCIPLE	*seize*	**THEIR—THERE**
pronunciation	*sense*	**TO—TOO**
prophecy—prophesy	**SEPARATE**	*truly*
psychology	*sophomore*	*until*
questionnaire	*stationary*	*usually*
RECEIVE	*stationery*	*Wednesday*
recommend	*subtle*	*were—where*
resemblance	*syllable*	*whether*
reservoir	*temperament*	*writing*

Pay particular attention to the capitalized words on this list. They are the ones that cause the most trouble.

Finally, make your own list. Keep track of words you have misspelled on your essays or on early drafts of your papers. Learn these words. There is no excuse for misspelling "separate" twice.

EXERCISES

Correct any errors in abbreviation, numbers, and spelling that you find in these sentences.

1. The suspect lived at 901 West Blvd. for 6 months. He burglerized a jewelry store, taking stones valued at ten thousand three hundred and fifty dollars. He was indited and convicted, and his new adress is Rockway Prison, Temple City, Mich.
2. 15 percent of the students at the Massachusetts Institute of Technology do not plan to work in the U.S. Most want to get their doctor of philosophy degree, emigrate to Canada, and make fifty-five thousand a year working for the aircraft industry.
3. Your education allready has cost me thirty-six hundred dollars. By the time you get you're M.A. in math, I'll be bankrup.
4. Citizens of Washington, District of Columbia, love Pres. Reagan. 10,000 of them attended his speech praising the C.I.A. and its dedicated personell.
5. We watched TV from eleven ante meridiem until after midnight. No more than 10% of the shows, however, were worth watching.

Final Counsel

It's not creative unless it sells.

      AL HAMPEL, *Benton & Benton, Inc.*

The eight rules should help to make you an effective writer. You may be further helped by these six areas of general counsel.

CREDIT YOUR SOURCES

In general writing, you do not need formal scholarly documentation. But commonly, you will want to specify your sources. Don't use footnotes for this; few people read them. Put information about your sources in your text. Any of these forms is acceptable.

> According to Genie Hamner (*Bald Windows Revisited,* 1978), man has endured . . .
> In *Bald Windows Revisited* (1978), Genie Hamner argues . . .
> In her article "Decision Making in Washington Transportation Systems" (*Fortune,* June 1977), Kathleen Kelly describes . . .
> According to *Time* (February 15, 1981), President Reagan has . . .

This kind of informal documentation need not be elaborate. But it is good to give your reader enough information to be able to refer to the sources you used.

USE YOUR SPEAKING VOICE

Try to get your speaking voice in your writing. You would never say, "This radio needed repair from the date of purchase"; you would say, "This radio hasn't worked since I bought it." In talking, you tend to use short sentences, plain words, active voice, and specific details. You don't worry about beginning a sentence with "and" or "but." You don't use words like "shall" or "secondly" or "societal." You would never say "My reasons were the following" or "Quiet was the night."

Try to avoid long sentences full of paired or parallel constructions. Look at this example. (Italics and parentheses are added to show the pattern.)

> Children need generous amounts of *affection, guidance,* and *discipline* in order to develop into *intellectually* and *emotionally* mature adults. Children (who feel *rejected* or *unloved*) or (who are given *inconsistent* or *ineffective* discipline) tend to develop *serious* and *long-lasting* psychic disorders, such as *schizophrenia, alcoholism, drug addiction,* and *psychopathic personality.*

This is *written* language; nobody talks like that. Don't write this kind of social-science prose.

Trust your ear. What sounds like good spoken language—at a level suited to your subject and your audience—will be good writing. In this book, you have been advised to keep the same grammatical subject through a paragraph, to tuck words like "however" and "therefore" in the middle of sentences, and to avoid "there is" and "there are" forms. Whenever you think this advice would make your writing sound awkward, don't follow it.

GET HELP FROM FRIENDS

In all likelihood, you will never be asked to write an essay or letter that someone else will read and judge immediately. Impromptu themes may be assigned in college classes, but in the outer world you will always have time for reflection and revision. As part of your revision, have a friend or spouse or teacher or secretary or colleague read through your essay for clarity and correctness.

Correctness in matters of punctuation, italics, number, idiom, and spelling is important. A misspelled "their" or "it's" can make a well-informed paper seem illiterate. An omitted comma can make an important sentence almost unreadable. A "not" that is typed "now" can cause big trouble.

Of course, you should resort to a dictionary or an English handbook when you have difficulties. But serious errors may exist where you don't recognize a problem. If a particular piece of writing is important to you, invite a knowledgeable friend to look it over.

MAKE IT NEAT

Imagine you're applying for an executive position and are well qualified. Then you come to the interview chewing gum and wearing an old Batman sweatshirt. You're not going to get the job.

Similarly, if you write a first-rate letter of application and send it off in sloppy form (with bad handwriting, cross-outs, irregular margins, and on paper ripped from a spiral notebook), you won't get the job. If you send a messy-looking manuscript to an editor, forget it. Major publishing houses and magazines now receive so many submissions that they immediately dismiss those that are sloppily presented.

This is a reasonable response. The form in which you send out your material says something important about you and your attitude toward your reader and your subject matter. Make it look good.

Neatness counts.

REMEMBER YOUR AUDIENCE

Keep in mind the kind of audience you are writing for. It makes a difference.

There is a danger in assuming that your reader knows what you know. This can lead you to commit what Edgar Dale calls the "COIK fallacy" and to write casually about Ken Maynard or Riverside Drive or real time because these terms are clear and meaningful to you. They are *C*lear *O*nly *I*f *K*nown.

Addressing an educated audience, you can use words like "arcane" and "protean." Speaking to Southerners, you might venture "tump" or "cattywampus." Writing to a specialized group (scholars or athletes or priests), you can refer to Romantic poetry, a trap-play, or John 3:16. But don't use such terms with a general audience; they won't understand you. Don't say, "They can look it up." They won't.

A problem arises when you are forced to use an obscure term. Here, along with the word, you should include an explanation of what it means. But you don't want to sound preachy or condescending. ("I suppose I have to explain to you that a shard is a piece of pottery.") In such instances, you have to give the explanation in an indirect way. See how necessary clarification is included in these sentences:

> As spokesmen for the Jewish establishment, the *Scribes and Pharisees* were immediately hostile to the message of Jesus.
> The *trap-play* worked perfectly: the linebacker charged through the space we left open and was blocked out of the play.
> No one ever understood what motivated Lizzy Borden. She remains an *enigma*.

Always, the burden is on you to make your meaning clear and acceptable to your particular audience.

Remember that some audiences are sensitive in particular areas. Writing to a black audience, be careful about using words like "negro" and "boy." Don't tell Polish jokes in Milwaukee. Addressing women's groups, try not to say "chair*man*" or "spokes*man*" or to insist that "a surgeon really earns *his* money." Don't address a letter to "*Miss* Gloria Steinem" or to "*Ms.* Phyllis Schlafly."

REMEMBER YOUR PURPOSE

The motto of one New York advertising agency is "It's not creative unless it sells." There is a lot of truth in that. Keep in mind the purpose of your writing. (Remember what you're trying to "sell.")

The eight rules just given are based on the assumption that you want to communicate information, to make an argument in a clear, forthright manner. But this is not always the case

Sometimes it's best to say nothing. The past decade records a number of individuals speaking out forthrightly when they shouldn't have. When Democratic National Headquarters at the Watergate was burglarized, Republican spokesmen denied involvement before anyone had accused them of anything. When pro-life and pro-choice delegates conflicted at the 1980 Democratic convention, President Carter volunteered a middle-of-the-road statement on abortion. Addressing stockholders of Bendix, Inc., the Board Chairman announced that the young lady working as Vice-President for Strategic Services had won the job on her merits, not because of her personal involvement with him. In each case, silence would have been a more effective argument.

Any time you are involved in an adversary situation, that is, when you are responding to police officers, lawyers, newspaper and television reporters, relatives who enjoy lawsuits, an ex-spouse, or an insurance adjustor, don't be too quick to frame an argument, volunteer information, or write clever letters. They may return to haunt you.

In argument, it is always a mistake to lie. But there are instances where truth won't do you much good. Always consider the virtues of silence.

There are also situations where you will want to express yourself indirectly. You might want to spare the sensibilities of your reader ("By the time he was twenty, Dudley had demonstrated a range of sexual abnormalities"). You might want to discredit an enemy ("The initial response to his book seems to be fairly favorable") or to veil a threat ("If you pay this bill promptly, your credit rating will remain excellent"). Such situations are not uncommon.

Suppose, for example, you are obliged—in a school or business situation—to write on a subject you know little about. Now your purpose is to conceal your deficiency. You want to fill up a page, to sound fairly learned, and to avoid any specific assertion that could demonstrate your ignorance.

So you reverse many of the rules in this book. You will add "which" clauses and sprinkle modifiers (like "truly," "more or less," and "on the other hand") to ensure that no sentence has fewer than twenty-five words. You will write of *quintessential* issues and suggest that *procrustean* tactics are the *ne plus ultra* of folly. (This will obfuscate your message.) You can avoid proper names by using the passive voice ("a decision has been made that" or "word was received that"). You will write of vague entities like "business leaders," "the former," and "fair play." These can be described as "adequate" or "unfortunate"; but if you want to avoid even this minimal level of judgment, you can call them "impressive," "notable," "meaningful," or "significant." (These words don't mean good or bad or much of anything.) The resulting paragraphs will be fairly meaningless. But in particular situations—where you can't or don't want to communicate directly—this may be exactly the kind of writing you want.

Most of the time, however, you write to say something specific. You want to show someone you are overworked. You want to persuade your audience that marijuana should be legalized, that gas rationing is essential, or that Sacco and Vanzetti were guilty. You want to describe your new boat. You want someone to give you that job, to buy mutual funds, or to settle that insurance claim in your favor. In such cases, the eight rules will help you produce effective writing.

Anything that thwarts the purpose of your writing (misspelling, wordiness, errors of fact, or even direct and meaningful statements) should be avoided. And anything that furthers your cause with a particular audience (even such features as expensive paper, threats, folksy language, neat typing, and footnotes) should probably be used.

Good writing may not always win you the final effect you want—that job, that insurance adjustment, that sale. But it will do all that language can do to achieve that end.

In general, you will find it easier to be persuasive if you are right.

Appendix

Pliny leaves mankind this only alternative:
either of doing what deserves to be written,
or of writing what deserves to be read.

—LORD CHESTERFIELD

Exercises for Review

How valid are these arguments? Identify examples of induction, deduction, expert testimony, semantic argument, analogy, argument in a circle, post hoc, begging the question, argument ad hominem, extension, the either-or fallacy, and statistical manipulation.

1. Of course you support federal aid to education. You're a teacher; you stand to profit on the deal.
2. "Ever wonder why kids instinctively go for soft drinks in bottles?"—Glass Container Manufacturers Institute.
3. A Tampax poll found that 22 percent of the respondents thought that menstrual pain was psychological.
4. Register Communists, Not Guns!
5. If God intended people to go naked, He would never have made cloth.
6. Naval ROTC should be abolished. I'm learning nothing from it.
7. Everyone knows that America's greatest threat is not from foreign powers, but from the enemies within.
8. Read *One in Twenty* by Bryan Magee—an adult, plainly written study of male and female homosexuality.
9. It's not safe to walk on the streets in New York; I'm glad I live in Cleveland.
10. I disagree with Abby Van Buren when she says no woman should be forced to have a baby she doesn't want. A lot of people are forced to have parents they don't like, but we don't let them go around murdering their fathers and mothers.
11. "There is no proof that sugar confectionary gives rise to dental cavities."— *Association Internationale des Fabricants de Confiserie.*
12. You have no more right to blow smoke into the public air than I have to spray mace on you.
13. A *Saturday Review* article carried the subtitle: "Do the Arabs Have a Case?"
14. I never knew a University of Alabama varsity football player who could read or write beyond the eighth grade level.
15. "Seven out of every ten Americans cheat on their income tax."—Professor R. Van Dyke Ellington.
16. How can you argue that a fetus is human from the moment of conception? The law considers a person dead when his brain is dead. A fetus shouldn't be considered alive until it has a fully developed brain.
17. Athletics teaches our young citizens good sportsmanship and how to play the game of life.
18. "Obscene material is material which deals with sex in a manner appealing to

prurient interest."—Justice Brennan, delivering the opinion of the Supreme Court, *Roth* v. *United States,* June 24, 1957.

19. We scientists working with astrological data expect to be criticized. We know that Newton and Einstein were ridiculed in the past.

20. All this effort to register and confiscate guns will not help us fight crime. Violence rises from the souls of men.

21. *The Husband,* a novel by Sol Stein. "The dilemma of countervailing demands on the sensual man of good will . . . rich and true . . . modulated with a respectful reserve . . . handled with hardly a false note."—*New York Times*

22. On a typical television poll, an early-evening newscaster poses a yes-or-no question, asking viewers to phone one number to vote "yes" and another to vote "no." Then a late-evening newscaster reports the result (e.g., 71 percent oppose socialized medicine).

23. *Miss MacIntosh, My Darling* by Marguerite Young. "What we behold is a mammoth epic, a massive fable, a picaresque journey, a Faustian quest, and a work of stunning magnitude and beauty . . . some of the richest, most expressive, most original and exhaustively revealing passages of prose that this writer has experienced in a long time."—William Goyen, *New York Times*

24. Homosexuality is no illness. It is a widespread practice, like vegetarianism. The homosexual has a sexual preference for members of the same sex; a vegetarian has an alimentary preference for noncarnivorous foods. In neither case is there any impairment of function or any disease.

25. Charlie's a gorgeous, sexy-young smell. (Concentrated!) And full of surprises. Just like you.

26. If your name is Makay, Malloy, or Murray, beware of drink. According to John Gary, director of the Council for Alcoholism in Glasgow, Scotland, people whose surname begins with the letter "M" may be eight times more prone to alcoholism than others.

27. What I want to know is who masterminded the plan to get President Nixon impeached.

28. *Miss MacIntosh, My Darling* by Marguerite Young. "In fact, this is an outrageously bad book, written by an author with very little of interest to say, and very little skill in saying it . . . wholly unreadable."—*Time*

29. To find her [Lizzy Borden] guilty, you must believe she is a fiend. Gentlemen, does she look it?

30. The U.S. Supreme Court Has Ruled That *Carnal Knowledge* Is Not Obscene—See It Now.

31. *Hitler's Daughter* by Gary Goss. "A brilliant academic satire"—Dennis Renault, *Sacramento Bee;* "Raunchy and unfair"—*The Reading Intelligencer;* "A hilarious time"—Harry Cargas, *Buffalo Spree*

32. A clever magician can always perform his tricks; but a genuine mystic can sometimes produce paranormal effects and sometimes not. Uri Geller produced no effects at all when he appeared on the "Tonight Show." He is a true psychic.

33. *The Power of Prayer on Plants* by Rev. Franklin Loehr. "In 700 experiments conducted by 150 persons, using 27,000 seeds and comprising 100,000

measurements, prayer consistently made a difference, in some cases showing as much as 52.7% growth advantage for prayer seedlings. . . . I doubt if anyone who reads this book and sees the photographs of actual experiments can ever be complacent about prayer again."—Ruth Sheldon Knowles, *Tulsa World.*

Subjects for Argumentative Essays

Abortion
ABSCAM
Absurd drama
Academy Awards
Adoption
Afghanistan
Alcoholism
Amnesty
Antichrist
Antitrust laws
Arthritis cures
Assassinations
Astrological predictions
Atlantis
AWACS

Baldness
Bermuda Triangle
Bible
Bigfoot
Biorhythms
Birth control
Black power
Brainwashing
Busing

Capital punishment
Censorship of textbooks
Chiropractors
CIA
Civil liberties
Cloning
Cocaine

Communism
Computer games
Conspiracy
Creationism
Cryonics
Cuba
Cults

Day-care centers
Daylight saving time
Death wish
Deficit spending
Dialects
Disarmament
Divorce

Ecology
Ecumenism
Electoral College
El Salvador
Endangered species
Energy
Entrapment
Entropy
ERA
ESP
Evolution
Exorcism

Faith healing
Falkland Islands
Family life
Federal aid to cities

Fluoridation
Jane Fonda
Food stamps
Football
Foreign aid
Foreign cars
Freud

Gambling
Genetic engineering
Glossolalia
God
Gold standard
Good taste
Grade inflation
Gun control

Health foods
Patty Hearst
Heredity
Heterosexuality
John Hinckley
Homosexuality

Illegal aliens
Income tax
Infant formula
Inflation
Instinct
Interest rates
IQ tests
Iran
Ireland
Israeli wars

Jesus
Jews
Jogging

Kennedy family
Korea
Ku Klux Klan

Labor unions
Laetrile
Leash laws
Legal insanity
Libel laws
Lie detectors
Life in space
Literature classes
Lobbyists
Loch Ness monster
Love

Mafia
Man as animal
Marijuana laws
Marriage
Medical costs
Military-industrial complex
Miracles
Miss America pageant
Modern art
Modernism in the churches
Moonies
Moral Majority
Mothers
Muslims

Names
NATO
National Enquirer
Natural law
Nazi party
Neutron bomb
New morality
Nuclear power

Oil company profits
OPEC

Panama Canal
PATCO
Patriotism

Pay television
Playboy
PLO
Poland
Political appointments
Pollution
Polyunsaturates
Population explosion
Pornography
Prayer in public schools
Prison reform
Private schools
Prophets
Prostitution
Psychoanalysis
Psychobiology
Psychokinesis
Public smoking laws
Punk rock
Pyramid power

Quack doctors

Racial superiority
Reaganomics
Required courses in college
Rights of the accused
Right-to-work laws
Ritual
Rock music
Roman Catholicism
Rosenberg trial
Royal jelly
Rubik's cube

Saccharin
Sacco–Vanzetti
Salaries of professional athletes
Sex Education
Sexism in language
Sexual harassment
Shock treatments

Single parents
Smoking and health
Soap operas
Social Security
Solar power
South Africa
Space program
Speed limits
Speed reading
Standard English
Stonehenge
Strikes
Student rights
Supreme Court

Tabloids
Talking animals
Television
Terrorism
Test-tube babies
Third parties
Third World
Tranquilizers
Translation
Trickle-down economics
Trilateral Commission

UFO's
Unemployment compensation
Unions
USSR

Vegetarianism
Vietnam
Virginity
Vitamin C
Vivisection
Vote fraud

Watergate
Weaponry
Wilderness preservation

Witchcraft
Woman's role

X-rated movies

Yoga

Zionism
Zoning laws

Writing a Business Letter

Probably the main form in which you will write argumentative prose is the business letter. You'll want to convince someone you deserve a job or a raise. You'll want to make a sale or get a larger insurance adjustment. You'll want to pacify someone who has written an angry letter to you.

Business letters take a fairly standard form.

Read these two letters. Both are effective examples of business writing.

862 Callaway Drive
Medford, WI 54101
15 December 1981

Mr. George Blazdon, President
Silver Shadow Pen Company
1515 Vermont Street
New York, NY 10009

Dear Mr. Blazdon:

Last year I was given one of your Silver Shadow pens (Model 364A) for an anniversary present. I love its looks, but I'm having trouble with it. I wonder if you can help me.

After a few months, the point no longer came out when I twisted the pen. I had kept all the original papers and followed the warranty instructions. I sent the pen to your Atlanta office, and they fixed it and returned it.

At the same time, because I can't seem to find refills locally, I sent for half a dozen red-ink refills. You sent them, along with a bill for $18. This seemed pretty steep to me, but I had no choice if I wanted to use the pen, so I paid it.

Now the pen is broken again. When I twist it, the point doesn't come up. I phoned your Atlanta office to see if the pen was under warranty. They said it wasn't, but that they'd be able to fix it for $10.75.

I'm not sure I should have to pay this amount. Either the pen was defective in the first place or repaired poorly in the second place. Should I have to pay for your mistakes?

I'm not a consumer-crank, Mr. Blazdon, but I don't think this situation is fair. What do you advise me to do?

Sincerely,

Thomas Ridgeway

Thomas Ridgeway

SILVER SHADOW PEN COMPANY

1515 Vermont Street
New York, NY 10009

December 21, 1981

Mr. Thomas Ridgeway
862 Callaway Drive
Medford, WI 54101

Dear Mr. Ridgeway:

Thank you for your letter of December 15. I'm pleased you like our Silver Shadow pen, and I'm sorry it's giving you trouble. I hope this information helps you.

Your pen is indeed out of warranty. You have used it for over a year. I'm sure you understand that we cannot offer a lifetime guarantee with our products.

You can purchase refills for your pen at Redman's Office Supplies in Medford or at Quality Stationery Company (3201 West Lane) when you drive into Milwaukee. The refills do cost $3. each, but these are jumbo-cartridges containing 2½ times as much ink as usual ballpoint refills.

May I offer a compromise, Mr. Ridgeway? You don't want to be without your Silver Shadow pen, and we can't afford dissatisfied customers. I suggest you have the pen repaired in Atlanta and pay the $10.75. Thereafter, if the same problem recurs, send it to me and it will be repaired free of charge.

I hope you have a pleasant holiday.

Sincerely,

George Blazdon

George Blazdon
President

GB:dm

Now consider the seven parts of a business letter as illustrated in these examples.

THE RETURN ADDRESS.

Notice that this is omitted if you write on letterhead stationery. Always use the two-letter U.S. Post Office abbreviations to indicate the state. (See p. 272.) And always include the zip code.

THE DATE.

Either of the two forms shown is acceptable. Just be consistent.

INSIDE ADDRESS.

If your letter is at all important, send it to someone by name. On pedestrian matters, you can address "Subscription Office" or "Catalog Department," but never address anyone simply as "Personnel Manager," "Chairman," "Publisher," or "President." If you make careful use of your library and your telephone, you can get the name of the person you want to write to. (It is useful to have access to a WATS line.)

THE SALUTATION.

Write "Dear Mr. (or *Mrs.* or *Miss* or *Ms.*) Name." This is always followed by a colon. Writing to a friend, you can use "Dear Bill," but this too must be followed by a colon.

Try never to write "Dear Sir," "Dear Madam," "Dear Sir or Madam," or "Gentlemen." These forms, which prevailed some years ago, now seem offensively vague and sexist. If you don't have a name to write to, address a title. Possibly you can get by with "Dear Editor" or "Dear Manager." But it's always best to take that extra time and find a name to write to.

THE BODY OF THE LETTER.

Usually this has at least three paragraphs, with the first acting as introduction and the last as conclusion.

The first paragraph should be short and should define the issue. Your reader should never have to move on into your second paragraph to know what your letter is about. If you are answering someone, it is a good idea to begin, "Thank you for your letter of March 17." Giving the date lets the reader check his or her file and refer to the original message. Saying "thank you" sets a positive tone.

Through the body of your letter, use the forms that mark good writing anywhere. Use short sentences, plain words, active voice, detail, and so on. Sound like yourself talking. At all costs, avoid "letterese," the clichés of business writing:

> *am cognizant of*
> *are in receipt of*
> *as per your request*
> *at your earliest convenience*
> *do not hesitate to*
> *enclosed herewith*
> *thanking you in advance*
> *under separate cover*
> *with reference to*

Work particularly hard to avoid the words "advise," "acknowledge," "per," and "transmit."

It is often effective to repeat the name of the person you're writing to, particularly with critical lines. ("I am genuinely sorry, Mr. Metcalf, but there is no possibility we can give you a loan at this time.")

Never express anger in a business letter. You can feel it, but don't write it.

The concluding paragraph should be short, general, affirmative, and personal. Even if your letter expressed criticism and unhappy truths, finish on as positive a note as you can. ("I'm sorry I have to give you this bad news, Bill. But I know you can handle it.") And even if you've been speaking for your company and using "we" throughout your letter, use an "I" in the conclusion.

THE COMPLIMENTARY CLOSE.

A simple "Sincerely" or "Sincerely yours" is probably best.

THE SIGNATURE.

Always type your name beneath your signature. And put your title (if you have one) on the line below that.

If someone else types your letter, the typist indicates the fact by putting the author's initials, then his or her own, on the left margin below the signature.

> <

A final word about the overall appearance of your letter. Keep it on one page if at all possible. Center the writing so that the white space around it seems to "frame" it. And begin a new paragraph whenever it is at all reasonable to do so. All this will make your letter more inviting to read.

In general, your business letter will be most effective and persuasive if it is short, informed, natural-sounding, and marked by unrelenting goodwill.

Making a Speech

Another form in which you may have to make an argument is the platform speech. You may have to speak before a civic club, a church organization, a union group, or a town meeting to plead a cause. You may want to champion a school-tax referendum. You may favor a particular candidate for office. You may want to sell some product or service or idea. You're going to have to stand before an audience and talk.

It is not very difficult to make an effective speech if you're willing to give necessary time to the job.

WRITING THE SPEECH

Most of the suggestions about "good writing" apply equally to effective speaking.

In writing your talk, you need to choose a subject that lends itself to detail, get specific facts, narrow the topic, organize the material, and express it in an everyday "speaking" voice. But a speech is different from a written essay in several ways.

Here are rules to remember:

1. Make Your Organization Clear. Because your audience has no paragraphs to look at, you have to be more specific in announcing the outline of your talk. You might say, "I have three reasons for opposing the construction of a nuclear power station in Arneson," then follow this with markers "first," "second," "third," and "in conclusion." (This would be mechanically offensive in an essay, but it helps a speech.) You can get the same effect with a time reference ("Every day last week, I thought of a new reason to vote for the school tax") or with an extended metaphor ("If the Patman bill was a used car, you wouldn't buy it"). Your audience should always have a general idea of how far along your speech is and where it's going.

2. Make Your Introduction Short and Provocative. Don't dawdle around. Greet the audience. ("Good morning, gentlemen.") Add a note or two of personal goodwill. ("I'm pleased to be here with you today.") Announce your subject. ("I want to talk to you about our new turbines.") And make it interesting. ("They're giving us strange problems, and they're costing us money." Then get on with your talk.

In platform speaking, you have about 30 seconds in which to "catch" your audience. If you don't win them then, you probably won't do it at all.

Don't begin your speech with a joke unless it is particularly related to your topic. The isolated opening joke is now almost a cliché. It suggests the speaker has a frivolous attitude toward his or her audience and the subject. You can, of course, offer any amount of relevant humor as your speech moves on. But don't begin, "Being here today reminds me of the story of the monkey and the artichoke." Spare your audience that.

3. Refer to the Audience and the Local Scene. In writing the speech, remember that you're talking to somebody. Address the audience as "Ladies and gentlemen" or "gentlemen" or "friends" or "you" or "we" (meaning you and them together). Speak to them courteously and directly. ("Please follow this now; this is important.") Refer to people in attendance. ("Tom here can tell you what happened.") Never let your talk become so abstract and objective that it loses this "you and me" note.

Refer to what is going on around you. Mention other features of the occasion: the preceding speaker, the orchestra, the meal, the awards ceremony, a special guest, whatever. Use immediate objects as illustrative props. ("It's like this salt shaker; if you don't shake it, nothing comes out.") Mention things everyone is concerned with at the moment (Christmas shopping, unusual weather, inflation, a hit movie, an election, the Super Bowl, etc.). These things tie you and your audience together.

4. Don't Let Your Speech Get Boring. You know how quickly you lose interest in a sermon on "faith" or a graduation speech on "responsibility." When a book becomes dull, you can skim a few paragraphs and get on to the more compelling material. When a speech gets dull, it just drones on, and you begin counting the bricks in the wall.

In writing your talk, therefore, it is particularly important to narrow your subject to a richly specific topic. Then talk about real things and use proper names. Say "for instance" and "for example" a lot.

Don't give long lists of names, facts, or statistics. These might be acceptable in an essay, but they're deadly in a speech. Put such material on a handout sheet; then distribute it and refer to it.

Always edit your speech to make sure you're not saying the same thing over and over again.

Unless you are singularly eloquent, don't let your speech go beyond 30 minutes. And shorter is better.

5. Keep Your Concluding Remarks Brief. When you've said what you have to say, quit. Never pad out a speech in order to fill up some artificial time frame.

Have a memorable final line. Don't trail away with a dull sentence. ("That's pretty much what I have to say about those turbines.") Make it more dramatic: "We *can* make these turbines work, but it won't be easy. We have to begin now."

PREPARING FOR THE EVENT

Besides writing an effective speech, you can do other things ahead of time to ensure the success of your talk.

1. Rehearse. Practice your speech. Give it over and over. Talk to anyone who will listen to you: your spouse, your brother, your dog, anybody. If you plan to use an opaque projector or flip charts or a pointer, practice with these props.

You might even have a dress rehearsal. Invite over a few friends, ply them with food and drink, and make them listen to your speech. Pay attention to their response.

2. Make Yourself Look Good. In a speech, everything counts. The audience is looking at you and making judgments. Whereas a writer is happily invisible, a speaker has to be concerned about his or her appearance. A man might want to buy a new suit; certainly he should have a haircut and a shoeshine. A woman should never wear clothes or accessories that draw attention away from her message. For an important occasion, an overweight person might elect to lose 5 to 10 pounds.

These things may sound trivial. But they're all part of the total impression you make. They are part of the persuasive process.

3. Arrange the Setting. It's important to get to the speaking site at least a half an hour early and look over the scene.

Make necessary arrangements. Check the lighting. Make sure there is a speaker's stand and get it at the right height. See that the microphone works. Get props and audio-visuals ready. Make sure that you have a blackboard (or a flip-chart) if you need one and that there is something to write with. Sometimes you can even arrange the chairs so the audience will sit where you want them.

None of these happen by themselves. Many speaking problems can be avoided if you take time to check things out.

DELIVERING THE SPEECH

Finally, the moment arrives. It's time to stand up and give that speech. This counsel should help you.

1. Stand up Straight. Never give a speech or deliver a report sitting down. And when you stand, don't slouch in an effort to look supercasual.

Face the front. Don't make extended references to a blackboard or flip-chart and talk with your back to the audience. When pointing to things on a chart, stand directly beside it so you're still facing your listeners.

2. Control Any Nervousness. The best way to avoid nervousness is to write a first-rate speech and rehearse it a lot.

If you are especially nervous, you can tell your audience that, *once.* But use a line that keeps the emphasis on your subject matter. Say something like this:

> *It must be obvious to you I'm not a professional orator. I'm nervous up here. But I do have some important things to say.*

> *I'm a little nervous right now. I wish I were a better speaker because the things I have to say are important.*

After that, get on with your talk. Never mention your nervousness again.

3. Sound Natural. Don't be intimidated by a formal term like "platform speaking." You've been talking to people all your life. Speaking in public isn't that much different.

Always sound like one human being talking to another human being. In a formal speech, you'll want to talk somewhat slower than you usually do and, if you don't have a microphone, you'll have to speak somewhat louder. Nevertheless, keep your tone as conversational as the audience, subject, and occasion will allow. (Notice how skillfully Ronald Reagan does this.)

Never sound (or look) like you're reading a document to the audience.

4. Speak from Notes or from a Full Text. Once you have written your speech and rehearsed it for several hours, you can decide whether you want to bring the full text to the speaking event or whether you want to rely on outlined notes. Either way has advantages.

Never memorize your speech; you could black out in the middle of it. Because you want to look like you're "just talking" with the audience, however, you shouldn't keep looking down to card notes or sheets of paper you're holding in your hand.

If you are comfortable speaking extemporaneously, simply put an outline of your speech on the speaker's stand and resort to that when necessary. This allows you to sound conversational and to talk more directly at your audience. Not being tied down to the exact words of a written-out text, you're freer to modify your talk so it meets the responses of the audience.

If you need the security of the full text, you must take care that it's written to sound like natural speech and that it doesn't "freeze" you so you can't change your lines when necessary. With a full text, however, you can be sure you're giving your talk exactly as you wrote it.

If you elect to use a full text, type out your speech (triple space) and put it in a ring binder. Rehearse it until it is practically memorized. When you rise to speak, put the manuscript on the speaker's stand in front of you and look at it as little as possible. Talk directly at your audience and turn the pages unobtrusively. If you raise the stand enough and step back a bit, you can look directly at your listeners and still—with the slightest lowering of your eyes—read from your text.

5. Use Whatever Gestures Come Naturally. As you address your audience, don't simply stand motionless, and don't move in any way that feels artificial to you.

Remember you have many props to occupy your hands with. You have the speaker's stand, your pockets, a pointer, chalk, your glasses, and so on. Feel free to use these.

Be careful of mannerisms that draw attention away from your message. Don't fiddle with a paper clip or with your hair or tie. Don't click your ball-point pen. Watch out for those collapsible pointers: Almost invariably speakers begin opening and closing them and look like they're playing an accordian.

If you can relax and get involved with what you're saying, whatever gestures come naturally will be fine.

6. Use Common Sense. Sometimes all your preparations aren't enough. Before or during your speech, unexpected things happen. Here you have to make common-sense adjustments.

If you are one of a series of speakers and those preceding you have all run overtime, what do you do? If you rise at 5:10 p.m. and have a 15-minute speech to deliver, forget it. Say one or two ingratiating things, then sit down.

If your speaker's stand faces directly forward toward a room where all the audience is sitting on one side, turn the stand a few degrees.

If you discover your audience is more conservative or more hostile than you expected, skip over material they are likely to find offensive.

If you are in the middle of your speech and find you are taking longer than you should, paraphrase a long section into a sentence or two. If you find you're going to end sooner than you expected, don't pad. Let the talk end.

If you misspeak, correct yourself. ("Excuse me, I should have said *Henry* Kissinger.") Then go on.

Watch your audience. You can tell when they are with you and following your argument. You can also tell when they start to shift around in their chairs and the glaze comes over their eyes. If you feel you're losing them, you may want to insert a quick, stimulating line ("Now get this; this is important." or "Anyone who doesn't understand this next point is going to lose money."). You may also need to end your speech as soon as possible. An audience always wakes up when it hears, "In conclusion."

If during your speech a water glass tips over or your manuscript falls on the floor, mention the accident ("I'm sorry about that"), then get back to your talk. Don't panic or giggle or make jokes about the event; that just draws attention away from your argument.

These are just a few of the unexpected things that can happen during a speech. When they happen to you, make the necessary adjustments. Use your common sense.

> <

The best way to give a good speech is to have a good speech. When you stand before your audience, all that time you took researching and writing and rehearsing your talk will pay off handsomely.

82 83 84 85 86 9 8 7 6 5 4 3 2 1